Better
Living
Through
Birding

Better Living Through Birding

*Notes from a Black Man
in the Natural World*

Christian Cooper

RANDOM HOUSE
NEW YORK

Published in the United States by Random House, an imprint and division
of Penguin Random House LLC, New York.

RANDOM HOUSE and the HOUSE colophon are registered trademarks
of Penguin Random House LLC.

Library of Congress Cataloging-in-Publication Data

Names: Cooper, Christian, author.
Title: Better living through birding: notes from a Black man in the
natural world / by Christian Cooper.
Other titles: Notes from a Black man in the natural world
Description: First edition. | New York: Random House, [2022]
Identifiers: LCCN 2022050405 (print) | LCCN 2022050406 (ebook) |
ISBN 9780593242384 (hardcover) | ISBN 9780593242391 (ebook)
Subjects: LCSH: Cooper, Christian. | Cooper, Christian—Travel. | Bird
watchers—New York (State)—Biography. | Writers—New York
(State)—Biography. | Long Island (N.Y.)—Biography.
Classification: LCC QL684.N7 C66 2022 (print) | LCC QL684.N7 (ebook) |
DDC 598.072/347471 [B]—dc23/eng/20221129
LC record available at https://lccn.loc.gov/2022050405
LC ebook record available at https://lccn.loc.gov/2022050406

Printed in the United States of America on acid-free paper

randomhousebooks.com

2 4 6 8 9 7 5 3 1

FIRST EDITION

Design by Ralph Fowler

Frontispiece by Penelope Krebs

Bird illustrations by Miki / Adobe Stock

For Mom and Dad

I believe the best way to begin reconnecting humanity's heart, mind, and soul to nature is for us to share our individual stories.

—J. Drew Lanham, *The Home Place: Memoirs of a Colored Man's Love Affair with Nature*

Contents

Introduction

WITH CAMERAS ROLLING, we hold our breath. What would happen next?

A swath of the Big Island unfolds below us, in stretches of open fields and moss-draped trees whose green meets the blue and white of sea and sky at the horizon. It's not the sandy-beach tourist postcard one might expect of Hawaii, but from the small cliff where the film crew and I stand, it's perfection, with two rare Hawaiian Geese in the foreground, taking their first tentative steps to freedom.

These two Nenes ("nay-nays"), as they are known, have spent weeks at the Hawai'i Wildlife Center rehab facility after injuries likely sustained on golf courses. Now that they've been deemed healthy for release, we're watching their repatriation to the wild and hoping to catch a bit of magic on film. There's no way to know what the birds will do, and we have only one crack at capturing this moment for television— for a TV show I'm hosting.

Poised at the cliff's edge, the Nenes raise their heads high amid a tussock of grass to take in their surroundings, including the sweeping vista; they honk in high voices, tentatively, as if to say, "Well, this is new; how did I get here?" I know the feeling.

Unexpectedly, after years at a desk job, I find myself living a birder's dream: crisscrossing the continent in pursuit of iconic species like the Nene; having close encounters with the rarest birds (it doesn't get any closer than peering via endoscope inside the body of a Puerto Rican Parrot, or Iguaca, to check on its testicles); and having the privilege of telling the harrowing and inspiring stories of these birds' conservation—

and of the farmers, biologists, and just plain folks, truly extraordinary birders, dedicated to these efforts—in front of the camera to a mass audience.

And yet this hasn't come out of nowhere. Elements in my life going back decades to childhood have conspired in the alchemy of this transformation, galvanized by a moment two years prior to my Nene encounter, a moment early in the morning late in the month of May, in Manhattan's Central Park, and by a sentence uttered as agitated white fingers hovered over a cellphone, poised to dial 911 to summon the police: "I'm going to tell them that there's an African American man threatening my life."

Fourteen words, captured amid sixty-nine seconds of video, that would alter the trajectory of two lives.

I can only speak about one of those lives, that of the African American man in question: my own. Ideally I'd be writing about it not with a keyboard but in the graceful strokes of an inked quill, to match in script the way feathered creatures have drawn a steady line through the disparate aspects of my existence. As a Black kid in the 1970s, I was rarer than an Ivory-Billed Woodpecker in the very white world of birding; as I simultaneously struggled with being queer, birds took me away from my woes suffocating in the closet. A total nerd, I devoured superhero comics, sci-fi, and fantasy long before nerd culture conquered the world; my obsession with birds only ramped up the geek factor exponentially, and birding would lead directly to the confrontation in Central Park, a moment when my choices would be informed by a lifetime of being Black, queer, and even a nerd.

Of the many disorienting twists in the aftermath of that incident, one of the strangest is that I have been afforded an opportunity that better folks than me don't always get: the chance to tell those interlocking tales of my life in their full complexity. As I might lead a bird walk through the woods, this book will lead you through six decades of a Black gay activist birder's tumultuous past, pausing to observe all things most notable—things of interest even if you don't give one whit about birds (but of course, by the end of this, you will) and whether you are a longtime enthusiast or have never held a pair of binoculars in your life (but after reading through these pages, of course, you'll have to). And though this book isn't about how to bird, I'll offer some modest tips along the way for the uninitiated, as well as insights (seven very specific ones!) into why birding might be the next big thing to conquer the world—if the recently soaring number of people taking up lenses to point at feathered beauties is any indication.

All that, yes, and something else.

One spring day, maybe in a suburban backyard, or maybe in a random tree in a busy metropolis, you might hear something with a flutelike quality that makes you curious. So you investigate, peering through leaves, feeling a little foolish, until you see brick-red undersides; you never knew robins, so familiar from every patch of grass, made that sound. Now those flute phrases of triplet notes are stuck in your head; you hear it all the time in places you never paid attention to. Even in passing, these ordinary places get your attention now. Suddenly alert to robins, you notice that they hop or run, whereas pigeons only walk, but with the head bobbing with each step; it makes you wonder what else you might be overlooking, right before your eyes and ears.

Or maybe you'll find yourself atop a cliff in Hawaii, listening to the honks of Nenes and realizing how the sound is so reminiscent of the ubiquitous Canada Geese back home (but higher pitched, as if a Canada had been kneed in the groin); the close kinship of the two different geese stops being an abstraction, but rather something you can see and hear. You start to perceive the world as an interconnected ebb and flow of genes that take one gorgeous form in one given location but have drifted in a new direction someplace else. Yet for a moment all that is forgotten as a flock of Nenes careens overhead and splits the sky with cries of their own, answering the two newcomers, as if to say, "Welcome to our world."

Birding shifts your perceptions, adding new layers of meaning and brokering connections: between sounds and seasons, across far-flung places, and between who we are as people and a wild world that both transcends and embraces us. In my life, it has been a window into the wondrous.

Allow me to pull back the curtain and welcome you to my world.

Better Living Through Birding

An Incident in
Central Park

I AM A BLACK man running through New York's Central Park. This is no leisure run. I'm not pushing for a new personal best, though my legs pump in furious rhythm. I'm running as if my life depends on it. And though my heart pounds, it's as much out of mounting panic as it is cardiovascular stress. I know what this looks like. My sneakers are old and muddy, my jeans in need of a good washing, and my shirt, though collared, could at best be described as unkempt. I am a Black man on the run. And I have binoculars.

This is not how this evening was supposed to unfold. But all it took was a brief exchange of words to put me in flight. Twilight is racing along the horizon, and I've got half an hour of light left at best. As the sun sinks behind trees wreathed in its glow, so, too, does a feeling of desperation in the pit of my stomach. I'm running out of time.

I check the alert on my phone again and curse myself for turning it off for the entire workday. I'd faced several grueling tasks with hard deadlines and had found the constant vibrating notifications from the Manhattan Rare Bird Alert too indiscriminate ("rare" being rather loosely defined by some contributors) and too distracting during working hours. I preferred to do my birding early in the morning anyway. Then I would head directly to the office, where my colleagues have grown accustomed to my business-questionable attire this time of year (functional and subject to deferred laundering; the demands of my spring migration schedule don't permit much else). So it wasn't until 6:00 p.m. that I turned my phone on and saw the text from Morgan:

"Are you going to go see the Kirtland's Warbler?"

Amusement at what obviously had to be a prank quickly morphed into disbelief as I read the chain of alerts that had preceded it. "Oh my God, oh my God, oh my God!" I sputtered, snatching the binoculars off my desk and hurtling out of the office without explanation. At least one co-worker would tell me later that he was certain someone had died.

Now, having sprinted from my office in midtown to the west side of the park near the Reservoir, I slow as I near where I think I need to be. After a few minutes a sinking feeling settles in that I must be in the wrong spot. But as I round a bend in the path, I see a mass of people—nearly all of whom I recognize—and know I've found the place.

Birding Tip

The fastest way to find a widely reported rarity is to look not for the bird but for the coagulation of birders already looking at it.

Reading my stricken expression and ragged gasps as the cocktail of panic and exertion that they are, Mike peels off from the crowd and intercepts me. "Breathe," he says, calm, compact, and dryly British as always. "It's still here; we're looking at it right now." And with a little help from my friends, I find the right spot in the right tree; lock onto the motion among the leaves; and raise my binoculars with hands shaking with anticipation. A bird, slate blue and yellow and smaller than a sparrow, moves from branch to branch with a pump of its tail. I see a unicorn, come alive before my own eyes.

In order to truly appreciate that moment, you must first understand something about this particular bird. The rarest songbird in North America, Kirtland's Warbler is a creature even more unlikely to be spotted in Central Park than the gay Black nerd with binoculars looking up at it. It nests strictly in jack pines of a certain age, habitat requirements so specific that in all the world there are only about six thousand of the birds, restricted to a breeding range that consists almost entirely of a small patch of Michigan. Kirtland's Warblers return there every spring from their wintering grounds in the Bahamas, traveling hundreds of miles to do so. Yet in that routine annual journey, one of these tiny bundles of feathers happened to wander a bit off course, or maybe, like me, this rare bird yearned to taste life in the big city, where freaks of nature of every kind are welcome. It would end up somewhere in the eight hundred acres of Central Park, a tiny thing flitting behind the leaves of the park's eighteen thousand trees teeming with a million or so other avian visitors, including other warblers from which, to the untrained eye, a Kirtland's is indistinguishable. In the words of Captain James T. Kirk, "Finding a needle in a haystack would be child's play by comparison."*

Enter the birder Kevin Topping. He happened to be at the right place at the right time, but though luck plays a part in any sighting, there's so much more to getting the bird than that. A birder is alert to the presence of creatures that "civilians" would likely never even notice; they'd just walk right past. A birder's eyes lock onto a particular kind of motion in the trees, distinct from that of leaf movement in the wind, or to a particular shape that, motionless, is meant to camouflage

---

Star Trek (the original series), "The Galileo Seven," as written by Oliver Crawford and Shimon Wincelberg. Use your best Shatner voice.

into its surroundings. And a birder's ears never turn off, akin to a police scanner that snaps the attention into focus and sends one springing into action when, from amid the constant chatter, an urgent message (a distinctive bird vocalization) comes through. Then there's the accumulated knowledge base that an experienced birder brings to bear—a familiarity with what to watch for in what habitats, and an almost intuitive grasp of the subtle details of behavior, of plumage, that let you sort one kind of bird from another. Kevin Topping not only had the skill to find the bird but knew enough to know what he was looking at, and he had the presence of mind to get the word out to the broader birding community in a timely fashion.

That's how, for the first time in history, a Kirtland's Warbler was recorded in Central Park. It's as if you stepped into your backyard and saw a wild tiger prowling your lawn, or as if you looked over the side of a boat to catch a wink and smile from a mermaid before she dove beneath the waves. Or as if a real live unicorn stepped out of the forest.

This, then, is the seventh of the Seven Pleasures of Birding, and perhaps the greatest thrill of the pastime:

Seventh Pleasure of Birding:
The Unicorn Effect

It's the thrill of seeing at last for oneself a creature that until then has existed only in the imagination. But while number 7 is the high-octane moment, other pleasures make birding a joy for almost anyone, as I have tried to tell my feckless friends; they wonder why I abandon them every year in May, the peak of Central Park's spring songbird migration, when I become an early-rising, sleep-deprived mess of a man instead of carousing with them. After one too many attempts to explain, I codified those aspects of the birding experience into the Seven Pleasures of Birding, for ease of dissemination to the uninitiated, and of those seven pleasures, this comes first and foremost:

First Pleasure of Birding:
The Beauty of the Birds

If you've never seen a male Scarlet Tanager in full breeding plumage—a bird of such incandescent hue, set off by jet-black wings and tail, that it makes a stoplight look dim—then a knock-your-socks-off experience awaits you. And that's just the beginning of the show, from the gaudy, Technicolor riot of a Painted Bunting to the serene, pristine grace of a Great Egret; from the effortlessly soaring majesty of a Golden Eagle to the fierce frenzy of a hummingbird; from the bold color blocks of a Red-Headed Woodpecker to the exquisite nuance of pattern and muted tones of a Lincoln's Sparrow . . .

But most people don't realize the reasons why, of all the spectacular creatures with which we share this planet, birds captivate us as no others can.

What makes birding such a phenomenon? Why not "mammaling" or "insecting"? Certainly those pursuits have their adherents, as the thousands who visit Africa on safari or who catalog butterflies can attest. And in fact, there's a large degree of overlap among all these obsessions, counting myself as one of the multi-obsessed; once you tune in to one aspect of nature, you eventually become aware of the whole connected network of life around us.

Birding, however, occupies a sweet spot of accessibility: The variety of birds, no matter where you are around the globe or what kind of place you're in—city, suburb, country; mountains, woodland, field, swamp, shore, or out to sea—greatly exceeds the limited number of species of mammals in the same area; and many of those mammals are nocturnal and/or hidden beneath the soil or under the sea, restricting observation. Bugs, on the other hand, present the opposite problem: The crazy profusion of insect species is nigh impossible to master, or else, in temperate climes in the wintertime, there are almost none at all. With birds, no matter the time of year, there's always something to see.

But the appeal of birds runs far deeper than just numbers of kinds. We can relate to birds, warm-blooded vertebrates like ourselves, far more easily than any other class of animals besides our own, the mammals. But even there, birds boast one big advantage.

Certainly we humans bond uniquely with other mammals; the relationship between us and dogs—an unlikely symbiosis between apes and wolves—goes back millennia, cemented by the traits of both species as social animals. Dogs can tell when we're happy, angry, excited, sad, and for the most part we know the same things about them. We share the same emotional palette, but we don't share the same primary senses. Dogs, like many other mammals, rely first and foremost on their sense of smell. They've got about fifty times more olfactory receptors in their noses than we've got, and a dog's brain devotes a far greater proportion of its real estate to analyzing odors. Where we might smell liquor on someone (given sufficient ingestion and unfortunate proximity), dogs can smell cancer. As close as you feel to Fido, unless you're planning to start peeing on trees and sniffing ass, you'll never experience the world quite the way he does.

Most birds, it is generally believed, have a very limited sense of smell (which is no doubt why a Great Horned Owl can happily make a meal of a skunk without losing its lunch). Instead, birds communicate the same ways we do: through sight and sound. So they've evolved a stunning range of patterns and colors and, among the songbirds, an astonishing musical repertoire, and we humans are equipped to revel in all of it. Our vision and our hearing are our go-tos for interpreting the universe around us, and the birds oblige by filling our little corner of the universe with living, singing vibrance.

With birds, revelations of sight and sound can come at any time. On an early summer hike in the foothills of the Catskills, where Scarlet Tanagers can flash through the trees like signal flares, I blundered into an overgrown gap in the forest to hear a tinkling, rambling melody. It was as if the Herbie Mann of fairies were riffing nonstop on the tiniest possible flute; no fantasy tale could conjure a more delicate enchantment, peals and peals of it wafting from . . . somewhere. I peered around, and peered some more, and peered again, and finally, on the end of a log, spotted a tiny dark brown ball of a bird with its tail cocked upright. I had seen Winter Wrens before—a bird that in the eastern United States is more commonly found in winter, as the name suggests—but I'd never heard one sing until that moment. Then and ever since, for me that song transforms a walk in the woods into something magical.

But beyond even that shared axis of communication, we love birds for a simple reason: They can fly. No other creature on our planet has ever had their mastery of the air. We see them launch themselves effortlessly up into a medium with no boundaries, while we remain earthbound, and we are inspired to dream. Imagine watching land and sea unfold beneath you, not through the windows of an airplane, but under your own power. The things that you've left behind recede to insignificance, put into new perspective by a towering vantage point. What it must be like, to hang suspended on the wind; how radically different, to conceive of movement not in a flat plane, not just as backward and forward, left and right, but in three dimensions always, infinite possibilities of direction, the body rising and falling at will. We lift our gaze skyward to the birds and see what it means to be free.

These passions and more inform the half hour we spend in the dwindling light drinking in the Kirtland's Warbler that has strayed into Central Park. It is by no means the most dramatically colored bird anyone has ever seen, and yet the context—that something so rare should appear miraculously on our home turf—makes the sighting unparalleled. A combination of satisfaction and amazement settles on us fifty or so birders, gathered like fan geeks staking out a rumored hot spot for a glimpse of their favorite celebrity; with high-end cameras poised in several birders' hands, we are in fact mistaken for such a gaggle of groupies more than once. We know none of us are likely to see this species here again in our lifetime, unless the bird sticks around for another day (it would, and into the following morning, to the delight of birders across the tristate area, and the woe of those who would get there too late). The camaraderie of this shared knowledge and experience is palpable.

We are a strange breed, we humans gathered by this small bird flown off course. We have feathered dreams, dreams that have filled my head from earliest youth. Birding served as a refuge as I struggled with being a queer kid in an unwelcoming world, and it simultaneously compounded my Black outsider status while setting my complete and utter nerdiness in immutable concrete. Birding had put me on the path to this once-in-a-lifetime sighting, and it would lead me, years later, to another life-changing incident in Central Park, on a day that would reverberate through a nation's conscience. But before that, it was these feathered dreams that would carry me across the globe on adventures, in search of birds in faraway places.

I believe that birds in the wild are meant to inspire such passions in us all. They are for everyone to enjoy and belong to no one group of people. And best of all, the wonders they offer are always available, freely given, to anyone willing to partake. All we have to do is step outside, look, and listen.

As the light fails and we birders start to disperse, a pair of cyclists zooms past, offering a snide remark about the ridiculousness of our assembly. They pass having no knowledge of what we're looking at or of its significance, nor do they care. They disappear from view none the wiser.

What wisdom I might have gained from years spent looking up in awe, from my earliest youth through seasons in Central Park to this very moment, I offer in these pages.

2

Blackbird

O UTWARD APPEARANCES CAN deceive. Take the blackbird, for example.

My "spark bird"—the bird that first ignited my interest in all things feathered—was the Red-Winged Blackbird. When I was nine years old, my parents enrolled me in a summer woodworking class; perhaps because my parents had sensed something was askew with their little boy, they might have thought it would butch me up. When faced with the Sophie's choice of building either a footstool or a bird feeder, I picked the feeder. No sooner was it up in our backyard than the cracked corn it dispensed lured in a nearly all-black bird with a red patch on the wing; I had discovered a new species of crow! Or so I thought. But it didn't take long to learn the bird's true identity, or for my disappointment that I hadn't accomplished a preteen scientific triumph to be replaced by a particular fondness for the species. Over the years, when I was growing up in the Long Island suburbs of New York City, the Red-Winged Blackbird's raucous territorial cry would become the voice of a familiar friend. To this day, that sound when the males return after being away all winter remains my definitive first sign of spring.

In the Americas, about two dozen species bear the name blackbird, the red-wing included, who with their relatives make up a sprawling family (the icterids) of medium-sized sharp-billed birds that mostly are black or black and yellow/orange. But mention the blackbird in Europe, and you're talking about a completely different bird from a completely different family. The problem arose when English settlers arrived on American shores, saw birds that superficially resembled a bird they knew from back home, and slapped the same name on it. The Eurasian Blackbird is indeed all black, but it's not an icterid; it's a thrush in the genus *Turdus,* which puts it on the same branch of the bird family tree as another *Turdus* thrush, the American Robin, that red-breasted icon of suburban lawns, which is not to be confused with the Robin in the U.K., which is not a thrush at all. (Again, English settlers noted the vaguely similar appearance—the color of the breast—of an American bird to one in the old country, named the "new" bird accordingly, and another confusing misnomer was born.)

As for the Red-Winged Blackbird, the possibility for confusion is doubled, since by European standards not only isn't it a real blackbird, but they already have a bird called the Redwing, which happens to be another *Turdus* thrush! That makes the Redwing a stranger to New World blackbirds like the red-wing but, as it turns out, close kin to the Eurasian Blackbird and the American Robin (but not the U.K. Robin).

With so many confusing labels to sort through, and the mistaken assumptions people make based on how things seem at a glance, it can take awhile to understand and appreciate a thing for who and what it truly is.

I am no exception. Like everyone else, I had to sort through aspects of my identity and where I fit in the social taxonomy, which labels fit and which chafed, and how the world might have misidentified me and pegged my kind all wrong. I had to grow comfortable in my own

Black skin in a white world, in my own rainbow-queer body in an era when sexuality was only seen in black and white.

Near as I can tell, I was born that way: as queer as the Alaskan summer day is long. It was conspicuous to me from the age of five, when I developed an erotic attachment to a comic-book superhero; one look at that male physique bulging with muscles, and something deep in my psyche said, "Yes, please!" It became conspicuous to my parents not long after. I'd been thinking superhero thoughts and got what must have been my first full-fledged boner, which terrified me at that young age.

"Mommy, Daddy!" I howled as I fled to their bedroom for help. "It won't go down, it won't go down! I think it's broken!"

I was too young at the time to be able to remember today the incident with clarity, so I can only imagine the bemused smirks suppressed on their faces. Now imagine those smirks morphing into worried frowns, if I had truthfully answered my mother's next question: "Well, Christian, what were you thinking about?"

"Nothing," I said after a considered pause. Somehow, even at that tender age, I'd sufficiently metabolized the cultural taboos around sexual desire to know enough to lie about it.

In the largely conservative suburban communities of Long Island in the late 1960s and the 1970s, there were few other options if you wanted to survive. There were no gay people, not that anybody knew, not that everybody didn't scorn, and if it was suspected, it was a character flaw that was whispered about, perhaps tolerated if the individual was discreet. The Stonewall rebellion would happen a stone's throw away, not that I would know about it then, but the forces of change it would unleash had yet to gather momentum. Gay characters were virtually absent from movies and especially TV, except when homosexuality was hinted at to make a villain extra villainous, or trotted out as an object of ridicule, or featured as the pathetic tragedy on a very special episode of *Dallas*. Openly gay celebrities didn't exist. The anti-gay leadership of the Catholic Church would keep a stranglehold on

New York's political scene for decades to come, and even if the laity ignored that leadership on most matters of human sexuality, on this the hierarchy still commanded some moral authority (ironically, considering the church pedophilia scandals yet to come to light). Even with my parents, nonreligious and liberal, I remember the distinct moment when the term "homosexual" first came up at the dinner table, and I asked what it meant; they told me, not without a subtext of disapproval.

After dinner, my brain still churning with this new information, I retreated to my bedroom. I closed the door with five words in my head but not on my lips, never on my lips, and locked the proverbial closet door tight with what was left unspoken: "But that's what I am."

The worst part: As a kid in those days, there was no way to know that others were going through the same thing. You were doomed to be alone, the only one with this terrible secret.

Confessing my urges to my parents was out of the question. My relationship with them fit the stereotype of "what would make a boy gay": close to Mom, with a distant dad. My mother, a chocolate-brown-skinned, beautiful, and charming English teacher, was to all appearances a model wife with a fierce belief that whatever her daughter and son decided to do in life, we were destined for greatness, but I was certain that me dating other guys fell outside the scope of her fantasies. My father, with a goatee of red hair and skin so light he could "pass" for white, presented a big, gregarious persona when outside the wood paneling of our modest suburban home (he built the dormer himself), but inside, with his family, he transformed into a taciturn, glowering presence. We all lived in fear of his black moods, which could last for days. I was confident I wouldn't last five seconds if I were to tell him I was gay.

Some young people under similar stress channel it into overachieving, and I suppose I did that, to an extent. Many others would graduate to alcohol or drugs to numb the pain. I never fell into that trap, principally because I had two refuges of my own to escape to.

The first was the natural world. Nature always held a special place in our household, since my dad taught science generally and biology in particular. To this day Black people visit the national parks at a depressingly low rate to our numbers in the population, but half a century ago when we were even fewer on the campgrounds, my Brooklyn-bred father routinely took his very brown-skinned family to the wild places of America. We went tent camping in Maine and later upgraded to a Volkswagen Westfalia camper—little more than a van with a pop-up roof. Since, as schoolteachers, both my parents had the summers off, after my sixth-grade year ended, they crammed themselves, me, my sister, and the family dog into that little camper for a cross-country odyssey. And in doing so, they inadvertently created a birding monster.

We left, as we always did for a camping trip, in the starry darkness just before dawn to beat traffic and maximize the day's driving time; my sister and I lingered in a zombielike, barely conscious state as we hit the road. "The road" this time would carry us up through Canada: across the prairie provinces to the glacier at Banff National Park and the turquoise serenity of Lake Louise, where swooping gray-and-black blurs (Clark's Nutcrackers, I would later learn) would delight us kids by snatching peanuts held aloft from between our little kid fingers; across the Rocky Mountains, the first sight of which seemed surreal, a backdrop to an American Museum of Natural History diorama come to life; back into the States to the Hoh Rain Forest on Washington's Olympic Peninsula, where conifers shade a landscape mystically drenched in mosses and ferns; down the West Coast through giant redwoods (literally *through* one, in that classic tourist move), the tallest living beings I will ever meet; across the desert Southwest to the wonder of them all, the Grand Canyon; and home, eventually, to Long Island. All in the space of two months.

It was a spectacular gift that my sister and I carry with us to this day. It was also a grueling ordeal, dominated at times by my father's bullying rage at all of us for the littlest things gone awry, often beyond anyone's control, and at other times by his bliss at seeing elk, moose, and bears in the flesh for the very first time. The last a little too closely; when Dad stopped the camper to observe a black bear begging for a handout alongside the road at Yellowstone, it made a beeline for the passenger side as my mother frantically cranked up the window. Our dog was perched on Mom's lap, making the situation all the more dangerous, since bears can become enraged in the presence of dogs. Mom got the window up just in time for our diminutive English cocker spaniel to growl in the bear's face, and taking to heart that discretion is the better part of valor, Spanky then hid in the back of the camper. I can still see the breath from the bear's nostrils condense against the glass.

Space was tight, with the four of us plus Spanky, our clothes, and our food stores packed into that dowdy VW Westfalia, but my biology-minded dad made sure that the birder's bible for many generations, Peterson's *Field Guide to the Birds,* was among our limited cache of books, and later I got him to add the relatively new *Golden Field Guide* as we entered the West. With little else to do during the hours of driving, sometimes with only monotonous farmland for miles, I pored over the guides. The birding spark had only just been lit by that Red-Winged Blackbird at the feeder I'd built; as I digested the illustrations of each new, unfamiliar beauty and imagined what it might be like to actually see one, the spark caught fire.

By the time we hit the West Coast, I must have flipped through the guides a hundred times. When we stopped one day for a restroom break at a small park in British Columbia, we were startled by a dramatic bird that was new to us all: bold blocks of black and white, of robust size, and with a lovely long greenish-blue tail.

"Look, Mom and Dad," I shouted with joy, "a Black-Billed Magpie!"

They eyed me with disbelief, because they had no idea what they were looking at—neither the bird nor their strange son.

"How the hell do you know that?" my dad asked, I think with some barely concealed science teacher's pride.

I shrugged. "I've seen it in the book." My impressionable young brain, as yet uncluttered with all the things life throws at us, had inadvertently absorbed most of its contents. I would never be the same.

Once back on Long Island, my father found a local group that was running a bird walk on an upcoming Sunday and marked his calendar; we didn't do a lot of father-son activities back then, so this would take us into new territory. That morning he drove us the half hour or so to Jamaica Bay Wildlife Refuge, a sprawling series of trails through freshwater and saltwater habitats on the very edge of New York City, for what would be the first of many bird walks with the South Shore Audubon Society and its walk leader, Elliott Kutner.

"Exuberant" isn't the only term to describe Elliott; plenty of accolades could flow for this air force veteran awarded the Distinguished Flying Cross in World War II, a man who afterward owned and ran a corrugated cardboard container factory that kept scores of unionized workers employed over the years. But with anyone he met, Elliott's exuberance burst forth as irrepressibly as springtime music from a Song Sparrow's throat. He was one of the founders of the South Shore chapter of Audubon and served as its president for many years, and long after that tenure he would remain deeply committed to the organization. Particularly on weekends: As an observant Jew, Elliott strictly kept the Sabbath on Saturdays, but on Sunday mornings he spread the gospel of birding on the walks he led, on outings to the ponds and gardens of Jamaica Bay and the windswept dunes of Jones Beach, in the spring and fall during the bonanza of migration and in the frigid depths of winter. He did this for decades, inspiring a passion for all things feathered in a large if not especially diverse group of people.

But on this sunny October morning, my dad and I showed up,

maybe the first Black people ever for a South Shore walk. If we were, you'd never know it; everyone seemed friendly enough, and Elliott was Elliott: exuberant. His voice rang out with a preliminary tutorial for us newcomers, on how to use binoculars effectively—something I'd been struggling with through my battered pair of hand-me-downs:

Birding Tip

"First, find the bird with your naked eye; then, KEEPING YOUR EYES ON THE BIRD, bring the binoculars to your eyes— not the other way around!"

We'd taken only a few steps before I'd put this new technique into successful practice: Small birds were flashing from shrub to shrub across the path in front of us, pausing on the open ground so that we could see the bright yellow patch on the rump, just above the base of the tail, amid its brown markings.

"Myrtle Warblers!" Elliott announced, since that was what the Yellow-Rumped Warbler was called back then. My heart jumped: I was seeing my first real, live warbler! I knew of the family from the guide, small birds in a dazzling array of colors, but I hadn't imagined just how small nor how active, couldn't imagine that something as exotic as a warbler could be seen right in Queens. Nor did I imagine then how in my birding years to come, warblers would transmute every spring in the East in general, and in New York City in particular, into a combination of pageant, treasure hunt, and symphony.

Farther along the path, with a spotting scope on a tripod to observe the distant shore of the refuge's West Pond, Elliott called out another find. "We have a pair of American Woodcocks in the scope! American Woodcock! Take a look!"

Everyone lined up for their turn, none more eagerly than me. As with so many species back then, a woodcock—a plump, weird-looking bird that probes the mud for food with an out-of-proportion long bill—would be new to me: a "life bird" (or "lifer"), in the birder parlance for a first sighting of a species one has never seen before.

My turn came, and after peering through the eyepiece, I walked away troubled. The birds were distant and therefore small and hard to discern clearly even with the scope, but blessed at the time with the fiendishly keen eyesight of youth, and after consulting my trusty field guide, I thought I'd noticed something amiss. "I don't think those are woodcocks," I said quietly to my father, apart from the group.

"Go tell him," my dad encouraged me and gestured toward Elliott.

Meekly, afraid I'd embarrass myself or be booted from the group, I approached Elliott. "I don't think those are woodcocks."

Elliott's eyes sparkled. "What makes you think that?"

"Well, uh, I think the pattern on the head looks more like a snipe." Since I'd never seen a Wilson's Snipe either, this was going out on a limb.

Elliott took another look through the scope while I held my breath. Then he fixed me with his gaze as if he were peering into me. "What's your name, young man?"

"Christian." I was about to shrivel and slink away.

"Well, Christian, you're right!" Elliott practically bellowed with glee. "Correction, everybody! As this young man has noted, these are actually Wilson's Snipes! Take a look!"

From that moment on, Elliott made it his mission to see to it that the nascent bird craziness of this kid he'd only just met was nurtured to its fullest. Over the years he schooled me on gulls ("There's no such thing as a seagull!"), continued my introduction to the wonderful world of warblers, and taught me to tease out the Sharp-Shinned Hawks from their nearly identical cousins, my namesake, the Cooper's Hawks, by noting the degree of head projection in flight. From Elliott

I got the trick of propping up a dripping garden hose above an over-turned trash can lid and digging a trench in the backyard into which the lid could overflow so that the sight and sound of refreshing water would lure in migrants; he'd done it in his own backyard (no doubt with similar forbearance from his wife, Shirley, as my parents showed).

Elliott saved any abandoned eggs he found and painted them with clear nail polish to protect and preserve them, to form a sprawling collection he would later donate for the education of children. He filmed every bird he could—on Super 8—and was especially proud of his astonishing close-up clip of a Rough-Legged Hawk, a rare winter visitor to Long Island that he encountered on a Jones Beach roadside; Elliott was partial to raptors. He loved birds, he loved people, and he lived a life indulging in both, full of family and his faith. Over the span of my junior high and high school years, this exuberant Jewish World War II vet gave his friendship to a Black kid who unbeknownst to all was struggling with himself, and he passed on a love of birds that transcends all struggle and will last my whole life. For that gift, accolades fail, except perhaps one appropriate for someone whose religion was writ large in how he lived: Elliott Kutner was a mensch.

The suburbs can seem antiseptic, nature mowed and manicured to *Better Homes & Gardens* conformity, but wild things roam there that can't be tamed. American Robins hop on lawns looking for wormsign; fire-truck-red cardinals adorn backyard shrubs; mockingbirds would take to TV antennas (cable wouldn't arrive in most homes for a few more years) to belt out a medley punctuated with leaps into the air, feathers of gray and white flashing against an Ansel Adams sky. For a moment, a Long Island rooftop would become as boundless as the West.

Where the suburbs of New York City fell short of Montana and failed to give me a backyard stream, I made my own using Elliott's garden hose trick. The feeder from wood shop was not enough; as I learned that not all birds ate seeds, I had to find a way to attract the ones that didn't. The sight and sounds of water invite birds to drink and bathe, including migrants that might otherwise pass you by, migrants that are largely insectivorous and wouldn't visit a feeder. My muddy trench ran for a few feet outside my bedroom, so I sat at the bedroom window and waited. I would crank the window open so that nothing would be between me and the birds, then perch motionless for hours, watching and waiting. Patience was rewarded with revelation: a tail-bobbing waterthrush, a black-and-orange redstart fanning its tail as if the delicate little thing were under the delusion it was a peacock. On the banks of my mini Mississippi, the neighborhood robins could be studied in detail, from the darker charcoal feathers on the head and the broken white around the eyes, to the white spots at the corners of the tip of the tail. These were ambassadors from another world, and I had a window on it.

For a bit more "wilderness," I'd walk to Mullener Pond—or just the Pond, because I wouldn't know its proper name for some time yet. Blackbirds thrived here among its reeds, thrusting out their red shoulders as they announced themselves with ringing voices; muskrats swimming through its shallows remained muskrats despite my best efforts to turn them into beavers or otters. Wedged against the intersection of two highways, in retrospect the Pond wasn't much, but to me as a child it was magic, from the moment I peered through leaves to glimpse grace personified: a Snowy Egret clad entirely in lacy white, its long neck held in elegant turns, stepping along the Pond's edge in slow motion to show off the yellow slippers only its feet could wear.

For as much as birding is about seeing and hearing amazing birds, it's also about the places these birds are a part of; otherwise we could just visit the birds in a zoo or an aviary and be done with it. Hence the second of the Seven Pleasures of Birding:

Second Pleasure of Birding:
The Joy of Being in a Natural Setting

A morning going birding in Central Park might reveal a large wading bird perched motionless along the shores of the Lake, the fierce red of its eyes the only violation of the Black-Crowned Night Heron's monochrome palette; and it will also show the Lake shimmer, daybreak dancing off its surface to send patterns of light undulating across the leaves of the trees leaning over the water. Watching a raven soar over the Coachella Valley, one can't help but take in the cloudless blue its black form traverses, the backdrop of barren mountain rock, the stillness of the desert. Navigate a perilous gorge in Ecuador chasing after a glimpse of the orange otherworldliness of the Cock-of-the-Rock, and pass underneath a tropical waterfall along the way.

Transported to such places, we reconnect with something deep within ourselves. The myopia that lets us see only our woes falls away for a little while. Suddenly we can breathe again.

This experience isn't unique to birding, of course; hikers, campers, park lovers, and other outdoor enthusiasts feel it too. But while birding, you consider it a bit differently, perhaps. By focusing on particular denizens of a habitat, you get a broader and deeper understanding of that environment, as counterintuitive as that may seem. A new dimension of a natural place is revealed as home to this other being, of providing everything it needs, and maybe something we need as well. Through birding, such realization can happen even in the densest urban setting; a sharp *K'LEE-K'LEE-K'LEE!* cry amid downtown Manhattan's sea of concrete makes the eyes dart skyward for a glimpse of an American Kestrel, perched on high or flying by on tapered wings. And knowing that this small, colorful falcon makes its home here, feasting on sparrows, big bugs, and little rodents, puts even the Big Apple into context as just another part of a wild world, for all its man-made interventions.

Looking for birds got me out there and engaged with rhythms of life that transcended my own sad particulars: searching the March woods for returning Eastern Phoebes and finding amid all the bare trees a lone serviceberry bush festooned in white blossoms, as if it had snowed briefly here and only here; scanning for a Snowy Owl on the winter dunes of Long Island's South Shore beaches, where the sky, sea, and sand stretch on forever; watching a mockingbird on a TV antenna jump for the clouds.

A mockingbird would have the final say about Elliott. When he died in 2012 at the age of eighty-eight, South Shore Audubon members past and present turned out in droves for his funeral. During the ceremony at the cemetery, a Northern Mockingbird—its scientific name is *Mimus polyglottos,* meaning "mimic of many tongues"—briefly alighted next to his grave site, sang a few varied phrases, and flew. Someone somewhere was letting us know that Elliott, far from being silenced, now speaks with many tongues through all of us he inspired, his passion now communicated through a host of voices.

3

The Book of Яamus

I'VE NEVER HAD the good luck to see Eleonora's Falcon, a particularly elegant, tapered-winged hunter in a worldwide family of such birds. I've also never witnessed the gruesome behavior ascribed to populations of the bird living on some Mediterranean islands. These craggy, barren rocks don't have a lot on them, but songbirds migrating south from Europe in the late summer and autumn pass through. This makes a great food supply for the falcons during their well-timed breeding season. But the falcons also have a way of making sure that supply lasts a bit longer: They don't kill all the birds they catch at capture. Rather, they save some for later by ripping out their tail and flight feathers and partially entombing them alive, wedging them into cracks and crevices on the stony islands. The songbirds are trapped that way for days, a source of fresh food for the falcon when it finally retrieves it for the kill.

Imagine being trapped like that, meant to be free but instead rendered a helpless, hapless victim until your merciless end.

Been there. Done that.

I played it straight through grade school, junior high, and high school, lying for a dozen years, which, when you're a kid, is your entire life and therefore an eternity. Back then, to be identified as gay at school meant death—social death at least, and maybe physical harm that could end in the real thing. The worst insult someone could level at a boy was "faggot," which is all the more devastating when it's true. I put up a brave front, convinced myself I was romantically interested in my female friends (to whom I was always closer than to other guys), and had zero opportunity for the sexual discovery most teenagers fumble through as adolescence brings on a raging hormonal storm.

Everything seemed right with me. No one had a clue about the despair I felt inside; I made sure of it, because any suggestion I might be troubled would invite questions that I could never, ever allow. So I presented as a happy-go-lucky guy who aced all his classwork—even if he was a little odd about this birding business.

But the truth was more complicated. The essential me—the part that hungered for honesty and intimacy; for raunchy, pulse-quickening encounters and, yes, true love; to not be so terribly alone and so constantly afraid—that real me spent that dozen-year eternity buried alive. I felt as if I were locked inside a coffin under six feet of earth, in utter darkness, slowly suffocating. I pounded on the inside lid desperate for someone to let me out, but no one could hear my screams. No one knew there was someone alive down there. Friends and family walked over my grave, oblivious.

That's the only way I can begin to convey how that life felt.

Some African Americans—some of the ones who aren't LGBTQ—dismiss the gay experience because, unlike Black folk, gays can blend in at will; sexual orientation, unlike skin color, can be disguised so that we may enjoy the full benefits of society without suffering discrimination. This is largely true, but it's anything but a plus for LGBTQ people; I can attest, after my stint locked inside that closed coffin, that life in the closet is no blessing. Coupled with the constant terror of discovery, the closet is the most baleful curse.

And more to the point: LGBTQ folks shouldn't have to bury ourselves alive in our own graves, just to be able to live.

The other key difference between the Black experience in the United States and the LGBTQ experience lies in the centuries of systemic oppression aimed squarely at African Americans. Our long struggle from the horrors of slavery and being constitutionally deemed three-fifths of a person, continuing through lynchings, segregation, and the civil rights era, to the current legacy of economic disparity and outright and implicit bias that leaves Black folk disadvantaged in life, or lifeless at the hands of police, has nothing remotely comparable in gay history.

That said, throughout that struggle, we African Americans have had each other: our families (at least when slave owners weren't selling them away like used furniture), our community, and, for those who are religious, the church and the faith that goes with it. The fresh horror LGBTQ people face is precisely the opposite: the very real possibility of family, friends, church, and community turning against you at the very moment you need them most. Instead of supporting you through a trying time, they can become the source of greatest pain, leaving vulnerable people abandoned not only by the ones they love but, according to some, by God himself. When some white schoolmate shouts "nigger!" there is at least comfort and shared understanding to be found in Mom's arms when you get home; what happens when the one shouting "queer!" is your very own mother as she kicks you out of the only home you've ever known?

Being Black and gay, I find the "Who's More Oppressed?" sweepstakes exasperating. There can be no winner, and it creates the false impression of a stark divide between communities. (It also ignores a special case where the gay and Black experiences are remarkably similar: the situation of light-skinned African Americans who hide their heritage to "pass" as white, which maps closely with the experience of being in the closet.) The reality is that these experiences live together in the brown-skinned, queer bodies of hundreds of thousands of people, including me.

And as a queer kid, I desperately needed to find a way out of that tomb, even temporarily.

When I couldn't escape to the outdoors, I fled in the opposite direction—internally—to my second great refuge: science fiction and fantasy. Science fiction in particular is the lifeblood of the Cooper line, but both fantastical genres, along with supernatural horror, find favor in our family. My aunt Audrey had a strange set of paperbacks on her shelf whose stylized cover art of writing monsters on the march inspired both fascination and fear. And what kind of name was J.R.R. Tolkien anyway? What could a Lord of the Rings be? It all struck me as something forbidden. When at last my preteen self summoned the courage to borrow the books (Aunt Audrey had the good sense to start me off with the more kid-friendly prologue, *The Hobbit*), I was lost to Middle-earth for weeks on end. To this day, the smell of yellowing paperback pages summons the Shire, the Lonely Mountain, the golden woods of Lothlórien, perilous quests, and glorious adventure.

Arthurian legend, the masterful short stories of Ray Bradbury—I devoured these and more. I white-knuckled my way through nights reading Stephen King's *'Salem's Lot*. Mythology struck a unique chord: fantastical yet quasi-historical, metaphysical and metaphorical, offering insights into the human condition from a shared, centuries-long story tradition grounded in a culture, its values, and a people's view of our world. I couldn't articulate these elements of its allure at the time; my grade-school brain couldn't even digest the "American Pie" lyrics the radio served up in constant rotation back then. But I knew I wanted to know myths, every one of them, from every part of the world (and still do).

When the standard elementary-school assignment to create your own myth arrived, I eagerly dove in, or rather, I soared up, where a youthful goddess dwells in a castle in the clouds. She looks out her window and weeps in dismay as her prince-god suitors battle for her favor, transforming themselves into rams to butt heads with a tremendous "crack!" Meanwhile, her father hurls spears from the tower above to try to separate them, and a thunderstorm is born.

Crafting such tales and creating whole worlds in my head allowed me to escape the suffocating confines of my closeted existence, at least for a little while. As the brooding, shape-shifting Ninth Lord of Arcadia, I had the unswerving devotion of the Seventh Lord of that lost, timeless land, finding in fantasy the romance I wasn't allowed in real life. Among the star-faring Nomads—often hideous human beings thanks to their chaotic, mutating genes—there was unconditional community and no norm to transgress; no one was deemed an aberration, and every variation of humanity was embraced. I spent hours in my bedroom, alone except for pen and paper, conjuring such people and places in great detail.

When books and my own imagination failed, the screen came to the rescue.

My sister and I were among an entire generation that raced home after school each day to watch *Dark Shadows,* the supernatural soap opera that implausibly became a daytime TV sensation. We ingested every cheesy minute of the adventures of the tortured vampire Barnabas Collins as voraciously as we did the Oreos and chocolate milk we snacked on as we perched on the foot of Mom and Dad's bed, riveted to the television. But *Dark Shadows* paled in importance in our household compared with *Star Trek.* That original series, flinging Captain Kirk and Mr. Spock from planet to planet, predicted a future where everything our parents had raised us to believe—racial equality, peaceful cooperation, the promise of a better humanity—had been fulfilled. It didn't hurt that its timely messages were bundled into some damn good stories, as when an acid-spewing rock monster on a murderous rampage turned out to be a single mom with child-care issues. How can you beat that?

Sure, my nascent gay self cheered on the inside every time Kirk's shirt got torn, and when the crew of the *Enterprise* met the Greek god Apollo, I swooned right alongside Lieutenant Carolyn Palamas. But hormones aside, for me *Star Trek* was first and foremost about Spock. His incredible intellect and devotion to science and knowledge embodied everything a smart nerd kid could dream of. What's more, I aspired to his Vulcan mental discipline; even as a child I didn't trust emotion, not as a basis for action. It just seemed to lead people to do stupid things—get violent, go off half-cocked, surrender to despair. A grade-school classmate named Andrew, smart but clearly with emotional issues, would explode into rage with the least provocation; my father's long stretches of sullen menace and my mother's tendency to react emotionally to that, and seemingly everything else, were further red flags about emotion to me. And since I was in the midst of a childhood spent carefully repressing any outward expression of gayness, tight emotional control became a critical survival tool. Spock, thriving in Starfleet while steadfastly keeping his bothersome human emotions under lock and key, offered a way forward. I idolized him to the point that I spent hours in front of the mirror pushing one side of my forehead up and down with my fingers, hoping to learn how to raise one supercilious eyebrow the way he did.

The big screen was an even bigger comfort. I joined the millions before me for whom cinema constituted an immersive getaway— a couple hours spent in someone else's reality, so you could forget about your own grim one—and I was a platinum-level Frequent Getaway Awards Club member. Put me in the dark with a bucket of popcorn in my lap, and the fake-buttered aroma alone primes my mind for the visual storytelling feast to follow. It really doesn't matter whether the flick is any good (in fact, sometimes really bad is better! *Plan 9 from Outer Space,* anyone?); the shift in consciousness, the receptiveness to a tale retold in flickering light, the suspension of disbelief just long enough to go someplace else—for me, that's enough.

The first movie I ever saw, at least that I can recall, was *Barbarella* at the Westbury Drive-In. My parents took my sister and me, barely six years old, thinking it was just another science-fiction film; they remained blissfully unaware of the truckload of sexual innuendo and outright fornication in this 1968 tongue-in-cheek flick, starring a very young and voluptuous Jane Fonda, until it was too late. Whenever things got too racy, Mom and Dad would order us to look away to the back of the car. "Do we have to? Okay," we whined but readily complied, because our parents remained blissfully unaware of something else: The screen was reflected perfectly in the car's rear window. Jane Fonda's zero-G striptease, the overloading orgasmic organ—we saw the whole thing.

I wouldn't see the movie again until college, where it played one Saturday as the midnight show at the Harvard Square Theatre. I was shocked—not by the bawdiness, but by how I'd remembered the film practically scene for scene and in some instances word for word, and yet all the sexual stuff had gone right over my head. It was the same movie, and yet a whole new movie experience.

Other science-fiction films were hard to come by. It's difficult to imagine it now, but the genre met mostly disfavor through most of the 1970s, perhaps bearing the stigma of too many silly B movies in the 1950s. There were occasional gems like *Planet of the Apes* (also its less lustrous sequels) and *2001: A Space Odyssey* (though many found that story impenetrable), but Hollywood was mostly consumed with gritty and downbeat tales that wrestled at least indirectly with the country's disillusionment and emotional wreckage from Watergate and the Vietnam War. Finding the essential sci-fi nutrients scarce on the silver screen, I was subsisting on a TV diet of *Star Trek* reruns, *Space: 1999* (the moon blasts out of Earth's orbit! Adventure ensues!), and old Flash Gordon serials on PBS.

Then *Star Wars* changed everything.

The sci-fi-crazy Coopers went as a family, of course, on a Friday, the third night of its opening, since our working parents couldn't get to the movies any sooner. The buzz for the young director George Lucas's space epic was already big, so when the 9:30 p.m. show sold out before we could get tickets, we waited on line for the midnight show. We were hyped up with anticipation but didn't know what to expect, and when the theater handed out buttons emblazoned with "May the Force be with you," I sniffed indignantly at the meaningless message.

After hours of waiting, we settled into our seats, me with a bucket of popcorn in my lap as the house went dark, my eyes went wide, and my ears met the first fanfare of John Williams's glorious score. My heart leaped as the preamble scrolled up the screen, just like in those old Flash Gordon serials I loved. This movie had me at "Hello."

Suddenly a starship zoomed overhead from off screen. And then another, and this one kept going, and going, until it had passed in all its immensity, leaving the entire sellout crowd with mouths hanging open. We had never seen anything like it.

By the end of the summer of 1977, I had seen *Star Wars* nine times, and it's no exaggeration to say that George Lucas saved my life. By age fourteen I'd begun to feel hopeless, convinced that I would have to take my sick secret with me to my grave. I spent an evening home alone sitting on the floor of the den cross-legged, with a big carving knife in my lap, waiting for the courage to put an end to my misery by putting an end to myself. Then Lucas unwittingly threw me an escapist lifeline, one tailor-made to my passion for mythic storytelling, fantastic adventure, and all things science fiction. A long time ago, in a galaxy far, far away, I was happy.

But I couldn't live in a movie theater forever. At about that age, in a desperate bid to achieve heterosexual "normality," I sat my parents down one day to make an unusual request.

"I want to see a psychiatrist," I blurted out.

They looked at me with baffled expressions. From their perspective, this came out of nowhere.

"Why do you want to see a psychiatrist?" my mother asked.

I was at the same juncture with my parents at that moment as at age five when, confused and panicked in all my tumescent glory, I'd faced revealing what I'd been thinking about. The outcome of my mental calculus was the same in both instances.

"I just need to see a psychiatrist." I dug in my heels without further explanation.

To their credit—since it couldn't have been easy on my family's lower-middle-class budget—they obliged without pushing too much harder. For all the good it did: In a handful of sessions with a therapist, I never told her why I'd sought counseling; the risk to me of speaking the unspeakable was just too great. So she had me draw pictures of people and arrived at conclusions from the fact that I didn't give them hands or feet ("feels disempowered"), when in reality I just found appendages too artistically challenging. I can't blame her; I gave her nothing.

So my secret was never discovered. Throughout my years in junior high and high school, I made sure there was nothing to discover: I had no secret stash of gay porn, and the idea of reaching out to another guy for a tender touch or passionate kiss was so fraught with danger as to be unthinkable. No one had to tell me any hint of being queer would derail my life; on Long Island in the 1970s, that message was abundantly clear in snide asides about those unmentionable people, in the locker room jokes, in the scorn aimed at boys who were effeminate. The disdain in my parents' voices when they'd first explained to me what homosexuality was still rang in my ears years later.

Only my sister, immersed in the very implicitly gay world of theater in high school, might have figured out what was going on with me. She cornered me one afternoon to ask, out of the blue, "Is there something you want to tell me?" In a panic, I grabbed Spanky and thrust her between us as a not-quite-human shield and then bolted out of the house to take the dog for a walk.

By that time, adolescence had given such force to my attractions that I couldn't fool myself about them nor cling to hope for a quack psychiatric cure anymore, regardless that I hadn't acted on those attractions, except in that way that guys do in private with themselves. For me that was early and way too often, and always with distinctly male icons in mind. (Robert Conrad on *The Wild Wild West*, Ken Norton and Perry King naked in *Mandingo*, Mike Henry or almost anybody else as Tarzan. In a scene in the 1980 spoof film *Airplane!*, the pervy pilot asks a young boy visiting the cockpit, "Joey, do you like movies about gladiators?" My answer would have been emphatic: Most definitely!)

Those attractions weren't just impossible to act on. They couldn't even be acknowledged to myself except with shame. I didn't dare check out another guy the way a guy checks out a girl. (Here, oddly enough, birding saved me, because it had led to a highly developed sense of peripheral vision: useful for spotting birds in the field and for scoping a room surreptitiously.) And I couldn't vent verbally in sharing with other guys.

Ironically, high school finally brought me a like-minded group of nerd friends. For this racially mixed bag of guys, conflating *Star Wars* and *Star Trek* was as anathema as it was for me. But as close as we might grow, my certainty that they'd reject me if they knew the truth about me crept silently behind the friendships.

About this same time, I rediscovered superheroes, comics having fallen into neglect somewhere along the way. I stepped into the local 7-Eleven, and the spinning rack by the front door grabbed me by the throat with its riot of colors, dynamic depictions, and bold titles promising strange adventure. "Save us from the Knights of Hellfire!" proclaimed the cover of *The Uncanny X-Men* #129. As a kid I'd read *X-Men*'s tales of persecuted teens gifted with superpowers by a twist of genetic fate, but these were no X-Men I'd ever seen before; and was that a Black woman among them, incongruously with a mane of flowing, platinum-blonde hair, shooting lightning bolts from her hands? I cracked the comic book open to find out, and I was hooked.

Originally conceived rather daringly for the time as a metaphor for the nation's racial and religious bigotry, the X-Men ended up mapping even more closely with the queer experience. The comics' unique setup in the superhero landscape—a group of people born different from everybody else, only discovering their terrible secret in adolescence yet trying to survive in a world that hates them—spoke to me as if I had written it. These were stories I could get behind.

Happily, Mario, Phil, Ulie, and Chris shared that love of comics, along with sci-fi and fantasy. With movies, it went a step further: Chris masterminded his own postapocalyptic sci-fi kung fu epic, to be shot on Super 8 film. Naturally, the rest of us would later be recruited as the on-screen talent.

Along with male friends, high school brought a new route to school and the discovery of a new favorite place to bird. Where the junior high school building was across the street from home—next to a still-working farm that was a relic of Long Island's agrarian past—the trip to the high school meant a twenty-minute walk past the farm and through a woodlot where the town's water tower stood. That twenty minutes would take me more than two hours, once I discovered how the trees came alive during migration.

Those woods absorbed me. I spent an hour searching for the songster when I first heard an increasingly explosive *cher-tea-cher-TEA-CHER-TEA-CHER-TEA!* echoing there. I had to lie on my belly to peer through the underbrush, before I spotted an olive-above, streaked-below bird with a cute-eyed look and an orange stripe on its head; I never forgot the Ovenbird's song after that (nor has it become any easier to find them when they're singing from their deep-woods breeding grounds). I learned other warbler songs that same way, through dogged pursuit in that little patch of woods: the *Wichita-*

wichita-wichita of the little masked bandit, the Common Yellow-throat; and the haunting, dreamy "trees, trees, murmuring trees" of my first Black-Throated Green Warblers. That pair of males led me on a maddening chase before deeming me worthy of a full-on view, golden faces shining above their black bibs. My solitude for these revelations thrilled me; it felt as if the secrets of the woods were unfolding for only me.

Birding Tip

Your skills will progress faster through a combination of birding with others and birding on your own; the synergy of helpful hints and knowledge transmission from your fellow enthusiasts and the indelible impressions from solo discoveries will increase your birding power exponentially.

Similarly I would learn something fascinating while birding solo in my twenties, something that puts a spasm of creativity in my teenage years in perspective. On a hike in the Hudson valley one day in the early summer, I flushed an Indigo Bunting from the shrubs. Sparrow-sized, Indigo Buntings breed throughout the eastern half of the United States, and in this rural area in particular you need only find an open stretch bordering the forest, and a bunting would be there. I got lucky with this one; he perched on a nearby oak branch where I could get a good look at him. This male wasn't one of those molting birds, with the blue plumage shot through with gray; the mid-morning sun showed his true blue throughout, from an almost electric blue on the body to a deeper ocean blue on the head. (Note that for almost all birds, there is no blue pigment in the feathers. The coloration derives solely from the structure of the feathers, which refracts light in such a way as to make the feathers appear blue, which is why, in bad light or on a cloudy day, everything from Blue Jays to bluebirds looks gray.)

The rich coloring wasn't the main thing that drew my attention, however. The bird kept doing something very odd: beating his bill repeatedly against the branch on which it perched. Not straight up and down like a woodpecker's hammering; more of a side-to-side motion. I thought maybe it was trying to get something off its beak, clean it somehow, and then it hit me, bringing me another of the Seven Pleasures of Birding:

Third Pleasure of Birding:
The Joy of Scientific Discovery

The bunting, I realized, must be nesting nearby, a mere foot away, and he flushed because I passed too close to that nest. He was enraged that I was putting his family in peril, but I was way too big for the little bird to mount an assault. So he had to satisfy himself by beating the living crap out of the stick on which he stood, when what he really wanted to do was beat on *me*. I had heard about birds redirecting their aggression, but now I was seeing it in the flesh. This bunting needed an outlet for what it was feeling, and the branch bore the brunt.

In a similar fashion, Dr. Яamus was born.

He was a construct of frustration; that seems fairly obvious in retrospect. High school was winding down, and I was nearing the end of my rope with my stifled existence. Creativity would have to rescue me again, crafting my pain into something tongue in cheek. I didn't realize that was what was happening at the time, of course; to me it was just good fun, albeit of the dark, twisted humor variety. Inspired by the campy, macabre Vincent Price film *The Abominable Dr. Phibes,* I needed my own avatar of retribution, a nefarious being of indeterminate origin, one who taps into an offensive racial trope and the treacly children's rhymes of yesteryear, turns them on their head (hence the backward Я), and sets them loose with mock malicious joy:

See the bunny sit up yon
In the path of walk-a-thon
Bunny will not budge, anon
And therefore he gets stomped upon
March of Dimes saves human lives
But *Lepus* life it soon deprives

Boots and shoes and sneakers tread
Making bunny very dead
Blood and brains leak from his head
Making bunny's fur turn red
See Doc Яamus dance with glee
On rotting corpse of dead bunny

. . . the hallmark of a Яamus poem being the strictly observer status of its muse. Яamus doesn't get his hands dirty. And he's nobody's uncle.

I dashed off lots of Яamus poems in those days, scribbled idly in the corners of notebooks at lunchtime or after class. They amused in a juvenile way, and they expressed with a wink what my subconscious had processed from my own grim experience, to the point that my alter ego had earned a doctorate on the following thesis: No matter who you are, no matter how innocent, sweet, or pure of heart (*especially* if you're innocent, sweet, or pure of heart), the universe has you slated to "live short and suffer" for its own amusement. It's so wrong you can't help but laugh.

So I laughed, on the outside. Inside my heart was breaking. As the end of senior year approached, when I thought I might burst, I finally came out to someone: my friend Deb, in a note passed in computer science class (where we learned the programming language BASIC, which now seems as relevant to the world as trilobites). I'd teased it out over weeks of such notes, unable to just spit it out, by which point Deb had concluded I was either gay or had cancer.

It was a huge step for me, admitting that I didn't have cancer! I needn't have worried about Deb, a trusted ally since junior high and one of the worthiest souls I'll ever know. Plus she's Catholic, and I knew from growing up my whole life among Catholics—including my own grandmother—that while the leadership of that church is dogmatic, the ordinary folks are pragmatic, make up their own minds, and tend toward kindness. There could be no finer example of that than Deb. My confession was safe with her.

She would remain my only friend who would know for the short time we had left in school. Yet even that little crack in the wall, a defensive perimeter I'd carefully maintained for years, allowed enough daylight in that I could see my way to a better life.

Another sign of a better life to come: I'd been accepted to Harvard. I tore open the too-thin envelope nervous that only rejections were so slender and blinked hard when I read the good news. I was thrilled, having set my sights on the university ever since I'd visited as a high school junior; and it didn't hurt that Harvard's early decision meant I didn't have to hustle applying to multiple colleges and fret during the spring waiting for replies. I spent so much time on cloud nine that I don't think I even noticed the reaction from my family. I know my beloved grandmother in particular was prouder than proud, and for both my parents, now split, the sense of achievement for a Black middle-class family must have been tremendous, even if a good outcome for their chronically overachieving son was somewhat expected.

When the advance welcome packet finally followed, I scrutinized the list of the official extracurricular clubs and activities until I found the entries for the Harvard Ornithological Club and, with a secret surge of anticipation, the Gay Students Association. There would be a chance to connect with others like me. There was hope. At Harvard, I was determined, as a gay person I would thrive. And find love.

That summer after high school graduation, Chris began filming his sci-fi kung fu foray into the world of cinema. All of our little gang of nerds was involved. My very minor nonspeaking role (best described as "Radioactive Goon #3") required me to perform a stunt for which I was ill-equipped: dangling from a rickety fire escape outside a condemned building, then dropping eight feet to land behind the leading man (Chris's friend Bob) and whack him with a fake lead pipe. Despite my complete lack of athleticism, I executed it flawlessly. Too bad a car drove by in the background at the very moment of filming. The postapocalypse did not have Hondas. We'd have to do another take.

I looked up at the rusted-out fire escape with foreboding.

For the sake of art, a.k.a. saving face in front of my buddies, I clambered up a second time, and when the fire escape didn't collapse as I feared, I dutifully re-dangled. Bob walked below me—Radioactive Goon #3's cue to drop to the ground and swing the pipe. I could hear the guys prompting me; in a moment it would be too late, and the shot would be ruined. I wasn't ready—my body was still swinging a bit—but I also didn't want to have to do this again. So I let go.

I landed off balance on my heel, toppled backward, and stuck my right arm out to break my fall.

CRACK.

The pain wasn't incomprehensible. But the sight of my forearm in a heretofore unknown Z shape was.

I freaked. Chris, Phil, Mario, and Bob freaked. The cops who stumbled on the scene freaked, though in that regard things only went sideways in a manner that would have seemed comical if I weren't busy convincing myself my arm would have to be amputated. Mistaking bloody postapocalypse makeup for grave injuries, the police rushed to help everyone except the guy sitting on the pavement cradling his arm.

An orthopedist, summoned to the emergency room from his Sunday on the links, would reset the bone with a hearty yank and twist worthy of his golf swing. I would spend the rest of that summer in a cast. The guys were very solicitous and, since I'm right-handed, especially curious about how I managed tension relief with the cast on. Because teenage boys.

"You just switch to the left hand," I said with a shrug, without revealing the nature of the thoughts I held in my head while exploring sinister pleasures. Because closet.

I would have one other encounter with the police not long after that—one that might very well have turned fatal. And once again, it would be in the company of my nerd pals.

Summer was winding down, and though I'd be heading to the Boston area soon enough to start Harvard, the guys and I took a quick trip to Worldcon, a big science-fiction convention that happened to be held in Boston that year. There, among the tables of vendors hawking everything from pirated VHS tapes of *Space: 1999* to back issues of Marvel Comics' *Tales to Astonish*, I found the holy grail: a guy selling sturdy life-sized replicas of medieval swords at a price that was just barely within reach of my teenager's wallet. The Arthurian and Tolkien fan in me swooned, and what would be the first of several swords I'd acquire over the years rode on the bus home with me to New York, perched in the overhead rack since it was too long to fit in my suitcase.

Getting from Manhattan's Port Authority bus terminal to the Long Island Rail Road for the final leg home required that the guys and I take a short subway ride from the Forty-second Street station.

"Hey," Phil said as we waited on the platform for the subway, "if somebody tries to mug us"—it was the bad old days of high crime in the city, or at least close enough that they were a fresh memory—"give me the sword, and I'll fight them off."

"Don't be ridiculous," I said. "*I'll* use the sword to fight them off."

Phil snorted. "You can't do that with that cast on your right arm."

"Oh yeah? Watch this!" And I pulled the sword out of its cloth scabbard with my right arm. I held it aloft like some hero of yore, feeling pretty pleased with myself.

I'd silenced Phil and the rest of my friends, their objections answered with my demonstration of dexterity, cast or no cast. Or maybe it was what they saw behind me that had stilled their tongues.

"DROP IT!"

I turned to find two uniformed cops approaching cautiously, white guys crouched with their hands on their holsters.

I gulped and, very slowly, knelt down to put the sword on the subway platform. For a Goody Two-Shoes like me, finding myself in this position with police was unthinkable; I'd gone from triumphant to publicly humiliated in 1.5 seconds. It didn't take long to sort things out.

"Where're you from, kid?" one of the cops asked.

"Long Island," I answered sheepishly, as if that explained everything, and to a pair of NYPD officers it probably did.

And that was it. I was sure they would confiscate my newly acquired sword before I'd ever had a chance to display it on my wall. But instead, they told me to keep the sword covered in its cloth sheath for the rest of the trip home and sent me on my way, intact and unharmed.

Even then, I recognized what a near miss that might have been, that I'd come close to becoming just another statistic, another young Black man dead at the hands of police. I could see the headlines: "Black Honors Student Shot Dead by White Cops Days Before Starting Harvard." Instead, I would live to see and make headlines forty years later, and in that context my future self would look back to remember this day.

College is supposed to bring new experiences. But to arrive as a Black teenager at Harvard to be greeted by a Confederate flag seemed a bit much.

There it hung, on the wall of the bedroom I was to share with this guy I'd just met named Mike. Chance had brought us together; five of us young men had been randomly assigned to share a dormitory suite, and when I arrived on move-in day, he and I ended up in the same room. He seemed like a nice enough guy—a slightly built Jew from

Minneapolis ("Land of the Frozen Chosen," his T-shirt proclaimed) who to this day retains a hint of the flat vowels of the Midwest, despite having spent a lifetime in the East. In fact, he turned out to be everything you'd expect from a Harvard student and seek in a roommate: friendly, charming, whip smart, considerate.

But that flag.

Who knows where it came from. It's not as if his family had transplanted from the Deep South, or that he harbored any yearning for a white supremacist world order; he's Jewish, for God's sake. But it was the fall of 1980, and the consciousness outside the Black community of what that flag embodies, of the blood of the enslaved and the repression of their descendants woven into its crimson field, hadn't matured yet. Indeed, a hit TV series, *The Dukes of Hazzard*, was pumping that image into millions of American homes during prime time every week, as if it were just an innocent symbol of the South. Look at those rascals Bo and Luke havin' a good ole time, their custom Dodge emblazoned with the sign of their youthful rebel yell! Who could object to that?

So I didn't make waves. Each time I returned to our room and passed that flag on the wall, I kept the scowl and growl on the inside. I lasted about a week.

"Mike," I said at last, "that flag has to come down."

"What? Why?"

"It's offensive to us Black people."

"Oh, come on."

"Mike, what if I hung a Nazi flag on my side of the room?"

I could see the dots connecting for him.

"The flag will be coming down right now." So ended the very brief Battle of Cambridge, Massachusetts, with another abject defeat for the Confederacy.

As it turned out, Mike had another unexpected experience in store for me: the Beatles' *White Album*. I'd thought I was familiar with the Beatles' oeuvre, but as I listened to that double record in his vinyl collection (in 1980, vinyl was all there was), it was all new. One song in particular hit home:

> Blackbird singing in the dead of night
> Take these broken wings and learn to fly

Paul McCartney crooned through chord progressions, nudging his gentle melody forward as if he were nudging me. It wasn't just that the song is ostensibly about a bird, and at the time I didn't understand that the bird in question wasn't my Red-Winged Blackbird, but rather the Eurasian Blackbird, whose midnight serenades I wouldn't experience until many years later, walking back to my crash pad from the bars of Berlin's gay scene. Nor did I know back then that McCartney had written the song as an ode to Black women ("bird" being British slang for a pretty girl) at the pivotal moment of the civil rights struggle. That would only deepen my appreciation for "Blackbird," but not yet.

I cherished the song for its insight. Like every other freshman, I had come to college full of hope, eager to launch a new life. But for me that need was imperative. Because while to all outward appearances I was thriving, I knew I was a broken-winged thing, stuffed inside a dark place where I wouldn't survive much longer.

How I would "arise" I had yet to figure out. Harvard presented a radically different environment from high school, including the sudden independence that comes with being away from home and on one's own for months for the first time. I relished it, but if I thought the change of scene alone would somehow spontaneously free me from my prison, I was wrong. In some ways my situation was more precarious, because now I was living full time with four male peers I didn't know.

The random combination of young men who formed our rooming group freshman year was something of an ethnic and U.S. geographic United Colors of Benetton ad: me, a Black guy from the suburbs of

New York; Mike, a Jewish guy from Minneapolis; Steve T., half Latino, from Los Angeles; Ken, a white-bread Quaker from Colorado;
and Steve P., another white guy, from the Chicago suburbs. Steve P.
was always his own man, but the other four of us, as different as we
were, quickly found how much there was to like about one another.

Steve T. introduced me to the Dead Kennedys, Wall of Voodoo,
and other hard-driving bands of the 1980s L.A. punk and alternative
scene. Ken's use of "thee" and "thy" with his Quaker family members
was startlingly anachronistic and yet somehow congruent with his
gentle disposition. I got everyone hooked on *X-Men* comics—easy to
do in the era of the Dark Phoenix saga and Days of Future Past, now
iconic story lines from the Chris Claremont/John Byrne creative
team—and like any good pusher I used that as a gateway drug to the
hard stuff. Our dorm suite was home to everything from Keiji Naka-
zawa's grueling *I Saw It: The Atomic Bombing of Hiroshima, a Survivor's
True Story* to the U.K.'s *Warrior* anthology, serializing the strange yet
compelling *V for Vendetta* from a then little-known comics writer
named Alan Moore, who would become the god of comics writers
with *Watchmen*. (The unexpected resolution of *V for Vendetta*'s gay
subplot, a rare thing for comics in those days, left me in tears, the only
comic ever to do so; I will not spoil it here.) It reached the point that
my roomies were almost as eager for Fridays as I was; that was the day
each week when the new releases arrived at the Million Year Picnic.
That warren of wooden bookshelves crammed with wonders remains
Harvard Square's premier comic-book emporium.

Despite Mike's laments about my alleged snoring—to this day I
maintain that his purported audio recording was a deep fake—he and
I became fast friends. The Confederate flag was long gone. (Decades
later, I learned from Mike its origin: An acquaintance gave it to him at
summer debate camp, and Mike thought it a cool memento.) Instead,
our bedroom's decorations included a poster of Edward Gorey's *Gashly-
crumb Tinies,* a primly illustrated *A* to *Z* of untimely demises among
the grade-school set. (My favorite: "N is for Neville who died of

ennui.") It dovetailed perfectly with my Яamusian sense of humor; Mike's own humor tended toward the well-placed casual remark. Mike was diligent about his classwork; I was an inveterate procrastinator, grudgingly plunking myself in front of my cheap, manual Royal typewriter to start work at midnight the night before the paper was due. Yet for all those differences, the Black kid from Long Island and the Jewish kid from Minneapolis had common bonds, a shared history of feeling socially marginalized, of being too smart for our own good. Only recently I learned from Mike's brother that when he wrote home about his first weeks of college, he said that in me he had "found someone exactly like" himself.

Well, maybe not *exactly* like him.

From the outset of my arrival on campus, as planned, I'd secretly been attending Gay Students Association meetings. I must have looked like a scared rabbit in that room, tentative about the other people in it and nervous that anyone outside it would find me out. I can't recall a single thing that happened there, only feeling exhilarated and terrified, yet not so terrified that it could stop me from going back, week after week. I would splash on a dash of aftershave before attending, as if a vaguely floral scent might lure in love like a butterfly; I lacked any understanding of the mechanisms of attraction beyond what one might glean from a Calvin Klein commercial. Half the room remained as skittish as I was, and I can't say I made more than one or two meaningful connections there, none of them romantic.

What mattered was that there was a room where the mask could be removed. That was something I'd never had before, and at that moment it was everything.

But not outside that room. In the middle of our first semester, I traipsed into the sprawling freshman dining hall with my roommates— by then we were a posse, enjoying each other's company so much we took most meals together—to find the Gay Students Association there too. I'd forgotten that this outreach was coming: A sign for the organization had been placed on one of the dining tables, and members had colonized it as a visibility effort. After weeks of meetings, everyone there knew me, and I them; it was pure cowardice to not sit there, to walk by them without so much as a friendly acknowledgment. Stronger than the sense of guilt that I was betraying them, though, was the sheer terror I'd be outed.

My Vulcan emotional control kicked in, and I marched past them without the slightest variance of step nor the merest nervous glance in their direction, and they didn't call me out. They knew I had been taking my first tentative steps out of the closet, and they had been there once themselves. As my roommates and I found seats at a different table from the gay one, just as I began to unclench and believe I was maybe going to survive this, Mike dropped one of his well-placed remarks.

"Chris," he said, fixing me with his gaze, "I'm really glad you didn't sit there!" He chuckled at the absurdity of the notion.

"Me too," I said with a matching chuckle through a grin I kept smeared on my face; I had had years of practice. If I was less than fine, if my insides at that very moment were in fact crumbling, it didn't show. Not even in the straining corners of my smiling eyes.

The grass was never greener in the cemetery in which I was buried alive. I'd meant to escape that place in college, had even seen shafts of daylight in those gay meetings, yet that moment made clear that with everyone I cared about and who cared about me, I was still right back in that same place I had been for an eternity. Mike had unknowingly spread a picnic blanket over the green, green grass of my grave and was having a nice lunch, and couldn't hear me scream from deep down below.

Right about then, as Halloween approached, I sat down at my clunky Royal and, by the time I stood up again, had composed the ultimate of Яamus poems. Consider it a giant eye roll in the direction of the slasher movie craze, which was peaking in that era: *Friday the*

13th, Prom Night, Motel Hell, Terror Train, and so on. ("The boys and girls of Sigma Phi. Some will live. Some will DIE.") It poured out of me as fast as this then-non-typist's two fingers could fly:

> You've seen it all in your good time
> From wanton sex to rampant crime
> Now come see the thing
> That will make you sing
> With joy and happiness sublime
>
> Yes, you knew them all in school
> The blonde, the jock, the brain, the fool
> The faithless love who made you cry
> But now—we're gonna watch them die.

The poem went on in hyperbolic detail as to how each of those young-sters met their end.

NOTE: This was well before our present era of school shootings; writing something like this today would likely get one expelled from any campus and certainly lead to mandatory counseling sessions with a licensed mental-health professional. To be clear, I harbored no actual murderous intent, which should be obvious since I included myself (the "brain," who gets plowed under a speeding car as he tries to cap-ture a mockingbird) among the roster of the doomed. Back then, I wouldn't even swat mosquitoes, only shoo them off my skin, because killing them would be wrong. The rhyme, like all the Яamus poems, was meant solely to amuse myself and others who enjoy taking the trite and making it twisted.

Like the outcome of a Яamus poem, but without the wink-nudge, things started to look bleak. Winter in Cambridge is a cold, dreary affair, and as it set in, I faltered. The term "seasonal affective disorder" (with the apt acronym SAD) hadn't been coined yet, but that didn't stop me from having it and knowing what it was I had, even if I didn't have a name for it. I hated winter in my native New York, and here it lasted appreciably longer on both ends. Worse, I slipped into that low-grade funk just as final exams for the first semester loomed, adding to the pressure.

Academically, despite my chronic procrastination, I was doing fine, but one doesn't know that with certainty before finals. Birding, my great comfort, was paused; I found midwinter outings unproductive, particularly for the songbirds I favor, and always unbearably uncomfortable, because I have little tolerance for the cold. And Harvard Ornithological Club trips were reserved for birdier times of year. Other extracurriculars, from parliamentary debate to announcing the news on WHRB radio, proved to be insufficient distraction.

The final straw was the housing deadline for the next academic year. Applications for where we students wanted to live as sophomores, and with whom, would be due soon; the five of us roommates were keen to stay together and were discussing which of the upperclassman houses were our top picks. And with that, I realized I couldn't go on this way. To keep this essential part of who I was sequestered away from these guys I loved and lived with day and night, and keep that going for another year, would break me.

I don't know where the courage came from; in 1981 homosexuality had barely moved from the "Unspeakable" column to the category of "Icky Things No One Really Has to Deal With." I was only seventeen and not at all wise. I had never had any sexual experiences with anyone, never even kissed a guy. But despite all that, in the course of a single winter's night I took each of my roommates aside individually and came out as gay.

Mike was last. At first he took the news as just another of our pranks on each other, and laughed.

I didn't.

He paused and regarded me. "Seriously?"

"Yeah." I felt as if I were teetering on a high wire.

He paused again and processed for a minute. Not connecting the dots this time so much as considering my unspoken question: Does this mean you won't have anything to do with me?

He shrugged. "It's cool."

No battle this time. Just the simple reassurance that my friend was still with me.

Indeed, Mike was mildly offended that I'd told him last. I parried that he could hardly be surprised, given that we shared a bedroom and what he'd said that day in the dining hall, at which he winced and apologized. (He's still wincing about it today.) Questions from all of them would follow, questions anybody would ask. The inevitable "how can you be so sure, when you haven't slept with anybody yet?" was probably the most pointed, to which any gay person can answer: the same way you knew, even when you were still a virgin, that you were straight.

So in our bumbling way, five teenagers from different backgrounds and from all across the country made room at our table for one more kind of diversity. Literally so: The next time the Gay Students Association staked out a table in the freshman dining hall, I took my place with them, and Mike led my four roommates in joining me there in a show of support. Mike and Steve T. would even back me up by accompanying me to my first gay bar, a seedy Boston dive called Sporters, where Mike would get hit on but gracefully deflect. We five remained roommates throughout our college days. And after that night I came out to my roomies, I never wrote another Яamus poem.

With graduation only a month away, I had one final mission I was determined to complete before Harvard kicked us out the door. It required retracing my steps from my inaugural Massachusetts birding outing, almost four years earlier when I'd first arrived on campus freshman year.

I'd been told that when I got to Cambridge, the place to bird was Mount Auburn Cemetery—something many non-birders find puzzling. The fact is, cemeteries often prove to be excellent birding spots, because of all the uninterrupted greenery. Spread over about 175 landscaped acres, Mount Auburn unfolds in rolling hills, shimmering pools, and lush plantings of trees and shrubs that form a fitting final resting place for Boston's elite—and a perfect migratory resting place for millions of birds. So alongside the classical columns commemorating Mary Baker Eddy, mother of the Christian Science religious movement, one might find one's first Bay-Breasted Warbler, a bird of the same browns as a commonplace House Sparrow yet that seems to pull together those hues with far greater elegance. The chance to find such striking travelers amid the tranquility of its grounds puts Mount Auburn on every Boston-area birder's map. Back then a lucky few of us even had keys to the front gate so that we could start birding right at dawn, before the cemetery officially opened. I'd spent many a late spring morning over the last four years combing Mount Auburn for interesting finds while simultaneously improving my warbler skills and reveling in the fact that New England had finally thawed.

But my first attempt at birding Mount Auburn turned into a disaster. I'd been in the college's computer lab the night before (the first primitive personal computers were still two or three years away from students' desks); fooling around on their system to familiarize myself with it seemed like a good way to cap off my first week of school. But my newfound freedom got the better of me; without Mom around to pull the plug at an ungodly hour, I'd ended up playing games all night. Being young and invincible, I decided that lack of sleep was no impediment: Since I was awake so early, I may as well go birding. I picked right then to finally check out Mount Auburn Cemetery.

From Harvard Square I headed up Mount Auburn Street as I'd been instructed, as the wind picked up and the dawn, obscured by brooding clouds, never really came. Though it was September, the day was blustery and cold, more like November, and I had underdressed. Bleary-eyed, barely conscious, and chilled to the bone, I trudged on. The walk seemed endless.

Just as I was about to turn back, I arrived at what seemed to be my destination, headstones and all, if somewhat less impressive than I'd been led to believe. Only after would I find out that this was Cambridge Cemetery, a public burial place immediately adjacent to vaunted Mount Auburn, and not nearly its horticultural equal. Where Mount Auburn is an Eden, Cambridge Cemetery is Everytown, U.S.A. That the divisions of class persist even after death is a fact as old as the pyramids; that the fact is old makes it no less irritating.

But at that moment I didn't know I was in the wrong cemetery, so I tried to bird in the gloom. Between the threatening storm, the less productive habitat, and my own compromised mental competence, I saw very few birds: some Cedar Waxwings keening in soft, high voices, a Tufted Titmouse as gray as the morning, and not much else.

Except that thing at the top of the hill.

From a distance it looked like the silhouette of a chair. It stood alone, framed by a roiling sky that any second now would crack open spitting electric fire. I couldn't figure out what a sturdy chair like that would be doing in the middle of a cemetery, though my sleepless body longed to sit in one. It seemed to beckon. Intrigued, I got closer to inspect it.

I blinked and shuddered, now close enough that even the dark skies couldn't disguise it: not a chair, exactly; a tombstone shaped like a chair. With the name "C COOPER" carved on it. And no dates.

I nearly ran all the way back to my dorm room.

That *Twilight Zone* moment had haunted me for four years, and in my subsequent visits to the actual Mount Auburn Cemetery, I'd avoided the public cemetery next to it as if my life depended on it. I'd come to almost believe the experience had been a hallucination brought on by sleep deprivation. How could anything like that be real?

But here I was, four years later having returned to the scene, staring at that tombstone. It was real, all right, if perhaps less dramatically situated than I remembered. Now in spring, in full daylight, it carried less power.

It would not get me. I was done with that grave. I stepped apart from it, turned my back, and walked away for good; I was never going back there. I was still a broken blackbird with a lot of healing to do, but the mending had begun. Commencement was coming, and a whole life afterward, and with that ahead I left the cemetery and hit the street for home.

4

Halcyon Days

GRACKLES ARE AMERICAN blackbirds that are hard to love. For one thing, they can be ubiquitous, a quality that is the opposite of what most birders prize; the rarer the find, the better the bird. They can be noisy, making harsh, strident sounds that wouldn't be out of place in a horror movie. They can be mean (by human standards), as if plucked from just such a movie: Grackles will sometimes kill and eat other songbirds, and they're known to dine on eggs and young snatched from other birds' nests. And their all-dark plumages and pale eyes can give them a cold, heartless appearance (again by human standards). Even the name "grackle" sounds ugly to English-speaking ears, fusing hard consonants in rough combinations more suggestive of construction surfacing compound, or clearing one's throat, than a bird.

Leave it to the innocence of youth to dispel all that human baggage.

On a walk through Central Park's North Woods leading fourth graders who were new to birding, I wasn't having much luck. At this point I was well into middle age and had been volunteer teaching about birds in my free time in the New York City public schools for many years; it was my way of giving back a bit of what Elliott had given me, and besides, it kept me young. Since it was spring migration, I'd hoped to knock the students' socks off with some spectacular transients: a male Scarlet Tanager, perhaps, whose incandescence would sear into the youngsters' memories; or an obliging American Redstart that in my mind's eye would flit nearly within arm's reach, fanning its tail to show off its color to the kids. After half an hour in the woods, however, it was clear that none of these fabulous sightings would come to pass. Whether because of the wrong winds or bad luck, it just wasn't that kind of day; we hadn't even seen a cardinal, a safe bet as one of the more plentiful resident species and a surefire crowd-pleaser. But not today.

The quiet desperation of an empty-handed bird walk leader began to set in. One can vamp for only so long—talk about the plants, tidbits of park history, interesting bird facts—in the face of the attention span of ten-year-olds.

"What's that bird?" Darwin asked, his face too wide open and innocent for a city kid. Even though, as was the case for many of the students, his family came from elsewhere (Ecuador), he was a New Yorker through and through, which made his unjaded, rapt attention to what he'd spotted all the more interesting.

I looked where he was pointing.

"Oh, that's a Common Grackle." I nearly expectorated the name, as if to underscore just how common it was.

"It's *beautiful*," he said with a reverent hush. He and the others were riveted.

Really?

Baffled, for the first time in many years I took the time to actually look at a grackle, really look at it: dark plumage throughout, yes, but with an iridescence to its feathers that gives its surfaces an ever-shifting rainbow sheen; those fierce yellow eyes; and a gloriously oversized tail with a pronounced crease down its length to give it a distinct V shape.

I was seeing the bird with new eyes instead of grackle-jaundiced ones, from the fresh viewpoint of kids for whom almost every bird was new.

And they were right. That blackbird is stunning.

Just as another blackbird had discovered in his own youth, many years before: To recognize something as beautiful, sometimes all it takes is a change of perspective.

I'd been in Buenos Aires for less than eight hours, but I knew what these two guys were up to.

Having secured a cheap room in a cheap *pensión* that catered to nearly broke Argentines trying their luck in the capital, I was prowling its graceful streets to get a sense of "the Paris of South America." I'd arrived that day with no plan, except to plant myself in the heart of Buenos Aires; the Hotel Maipu's rock-bottom price yet central location made that hovel the perfect home for a few weeks. Fresh out of college and all of twenty-one years old, I'd undertaken this journey through Latin America with a loose itinerary and even looser agenda propelled by fabulist literary visions because, like so many other recent grads, I had no idea what to do with my life after college graduation and I didn't have a clue what was next for me.

I'd decided way back in high school that I didn't want to turn my hobby into a vocation, to avoid the risk of leeching the joy out of birding. (And also to avoid the risk of being perennially broke.) And despite years as a successful debater in both high school and college— usually a good indicator that a career as a lawyer lies ahead—I'd quickly concluded in my freshman year that the practice of law was not for me. I had the good sense to recognize that my notion of lawyers as modern-day knights, rhetorically jousting in their championing of justice, was, well, perhaps more than a bit romanticized. And at the start of the 1980s, to my mind there was an insurmountable societal barrier to me being a lawyer: As a Black man I might (might!) have a decent shot at advancing in my career, but as someone who's Black and openly queer? Somehow I didn't see that going over well with the white-shoe set.

Rather than face my own monumental indecision about my future, I ducked the issue by hitting the road.

Among Harvard's many endowments are traveling fellowships, grants of money competitively awarded to graduating seniors so that they can spend time abroad exploring an issue or subject that has captured their imagination. Although I was a political science major (I'd stuck with the standard "pre-law" undergraduate path out of inertia, interest in politics, and the lack of a more compelling option), what had captivated me was a literary movement out of Latin America: magical realism. I'd been exposed to it in a single class junior year, but the likes of Jorge Luis Borges, Juan Rulfo, and Gabriel García Márquez had nonetheless seized me by the throat and wouldn't let go. And no wonder; for someone like myself steeped in fantastical storytelling, here was a tradition where fantasy and realism were yoked together to better plow into the truth. I wanted to experience the places and cultures that had spawned such fervent contradictions of expression. To my surprise, Harvard agreed.

So having never traveled farther than Mexico City on a brief family vacation, I headed overseas on my own for the very first time, on a months-long journey beginning in Mexico, stopping briefly in Venezuela before leaping to Argentina, then up through Brazil, over to Bolivia, and briefly into eastern Peru. The epic tragedy of the trip: In countries with some of the richest avifauna on the planet, I probably did the least birding I would ever do in my lifetime.

Chalk it up to budget—I was traveling on a shoestring, and remote birding hot spots can be tough to access affordably—but even more important, to lack of information. In 1984, there was no internet to put everything you need to know about birding a particular area at your fingertips, no eBird (the web-based birding records aggregator that today one can consult to find good locales), and no field guide apps to instantly download onto smartphones that not even *Star Trek* had dreamed up yet. The only Amazon was the real one (more of the rain forest was intact back then; I did not get there, sadly), so there could be no ordering of a hard-copy field guide for next-day delivery. In fact, field guides for much of the region did not yet exist, or if they did, they were tough to come by in a local bookstore. I was largely flying blind, in more ways than one.

Birding Tip

When traveling anywhere, do a little relevant birding research beforehand. You may find that a slight tweak to your itinerary lands you in a hot spot that will yield a bonanza of birds. Use a good field guide to the region to familiarize yourself in advance with some of the species you might see; even a little bit of such prep will make you much more effective in the field. Hire a qualified local guide if you can afford it, or enjoy the extra thrill of finding things on your own, but above all, with every trip, *don't forget to pack your binoculars!*

So on that first night in Buenos Aires, instead of retiring early so that I could bird at the crack of dawn, I found myself alone on the late-night empty streets of a city I didn't know, far from home, where even the stars overhead were unfamiliar. But I recognized the two guys following me right away.

For one thing, their attire spoke volumes. The austral summer breeze doesn't cool things off much, but even so, no machismo-minded Latino (except perhaps in Rio) would venture out on the town in short shorts and a tank top, no matter how hot it got.

And subtlety was not their forte. Admittedly, I could be oblivious to sexual advances, especially in those early days. But when two guys repeatedly sprint ahead of you and then pause to pretend to notice something in a shopwindow—all the while giving you sidelong glances to make sure that you're noticing *them*—even I eventually get the message. I cut through the coyness and said hello.

What followed was not a sexcapade, but rather a friendly conversation that constituted a rapid download about all things gay in Buenos Aires. For the first time, but not the last, I experienced how queerness can be a passport of its own; forging a common bond between strangers and across cultures, a gay identity gave me rapid access to a segment of the local population, an entrée into a society that otherwise might remain closed to the random foreigner. In an era of much less acceptance and no tell-all gay tourist blogs, I had offered the secret handshake to fellow members of the tribe, and I was in.

Twenty-four hours later I'd gone from knowing nothing and no one to meeting people and dancing until dawn in the hip gay club Contramano. Argentines were like kids in a candy store; after years of military dictatorship and thousands of dissidents made to "disappear," real democracy had just returned to the country when I'd arrived, and the joy of liberation was almost palpable in the air—particularly among previously repressed groups like the LGBTQ community. New friends were giving me an insider's view of Argentine life, its constant setbacks and disappointments, but also this heady new sense of freedom. They were also giving me a lot of attention.

I was greatly confused by this last part. And yet the evidence kept mounting: the aerobic maneuvers of the two guys that first night, the frequent propositions I received in Contramano; even random folks would sometimes stop in the middle of a busy street and stare as I went by, as if they'd just seen a superstar. At twenty-one I was a decent-looking kid, but I wasn't all that.

After a week of this, I was back in Contramano when I encountered Randall, the first Black person I'd seen in Buenos Aires without looking in a mirror. (*Porteños,* as the residents of Buenos Aires are known, are overwhelmingly white. Unlike in nearby Bolivia or Peru, European settlers swamped Argentina's indigenous peoples demographically and culturally, and the relatively small Black population, descended from slaves, was wiped out by a yellow fever epidemic in the nineteenth century; the rich white residents of Buenos Aires moved to safer ground, while the Black folk were left in the plague-ridden core of the city, a process that would be repeated more than a century later in U.S. cities during the COVID epidemic. As a result, today's Argentines have an ancestry that is some mix of mostly Italian and Spanish, with the occasional Welsh and a smattering of escaped Nazi.)

Randall was a pro basketball player from the United States who made it into a second-tier, overseas league whose off-season coincided with the Southern Hemisphere's summer. He'd chosen to spend his free months in Buenos Aires with his gorgeous girlfriend, and as any porteño with an ounce of cool could tell you back then, a new gay club like Contramano was the place to be, gay or straight. That's exactly where Randall and his girlfriend were, ensconced on a sofa in the corner. One look at each other, and Randall and I knew we had to talk.

"Just don't lose your head down here," he warned me. "You'll find you'll have a lot of opportunities, with both men and women."

"I'm starting to catch on. I was beginning to think I should hang some No-Pest Strips to keep so many from bugging me."

"Yup. They can't get enough of Black people."

There it was. In Buenos Aires, I had found myself in a city full of white folks who desired me *because* of my Blackness, not in spite of it. The difficulty I had wrapping my head around that notion revealed to me just what growing up in the States had done to me. I'd spent my whole life being told that as a Black person I was not quite as worthy as a white person, and on an unconscious level I had internalized that proposition.

Certainly that message didn't come from my parents. For all their difficulties with each other and their radically different parenting styles, they both were clear to me and my sister that being Black is something to be proud of. They made sure we knew Black history and that they expected excellence from us in academics and whatever else we chose to devote ourselves to. I never felt inferior to the white classmates who surrounded me in honors classes.

But American society in the formative era of my childhood—the late 1960s and the 1970s—was sending out a different message. Yes, this was the era of Black Power and Black Is Beautiful, but there's a reason those messages had to be deliberately cultivated, as if the slogans were needed to sell something new to the public. The dominant culture of the United States then and even now makes it clear that whiteness is the norm to which to aspire, and Blackness is that other thing that, well, if you had to be stuck with it, good for you!

In those days we didn't have characters like Kerry Washington's Olivia Pope on the TV series *Scandal,* or the protagonist of the spy movie *Tenet*—Black people in the lead role and at the heart of a story that wasn't specifically deemed Black. In sitcoms like *Good Times* and *The Jeffersons,* prestigious TV events like *The Autobiography of Miss Jane Pittman* and *Roots,* and cinema from *Sounder* to *Foxy Brown,* African Americans shone in stories that focused on the Black experience; we held the spotlight on that separate stage. Otherwise, Negro Sidekick Syndrome prevailed—we were the sassy neighbor, the cop's buddy partner, the helpful best friend—making it clear that as Black people we were fit to be supporting players on the main stage, but never the lead. This only confirmed what was obvious at the time from the complexions of the procession of U.S. presidents, the people to whom monuments were raised, who got holidays in their name and their faces on the currency. Smiling at me from every magazine rack, the Beautiful People, the objects of desire, were almost always white. Message received.

Far from being beyond such bias, my beloved nerd culture was a principal disseminator. Over at Marvel Comics, nothing screamed

Negro Sidekick Syndrome louder than the title of the series *CAPTAIN AMERICA and the Falcon.* I despised Falcon, a character that should have been tailor-made for me—Black, bird themed—for his tokenism and epic auxiliary uselessness. The ranks of the group Captain America led—"the world's mightiest heroes," the Avengers—looked like a meeting of an Aryan brotherhood: blond-haired, blue-eyed Steve Rogers (Cap); blond-haired, blue-eyed Thor; blond-haired, blue-eyed Hank Pym (Ant-Man); blond-haired, blue-eyed Clint Barton (Hawkeye); platinum-blond-haired, blue-eyed Pietro Maximoff (Quicksilver); and Tony Stark (Iron Man), poor guy. He was only white.

The *Uncanny X-Men,* phenomenally popular since its 1970s reboot, boasted a multinational cast of superheroes, including my favorite character in all of comics, Storm. One of the most powerful mutants alive, this African woman can hurl lightning bolts, summon hurricanes, and otherwise shape the weather to her will; she remains a pillar of the team and a champion of the forces for good. Her birth name, Ororo, means "beauty" in the fictional African language that's her native tongue. And no wonder: Along with the dark skin of a Black woman, she has straight platinum-blonde hair and blue eyes, the consequence of her mutation, or more accurately, the bias of the character's creators that a Black woman can only be beautiful when she has these white attributes. (To see that millions of Black women have internalized this particular pathology, one need look no further than their tresses, chemically "relaxed" to make the hair as straight as possible. The phrase "good hair," for that of a Black woman with enough European ancestors that her hair is textured similar to theirs, says it all.)

And then there's the original *Star Trek,* the TV show that held pride of place in my childhood home for its progressive vision of a utopian future for humanity where racial bias is a thing of the past. The show that featured a Black woman, Nichelle Nichols's Lieutenant Uhura, as a bridge officer and littered its guest stars and incidental characters with Black actors, in roles from a Starfleet head honcho to the galaxy's preeminent computer engineer. The show with the first interracial kiss on U.S. television.

Yet in all the travels of the starship *Enterprise*, virtually all the human-like aliens encountered are white. As if the entire galaxy were populated by folks who hailed from a stretch of land adjacent to the Caucasus Mountains.

Even a show as enlightened as *Star Trek* couldn't escape a faulty underlying assumption (gradually eroding but still holding sway today): that whiteness is the default setting. What's equally surprising is that it took decades for me, a reasonably intelligent, well-educated, racially aware Black person, to notice the alien whitewashing. That's how pervasive the bias is.

But maybe it's not surprising, considering how this implicit message bombards all of us in the United States from birth. One of the skills that makes a good birder—perhaps the most important skill—is pattern recognition. When you're at a certain level, it's not even conscious: You hear a snippet of sound or catch a glimpse of color or behavior, and your subconscious mind has already reached certain conclusions about what the bird might be, based on past experience. We birders call it "jizz"—the overall impression of a bird—and with enough years birding you pick up on it without even thinking. The great tragedy for me: That very skill, so valuable to me in birding, also had the awful consequence of helping me assimilate the rotten, racist undercurrents of American culture. I didn't consciously agree with them, but my subconscious recognized the pattern and without meaning to made them a part of my thinking.

Suddenly in Buenos Aires, all those assumptions were laid bare and turned upside down, as if inverted by the switch to the Southern Hemisphere. It was disorienting and exhilarating, and though this new status involved more than a little fetishizing of my Blackness, if Randall could kick back and enjoy it, I saw no reason why I shouldn't too. Being Flavor of the Month was a damn sight better than being

Uncle Sam's unwanted stepchild. Now Cinderella was belle of the ball, about to meet Prince Charming.

Handsome, hard-bodied, and haughty, Alejandro breezed through Contramano each weekend, greeting everyone who should be known, but had kept his hazel eyes on me through the smoke from his cigarette for at least the last two Saturdays. Finally we met on the dance floor; I'd become a regular at Contramano, and you couldn't keep me off it when the music was right.

"¿De donde sos?" he asked when he'd circled close enough to be heard over the music, meaning we ended up provocatively near to each other.

"Los Estados Unidos. Nueva York," I said, fudging the answer to where I was from; claiming the city, even though I had yet to live there, was simpler than explaining Long Island.

"Nobody says 'Nueva York,'" he said with a grin, flirting with that light jab as I shrugged and smiled too. "Welcome to Buenos Aires."

It was immediately clear that he was distinguished: an older man (thirty!), impeccable English, a hint of Argentine upper-class arrogance. At twenty-one, I had never had anyone like that pay so much attention to me. I was smitten.

So what was originally intended to be about three weeks in Buenos Aires turned into almost three months. We spent as much time together as his featureless, placeholder job as an investment banker would allow, with Alejandro picking up the tab at a chic restaurant or for a show in a supper club, since he was flush and I was traveling on a shoestring. Just as often we would simply stroll the city's broad boulevards or hidden plazas, or sit and talk in the park beside a sprawling *gomero* tree, ending up at his crash pad or not. He needled me regularly, as with his "Nueva York" comment; the ribbing fazed me not at all, since it couldn't disguise how he couldn't get enough of me. That was a feeling I'd never had before; it was intoxicating, and it was mutual.

I had no illusions, and neither did Alejandro. There was an expiration date on our affair, even if I deferred that date as long as possible; I would be leaving Buenos Aires and eventually returning to the States to start my life. And it was definitely an affair: For all his own wealth and family breeding, Alejandro was a "kept man," the life partner of a much older and even wealthier Argentine aristocrat who financed a lavish lifestyle. They had their arrangement; Alejandro had his own vast apartment overlooking train yards, where he could bring his paramours, preferably a steady flame rather than a succession of one-night stands. It was, after all, the mid-1980s.

"I'm terrified of getting AIDS," Alejandro would confide to me many times, between draws on an omnipresent cigarette; whether to dissuade me from trysting outside our relationship or simply to voice the angst of every gay man of the era, or both, I couldn't say. He could be impossible—arrogant, manipulative, demanding of my time when he himself was not a free man. (Admittedly, I had a lot of time to give; I didn't have anything on my plate, besides chipping away at my own quasi-fantastical epic and exploring the city of Jorge Luis Borges. At the time I'd never been to the Old World, so the city's European-style grace had me completely charmed.)

But much of Alejandro's hauteur was a facade, a defense mechanism to push aside the precariousness of his life. He was a gay man of a class and a culture that would still crush a man for that, and for all the comforts and freedoms afforded him, he wasn't master of his own destiny. He was like Argentina: caught between worlds, not belonging to the first world of the West to which it aspired, and yet disdaining its striving Latin American neighbors. I don't think he realized how he wore his vulnerabilities on his sleeve, at least to the eyes of this outsider. It made me tender toward him, even when he was being impossible. So as the trains pulled in and out of the yard outside his apartment, we'd lie arm in arm, together for this little while. I'd reassure him with a kiss, even if he did taste like an ashtray.

I said goodbye to Alejandro near the end of the austral summer of 1985. I'd see him about a year later, when he would visit New York for a week; of course, Alejandro being Alejandro, it involved hob-nobbing with the likes of Bianca Jagger and Richard Gere through some peripheral connection he had, and I can't say I complained as he dragged me along. After that we lost touch.

In the subsequent years my experiences on that first Latin Ameri-can sojourn would gestate and spawn a work of original mythology called *Songs of the Metamythos*. At the bottom of a file cabinet some-where I still have a scrap of paper torn from a pad in a Mexico City hotel, at the beginning of the trip, on which I scribbled the first kernel of an idea of what a new mythology that lives and breathes with the contours of today's world might look like. It's nothing more than a few connected symbols, inspired by the deep cultural roots of the place around me. It would take crossing the Bolivian Andes over four days on the back of a truck and the unorthodox perspective of looking down on the clouds to grasp the scope of the story I wanted to write; I'd have to watch waves of swallows blacken a tree on the edge of a Brazilian swamp for the evening's roost to glimpse life's magnitude that I wanted to capture. And I'd have to find myself anew reflected in a pair of hazel eyes in a foreign city, before I could put the proper pas-sion to the page. What is myth, if not these things on the grandest scale?

I'd return to Buenos Aires three more times, on trips for birding and pleasure and to revisit the city that had been my awakening. I'd come armed with the proper field guide, discover the city's Costanera Sur Ecological Reserve, and find bulbous-billed Coscoroba swans, alien-looking and alien-sounding Southern Screamers (not to be con-fused with a vocal Alabamian in the throes of excitement), and a plethora of stunning ducks; but I would not find Alejandro. Each time, I tried to track him down while I was there. I had no success the first two times, and on the third visit I learned through a chance encounter with a gay American who moved in Argentina's rarefied circles that Alejandro had died, not of AIDS, as he once feared, but of lung cancer. By that time I knew, from my own family, what kind of death that meant. I was glad I hadn't been there to witness it take Alejandro. He remains unchanged, the hazel-eyed man dancing all night with me in a city as giddy on possibility as we were.

5

In a Happy Place

IT STARTS IN Ecuador, or Costa Rica, or the Bahamas, with a slight lengthening of the days and a jolt of hormones. Gradually, small feathered things that have been content for months to feast on bugs in the forests of the American tropics find they can't hold still anymore. They're restless in their bones, and like *Star Trek*'s Mr. Spock in the episode "Amok Time," they are driven by forces they cannot control to return home and take a mate, or die trying. So one night, when the winds are right, they abandon the contentment of tropical forests and launch themselves skyward to undertake a perilous journey of thousands of miles. And whether they leave from Ecuador, Costa Rica, or the Bahamas, those winds may eventually carry some of them up the Eastern Seaboard of North America and over the bright lights of a big city, where smack in its middle a rectangle of green will beckon with the promise of water, cover, and food—an oasis in a sea of concrete, offering the chance to rest and refuel. They will pour through Central Park by the millions, unaware and uncaring that eager human eyes and ears await them there.

It starts sometime in February, a restlessness in the sleep of certain enthusiasts who have endured most of winter and long for what they know comes next. In a dream a bird, of real or imagined species, alights in the subconscious of the dreamer; they may pursue the bird, perhaps alongside the familiar faces of the equally obsessed, or the bird may do something dramatic, but always the bird is central to the dream. They awake with a fading memory of an avian encounter and a fresh, exhilarating certainty: The migrants will be here soon.

I pop awake at 4:20 a.m., which spares me the alarm, set to go off in the next ten minutes. Just as well; it means my body is adjusting to its new schedule, and I have a bit of an extra safety margin. No grogginess, no need for coffee—I never drank it in the first place, and the urgency to get out the door is jolt enough. It's May 1989. I checked the forecast right before bed, and a quick consultation with the all-news radio station confirms the current conditions: winds from the southwest. In theory, ideal conditions for pushing spring migrants traveling along the Atlantic flyway up and along the edge of the coast and right into our waiting arms. I have to move fast.

Everything is prepped: Last night, right before bedtime—an insanely early 9:00 p.m., which despite my best efforts turned into 10:30—I'd showered, laid out tomorrow's clothes based on the predicted weather, and concocted a protein shake to stick in the fridge for the morning. Under normal circumstances, the shake would be reserved for right after the gym; in a classic bit of gay overcompensation, I've developed a compulsion for weight-training workouts, and the shake consumed at the right time would maximize my gains. But for the peak weeks of spring migration, the gym has been sacrificed to a greater obsession, and the right time is now: I guzzle the shake before I rush out, chasing it down with half of a day-old bagel eaten on the run.

Cuisine isn't the point. Not when missing the subway, whose schedule I've so carefully timed, could mean a crucial half hour lost waiting underground instead of in the park!

The air is crisp, the sky still dark, and the Manhattan streets in a rare moment of near desertion as I take to the pavement at a brisk pace. I conduct a mental inventory along the way: keys, check; binoculars, check; food for later (a protein bar and the other half of the bagel; I don't bird on an empty stomach), check. I've forgotten any one of the three in the past, particularly as I get deeper into the season and my long-term sleep deprivation sabotages my brain's reliability. It's not pretty.

Neither am I. Personal neglect has taken its toll: my hair getting shaggy, face unshaven for several days, build eroding from lack of routine exercise maintenance. The dark circles under my eyes are somewhat less noticeable on Black skin, mercifully. My clothes consist of what little is left after a month without doing laundry, because who has the time this time of year? So I'm dressed in old rags and worn, muddy sneakers—whatever ensemble requires the least thought, provides freedom of movement for raising one's arms to use binoculars, and is expendable to prolonged outdoor exposure while still being passable, barely, at the office.

Fortunately, when you ride the rails at 5:00 a.m., no one cares what you're wearing. I manage not to miss my subway train—a first small victory for the day—and find it more crowded than most would expect at that hour. Crowded but quiet, besides the rhythmic rumble from station to station, punctuated by closing-door chimes, repeated seemingly endlessly. All the passengers pretend not to see one another, as is customary in the New York subway. We remain in our own private worlds and thoughts, in comforting silence perhaps born of exhaustion but maintained by unspoken agreement, as if preserving something sacred at that hour. The faces are largely brown and Black like mine, work-booted laborers and nurses and home health aides in uniforms, going to and coming from shifts with odd hours; their unseen and unsung efforts keep the City That Never Sleeps running smoothly. If not for the early start time I choose for my hobby, I wouldn't see them either, because my hours are otherwise conventional.

Like a large swath of America, I have joined the nine-to-five world.

(Though during migration, my start time gets pushed to 9:30 . . .
10:00 . . . 10:30 . . .) Upon my return from South America, after a few
months of temp gigs and crashing at my mom's on Long Island, I was
hooked up by a Harvard friend with an entry-level job in magazine
publishing in Manhattan—nothing glamorous, but a scrappy video
trade publication with a great group of young people putting it together. (The editor in chief, Juan Arroz, at age thirty, was positively
ancient to me.) That had morphed into a copyediting job at *Interview*
not long after Andy Warhol had died, and now I had moved to *Fame,*
a start-up *Vanity Fair* wannabe that stretched the concept of workplace civility to new lows. ("*Fuck you!*" the editor in chief and senior
editor routinely screamed at each other across the open loft space as a
trash can one had hurled at the other sailed over our heads.) With the
meager magazine salaries, I'd managed to get a room with two other
recent college grads (from—gasp!—Yale) across the East River in
Queens and eventually a share with two pals (one a Harvard classmate
this time—thank God!) in the last affordable downtown Manhattan
neighborhood, the cutting-edge East Village.

Living in New York as a twentysomething meant the usual complete lack of disposable income, because half the salary went to rent a
dilapidated closet to live in. And yet, like all the twentysomething
New Yorkers before me, I was still finding a way to dance until dawn,
at the cavernous Roxy on a Saturday night, where chiseled muscle
gods gyrated atop the bar for your viewing pleasure, or on Tuesday
night at Rock 'n' Roll Fag Bar at the World, where a six-foot-tall bald
drag queen presided over retro tunes in a converted old East Village
theater, and still I managed to fake my way through work on Wednes-
day. And if when Saturday night rolled around again the weather was
warm and I was in a raunchier mood, I could run the gauntlet of
probing gazes from the leather-and-Levi's-clad butch dudes who lined
the sidewalk along the West Side Highway on the one-block stretch
between the Eagle and its sister gay bar, the Spike.

But the Roxy, the World, the Eagle, and the Spike would have to wait until June. All of that had abruptly stopped for me in the middle of April, because unlike other twentysomething New Yorkers, I am a birder. I needed a place to bird in Manhattan, and I found it in what would seem the unlikeliest of places: Central Park. Consigned to a limited assortment of birds for most of the year—House Sparrows, Downy Woodpeckers, Mourning Doves, Northern Cardinals, for example—Central Park becomes a migrant trap during the spring and fall, concentrating the avian tourists in one spot just as effectively as it does the human ones. And since, unlike the fall, the spring features males in beautiful breeding plumage—I'm nothing, if not consistent— Central Park's unparalleled spring songbird migration, the peak lasting about six weeks, had become my holy month of Ramadan. Work, the gym, nightclubbing, eating, sleeping, friends, romance, all become secondary.

I emerge from the subway station at Sixty-eighth and Lexington, the stale underground air swept clean by a cool breeze. In just the time it takes to cross the few avenue blocks to reach the park, the sky grows lighter; daybreak is minutes away. I turn over the day's possibilities, trying not to get my hopes up; but I have a target bird, one I'd like to see, expected for this point in the migration, that I haven't yet found this spring: a Blackburnian Warbler.

Sure, I've seen them before, plenty of times. But each spring is a reset, when you start fresh seeing the roster of birds that come our way every year; it's part of the Fourth Pleasure of Birding:

Fourth Pleasure of Birding:
The Joy of Collecting

Some people collect stamps, some coins; birders collect not actual physical birds (anyway, not since the days of the old-time naturalists, who didn't count it if they hadn't blasted it out of the sky with a shotgun) but sightings. Every birder keeps lists, whether it's a life list (every species seen in one's life) or a day list (the birds seen today), a county or state list (birds seen in a particular jurisdiction) or a yard list (birds seen in one's backyard). For some, listing is primary; sadly, they hardly get to know a bird or appreciate it, just as long as they can check it off the list, and then they're on to the next one. And then there are the absurd lists: birds seen from the bathroom window; birds heard in the background during TV commercials; birds seen while driving on an interstate (not recommended for obvious reasons of highway safety).

Two things make listing during the East Coast's spring migration particularly compelling. First, there's a sequence to the migration that varies from year to year in its specific details but remains remarkably consistent: The Blue-Headed Vireo will be among the first birds back, arriving in New York in mid-April; the Red-Eyed will be the last vireo, beginning in mid-May and rapidly zooming up in numbers; the Acadian Flycatcher will close out the show in late May/early June; and so on. There is an order to this pageant, not inviolable yet reliable, so there are benchmarks by date to fulfill. Which makes the surprises— the right bird at the wrong time, or a bird one didn't expect for the park at all—that much more thrilling.

The second is the warblers.

Active and diminutive—smaller than a sparrow—warblers are the stars of the migration in the East. They are particularly thrilling in the spring, when the males are festooned in bold color patterns and belting out distinctive songs as they flit from branch to branch; think of warblers as butterflies with personality. And yet, because they're small and always moving, the ordinary civilian will likely pass through a park greening with spring and never realize these little beauties are dashing through the leaves around us, feasting on bugs.

But we birders not only know; we drool over it. All the more because the warblers' time with us is so fleeting: None have been known to nest in Central Park. In fact, in any given region a dozen or more species may be resident all summer long, but the full variety of warbler species that grace the East—some thirty-five different kinds—is something witnessed only in passage. (The West has a much more limited palette.) We measure our migration by them, both on a daily basis, where an unofficial "warbler index" rates the outing by number of species (twenty warblers or more in a single day makes a very good day indeed), and for the entire season, where a collect-them-all mentality holds sway. Heaven help the poor soul who comes between a birder and that last warbler they're missing for the spring!

So far this spring, we have yet to achieve a twenty-warbler day. It will take a fresh influx of arrivals to bump up our species variety; the southwest winds overnight might just have done the trick. As I step into the park, I listen closely for birdsong—not the chirp of House Sparrows or the triplet flutelike phrases of resident robins, but behind that, searching for the sonic signatures of migrants, each species distinct. Hearing them at the edge of the park would be a likely sign of a very birdy morning to come. But there's not much action here at the moment; a lone Ovenbird (a warbler, despite its name) belts out its crescendoing *teacher* cry from beneath some ground cover. As a predictor of things to come, that's inconclusive.

I catch myself still walking with the brisk strides I used to get from subway exit to park, and I force myself to take the pace off. These first moments of the day's outing are important; I almost have to learn how to see again each morning, not with my everyday eyes, but with the ones that are attuned to a particular kind of small motion: a quick, short burst of action, not to be mistaken for a leaf moved by the wind or an irritating squirrel's antics. ("Mammals!" I mentally huff and spit on the ground, as if I were better than my own kind.) If that mode of perception kicks in too slowly, I may walk right past some great bird at the outset.

So I go more slowly and take the time to actually get visual contact on the first migrants I hear, even if they're common species that I'm certain to see anyway in the course of the morning. Sure enough, the Ovenbird comes out from under a low shrub, walking on the ground like a miniaturized chicken. First bird of the day. Now I'm ready.

Reflected sunlight erupts across the cityscape along the south and west sides of the park, making spires gleam while the leafy expanse at their feet waits for its moment in the sun. The color is splendid this morning, an intense rose shooting up from the eastern sky. The glory of Central Park unfolds before me as only a few of us know it: nearly devoid of people. By midday it will be swarmed with tourist groups, lunchtime picnickers, Rollerbladers, rowboaters, street vendors, side-walk musicians, armies of grade-school students on expeditions, and thousands of others engaged in every conceivable permutation of human activity. But in the early morning, there are only four major constituencies: the birders, the runners, the cyclists, and the dog walk-ers. And at dawn, even these are in short supply. I relish this quiet time in the park, when you can fool yourself into thinking you're landed gentry and the rolling, landscaped hills are all yours. For at least the first half hour of my walk, I guard my solitude.

"Good morning, Chris."

Roger Pasquier is one of the few people who can violate my solo half hour without my minding it. Short of stature and towering of reputation, Roger has been birding the park for decades, though you'd never know it to look at him; his spry build and unlined face are those of a man of indeterminate age. He's dressed in the pleated khakis and button-down oxford shirt of a fastidious white guy because, well, he is. Erudite and of impeccable breeding, outside the park he glides through a stratum of the city's elite that will remain unknown to someone like me; inside the park, he's a self-confessed snob, only deigning to speak to certain other birders. That's partly a defense mechanism; as one of the most skilled birders I've ever known, he'd be plagued with basic questions newbies could easily find out for them-selves, or with entreaties to bird along with him that would ruin his own experience in the park, which he cherishes as much as I do mine. His aloofness forms a wall to shield this Master Yoda of Central Park birding. (When I first told him I'd dubbed him this, he looked con-fused: "Is that one of those J.R.R. Tolkien things you like?")

I'm not sure why Roger initially deemed me worthy of conversation. He might have been intrigued at the rare sight of a Black birder; it might have been the dedication I demonstrated by arriving at the park as early as he does, we being among the few on dawn patrol; or maybe my reputation as a careful birder who doesn't make unforced errors in identification—perhaps the single greatest qualification in Roger's eyes—preceded me. For in birding in general and in Central Park in particular, reputation is everything. When word arrives of a Cerulean Warbler or other rare sighting, the immediate questions are "Where?" "How long ago?" and "Says who?" Nobody wants to spend an hour chasing after a purported Yellow-Throated Warbler that's actually a Common Yellowthroat (also a warbler, with a confusingly similar name).

Birding Tip

Avoid rookie mistakes by taking an extra beat of considered examination before announcing an ID. All sorts of things can fool you, from poor lighting conditions to wishful thinking; that moment to make sure of your findings can save you from turning a Canada Warbler into a much more prized Kentucky Warbler, or a female Common Yellowthroat into a not-at-all-common Mourning Warbler, and save your reputation! And if you do make a mistake, don't beat yourself up too much; we all get it wrong sometimes—even experts like Roger Pasquier.

Once Roger talked to me, he must have found me passably amusing to chat with, since in several subsequent chance encounters the talk continued. And, Roger being Roger, once it came out in conversation that I'd gone to Harvard, I was in. Lucky for me, since I would go on to learn more about birds, birding, and Central Park in those moments of chatting and birding together with Roger than I would from anyone else. I was an eager Luke Skywalker receiving a bit of off-the-cuff Jedi training from Master Yoda himself; just replace the light sabers with binoculars.

I can imagine Roger's exasperated and uncomprehending eye roll at even the mention of light sabers.

"Did you catch the fragrance from the *Calycanthus* up on Strawberry Fields?" he asks me.

"Unmistakable," I parry, the dry edge in my voice meant to slice through his playful pretension. He smiles; as much as I know about birds, he knows full well I haven't got a clue about plants. He'll call out a bird of interest and say, "It's in the elm," and wait the several moments for me to glare at him for directions that are actually useful to me, the intended side effect being that I've started to learn to identify trees. That's opening up a new world for me: Yellow Warblers love willows in their habitat; Cedar Waxwings, as the name suggests, adore the berries of the eastern red-cedar (which is actually a juniper). The interconnectedness of living things comes into sharper focus. As Roger and I trade barbs, there is method to our banter.

We move quickly, faster than my preferred pace, but Roger's style of birding is to blitz through several areas as early as possible and hear what's around. It's a little frustrating for me, since I like to see the birds, too, especially at the beginning of my walk. But to be counted on Roger's list for the day, a bird need only be heard; I adjust my birding accordingly. Roger's company is worth the sacrifice; he's always got something interesting to talk about, in this case a book he's reading about 1960s girl groups. This sparks a heated discussion of the relative merits of Martha Reeves and the Vandellas' "Heat Wave" versus "Dancing in the Street," until we're interrupted by a different kind of song.

"Did you hear that?" I ask Roger, my ears perking up.

"You mean the Pine Warbler?" he says, evaluating the trilling without hesitation.

"No way. It's much too late for that." In the procession of warblers, the Pine is the first one back, sometime in late March or early April, and for all songbirds the males arrive in the spring before the females, to squabble over who gets the best territory on the breeding grounds. (The females arrive later to pick and choose, at least in part based on who has secured prime real estate; a tactic shared with some Upper East Side social climbers.) A female Pine this late into May would be unusual, but a singing male—and among warblers, it is almost exclusively the males that sing—would be unheard of.

Roger doesn't waver, even though one-note trills are a perpetual source of ID consternation for me and many others. Pine Warblers, Worm-Eating Warblers, Orange-Crowned Warblers, Chipping Sparrows, Swamp Sparrows, and Dark-Eyed Juncos all do it, and all might be found in Central Park in springtime. Superficially they all sound the same; factor in the regional and individual variations in each species' song, and teasing them apart by voice alone with any certainty can be daunting.

But Roger is not just the park's best birder; he's an excellent ear birder, someone who relies on what he hears to help him find the birds and identify them. We share that skill; blindfold us in a wild spot in the Northeast, and we can tell you what birds are there just from what we're hearing. That may sound superhuman, but everybody possesses the ability: When you hear a familiar pop singer's new song, or when some relative or close pal calls on the phone, you know right away who it is just from the voice. A dozen different cues tip off your subconscious, from the words they choose for the greeting to the pitch and quality of the voice. For ear birders like Roger and me, these birds are old friends, their voices often instantly recognized. And it's an ability that's always turned on: No matter where you are or what you're doing, your ears are feeding you a constant stream of avian information, as if a news banner were subtly scrolling updates across the bottom of your brain. It can make going to the movies, where careless use of bird vocalizations abounds, an ordeal, either for you or for the non-birder with you as you pound the armrest in outrage. (The Leonardo DiCaprio/Djimon Hounsou film *Blood Diamond* is the ultimate nails-on-a-chalkboard experience; it takes our heroes on a harrowing journey through war-torn Africa—not that you'd know it from the ubiquitous and unmistakable North American birdsongs in the background.) And it makes my and Roger's conversations a bizarre mix of normal sentences punctuated by "grosbeak" or "pewee" outbursts as we call out what we're hearing, as if afflicted with ornithological Tourette's.

The suspect bird sings again.

"It sounds musical enough for a Pine," I say, "but it can't be."

"Listen to the way it fades in at the beginning and out at the end," Roger notes. "Chipping Sparrows and Worm-Eating Warblers don't do that."

Once more; only this time not only do I hear the diagnostic fades, but the bird comes out into the open from the depths of the tree it was buried in. Sure enough, it's a Pine Warbler, greenish above with a lovely yellow hue below. I would never again confuse a Pine's song with any of the other trillers from this day forward. Yet another thing I've learned from Roger.

"By the way," Roger adds, "did you get the Hooded on Strawberry Fields?"

This is what you'd call burying the lead. We get several Hooded Warblers each spring in Central Park, but they remain one of the more uncommon species because New York sits just barely within the northern edge of the bird's range. The Hooded is a showboat: Bright yellow overall, the male sports jet black on the head that starts on top and wraps around the neck to conclude at the throat, forming a hood entirely encasing the yellow of its face. It repeatedly flicks its tail open to display white spots at the tip, and it tends to stay low—eye level or lower—unlike some of the other warblers that torture your vertebrae by sticking to the treetops. (The occasional ache of "warbler neck" is the birder's vocational hazard.) In short, the Hooded boasts dramatic flair in spades.

Not that Roger saw any of that. He heard the bird, and that was enough for him.

This is where Roger and I part ways. His walk will carry him north to Belvedere Castle, the folly in the center of the park with the regal views the name suggests. But I'm now quite determined to backtrack to find the uncommon bird I apparently missed out of inattentiveness, or else it just wasn't singing when I happened by. Roger has done his good deed for the day; he may not talk to every birder in the park, but he knows I do, so he's just disseminated important info. One nice thing about our little community: In Central Park, we all share the birds, pointing each other in the direction of good sightings by word of mouth. Even Roger. (This was in the years before wide cellphone usage; these days we tweet and text away.) I'm told not every birding hot spot is like that. But I'm glad it is here.

I settle back into my own natural birding rhythm, albeit with a bit of urgency in my step, because there's a Hooded Warbler at stake. The Blackburnian Warbler remains my big target of the day, but if I can get a Hooded, I'll take it! It's not that I've never seen one before, nor that I haven't seen one this season, but as far as the joy of collecting is concerned, my personal bias skews toward a big day list, racking up as many species in a single outing as possible, and a Hooded would be an addition that isn't easy to come by. Sometimes my day list ends up focused: For example, if I happen to have luck with sparrows early on, I may go for a clean sweep of sparrow species that morning, determined to get that last one of our expected species before I leave the park. And if that sounds a bit obsessive, yes—listing can definitely lead down that path.

Yet for most birders, the need to add another entry to one's list is tempered by something more fundamental. As I approach Strawberry Fields, I have the Hooded Warbler in mind not just to see it to list it but simply to see it for itself, because with a bird this striking, why *wouldn't* you want to see it as many times as possible? Even for birders obsessed with checking off another box, the first pleasure of birding—the beauty of the birds—still lurks at the heart of why we do this.

I climb a hill to reach a long, grassy expanse flanked by trees and plantings on both sides: Strawberry Fields, where to my knowledge you'll find no strawberries (but then, I'm still at the start of my learning curve about plants). The name for this spot in Central Park is of recent vintage, taken from the Beatles' song "Strawberry Fields Forever" in tribute to the man who wrote it, John Lennon. Lennon's murder nine years earlier is still a fresh memory here in the shadow of the Dakota building, where he lived and died, and here in liberal New York City, with the eight years of the conservative president Reagan and now Bush, it seems an era died with him.

But those gloomy thoughts can't prevail against a promising morning. One of the best things about birding is how it pulls you out of your inner monologue and forces you to observe a larger world. That aspect helped save me as a closeted kid, and it sets to work now. There's a Hooded Warbler to find here, and all my concentration pours into scanning the lower branches and listening.

Almost immediately I hear *weeta-weeta-weeTEEoh!*—the telltale explosive whistle—and follow the sound to a fenced-in, shaded, shrubby patch. Anticipation mingles with urgency and a bit of fear that the bird will manage to slip by me.

Not this time.

He alights onto a fallen log in full view, flicking his tail to show off the white in it as he forages. His yellow glows in the understory gloom, but it's the contrast of black on yellow of his head that's so striking. I'd joke that with that hoodie pulled up over his head, if he were brown instead of yellow, here in New York City he'd have been stopped and frisked by now. But the failings of law enforcement are the furthest thing from my mind; I'm too busy having my breath taken away. I am alone in the presence of this small, improbable creature to witness its remarkable show in silence, partly so as not to scare it away, partly out of reverence, and entirely overwhelmed with wonder.

He flits a little farther away, then dives into the undergrowth and disappears.

Still high on my Hooded encounter, I'm eager for more; birders are a greedy lot. I head for the Ramble, so called because this woodland section of Central Park was designed with a maze of twisting paths so that one might lose oneself in the woods and keep walking around each new turn. Once within the Ramble, the skyscrapers of Manhattan disappear from line of sight, and you can forget that you're wandering in the heart of one of the most urbanized metropolises on the planet.

The used condoms I stumble upon each morning serve as a reminder; the Ramble has long been a notorious gay cruising spot. That's diminishing now, with the horror of AIDS at its peak, killing gay men and chilling the scene, though for some a sense of looming demise drives them to reckless abandon. Not me; my somewhat prudish (by gay standards) nature, lingering self-esteem issues, and Vulcan-like devotion to rational behavior combine to act as a brake on any runaway sexual impulses. Nothing but safe sex for me, when sex happens at all; that and a bit of luck have kept my HIV status negative so far. But before that test result, I'd decided that the growth on my knee was a Kaposi's sarcoma lesion and spent months reconciling myself to my impending death, only to learn, when I finally went to the doctor once I felt I'd adequately prepared myself for the bad news, that it was just a wart (I didn't recognize it as such, because I'd never had one before). And quiet terror gnawed at me for a week after a chance encounter with a former one-night stand whose once handsome face and proud body had been so altered by disease that I almost didn't recognize him. When *Newsweek* magazine released a special issue devoted entirely to pictures and one-sentence profiles of those lost to AIDS, I pored through page after page, trying to imagine their lives more fully and wondering what my own single sentence would be. I don't remember what words I settled on, only that when I turned the next page, a Black man's face and nearly exactly those words stared back at me. My roommate came home that night to find me standing in the kitchen in the dark; I'd started washing the dinner dishes while it was still light out, and an hour later my hands were still washing the same single plate, over and over, while my mind was stuck among those faces, processing the unprocessable.

Despite the AIDS upheaval, shenanigans in the Ramble continue, if not apace, at a less than respectable clip. The AIDS crisis has inadvertently kick-started the mainstreaming of gay life, by bringing us as full human beings into the public eye, and that has opened possibilities for being gay that don't involve furtive park trysts. But we birders still occasionally stumble across more than just the condom aftermath, when some al fresco fornication in the wee hours of the morning has lasted past dawn. (In the years to come, social media and hookup apps would effectively put an end to the Ramble gay scene, and many of the bars as well.) The very thing that makes the Ramble a draw for the horny—the understory of leafy cover—makes it equally a draw for migrating birds and a habitat for wildlife in general. So the Ramble shares these dubious and glorious distinctions. Eyebrows always raise when I tell my non-birding gay friends that I go birding in the Ramble, but for me that's the only thing it's about. I don't shit where I live.

Except for once, almost, when a man with a come-hither glance and the body of a god expressed curiosity about the birds I was looking at. Of course I had to nurture that interest. So to help him get a better view, I let him use my binoculars, which required that—purely in the name of science—I press in close behind him, my hands on his, to help him aim his sights in the right direction . . . .

At which point I was interrupted by the arrival of the same two old codgers I run into now.

"Marty! Jack! Roger Pasquier found a Hooded," I say as greeting as we cross paths at the Humming Tombstone (so named by birders because a ConEd power transformer stands at that location: a rectangular monolith that vibrates with the electricity running through it). The sight of the two of them, as ever ambling through the Ramble together—strictly platonically!—pulls me out of my fond gay memory.

Marty Sohmer has the distinction of being the first Central Park birder I ever met; "Central Park birder" is too limiting for Marty, however, since he frequents both Central Park and Brooklyn's Prospect Park with equal ease. And I was far from either park, far from any sort of birding at all, when he came to my attention: I was underground, waiting at the Union Square subway stop for a train to the office, when some probably deranged guy whom it was better to ignore came shuffling toward me. Along with the gait came a stooped posture and thick, gnarled features like a Cabbage Patch Kid, crumple-faced dolls that were big that year. When he opened his mouth, a thick working-class Brooklyn accent tumbled out.

"Hey, yeah, you boid Central Park, dontcha?"

That was unexpected, and it blew past my New Yorker's standard deflect-the-crazies guard, though I was still a bit suspicious; I had only just started birding Central Park. I hadn't met anybody there, and yet this odd fellow recognized me when we were both way out of context. Marty not only introduced himself but would subsequently introduce me to other Central Park birders and to the park itself—all the quirky place-names that birders use to tell each other where to find birds, like the Humming Tombstone, Mugger's Woods, the Evodia Field—and then he went a step further. I had no idea where the Locust Grove was the day Marty told me that a Red-Headed Woodpecker had been hanging out there for at least a week, but I desperately wanted to see the woodpecker, since it would be a lifer for me. So Marty stopped his own birding to walk me up to the Locust Grove, and then proceeded to find the bird and get me on it.

Right now many of you may be thinking, "I've seen a Red-Headed Woodpecker! They're pretty!"

No, you haven't.

You've seen a Red-*Bellied* Woodpecker, the red-head's close cousin. The Red-Bellied is much more common and is often misnamed "Red-Headed" by the unwary, because the Red-Bellied also sports red on the head, a big stripe of it on the crown and the back of the neck. Its undersides are predominantly cream colored, its ridiculous name stemming from the fact that if the bird were stunned unconscious and fell on its back at your feet, you might be able to spy in all that creaminess a couple of reddish feathers in a small patch near the base of its legs.

I was looking at my first Red-*Headed* Woodpecker, and I gasped: head entirely blood red, an almost shimmering crimson that no artist has yet captured, and a back of solid slate, except for a huge white patch in the wings, as if someone had rubbed that part clean with an eraser. To watch it fly from trunk to trunk is to see crimson thrust forward by a cascade of white and dark, white and dark. I'd built a plastic model of one from a kit as a kid and carefully painted it, so I knew the bird, or thought I did. But I realized I'd known nothing, until seeing it that moment, in real life. Thanks to Marty.

I had learned nearly as much from Marty as from Roger, though in a markedly different manner. When I was stumped on how to tell the Northern Waterthrush apart from the Louisiana Waterthrush, two warblers that look nearly identical, Marty advised focusing on behavior. Both warblers pump their tails as they walk along the water's edge, picking their prey from the mud and leaf litter, but there's a difference.

"The Northern pumps its tail in a fast motion, straight up and down," he explained in his inimitable accent. "But the Louisiana is like a southern lady: It sashays—when it walks, the whole back end is moving!" He then pantomimed the motion with his own backside, his dumpy butt grinding lasciviously to and fro as he grinned and his eye gleamed with a little bit of excitement at the thought of such a lady. My eyeballs thus seared, I hadn't had a problem picking out the Louisianas after that.

I credit Marty with fostering the ethos that prevails among the vast majority of the birders in Central Park, of sharing the birds and our knowledge of them, of welcoming anyone with a pair of binoculars around their neck. He certainly had welcomed me. And we birders tend to keep mental tabs on who's done us a solid, who's given us a long-sought bird, and, though the information is freely given, we like to pay it back.

So I point Marty and Jack toward the Hooded on Strawberry Fields, and though neither man is young, they're off at the briskest pace Marty's shuffling gait will allow.

The Ramble is now my companion, and though it doesn't have more than twenty warblers for me today, it finds other ways to move me. The sun's morning rays, for one thing: They filter through the trees and suffuse the woods with older majesty than the light streaming down through any cathedral. And those twisting paths do exactly what they were intended to do, making the walk seem endless, with a new mystery just around every bend. In the Ramble in the morning, the heart of Manhattan is temporarily absolved of its worst sins; the crush of crowds and din of traffic are supplanted by room to breathe and birdsong.

Birding Tip

The best way to learn birdsongs is *not* by listening to recordings; with that method, they'll all start to blend together fairly quickly. A better method: When you hear something you don't recognize, spend the time to track it down! And don't stop, no matter how long it takes, until you not only see the bird but see its mouth fly open, its throat vibrating, and its tail shaking with the force of the sound (otherwise you may get faked out by a bird that's not actually the songster but happens to be in the same tree). This has two advantages: (1) You'll hear the song a ton of times before you actually see the bird, allowing repetition to aid with retention; and (2) you'll associate the sound with an experience in the field, rather than some abstract recording listening session, so you're much more likely to remember which one makes that sound.

You'll find it ever easier to learn new songs as your mental library of sound grows, building on your existing knowledge (for example, learning the song of a common bird like the American Robin is the key to that of the spectacular Scarlet Tanager, which sounds like a robin with a sore throat). And with time, you'll start to tune in to the aspects of the sound that help differentiate one bird's song from another: rhythm, tempo, pattern of notes, and—very important—voice quality (whistled, throaty, buzzy, and so on).

Use tricks freely to help you remember songs, like the singing of its "B—T—B!" initials for the Black-Throated Blue Warbler. Other potentially helpful mnemonics:

"Sweet, sweet, sweet, little bit sweet!"—Yellow Warbler.

"I'm singing and I'm singing and I'm singing and that's it!"—Warbling Vireo.

"Chicks! I don't think that's really for me."—the gay mnemonic for the Canada Warbler's explosive jumble. Not exact, but it gives you an idea.

A cheerleader singing paired phrases—"Cheer! Cheer! Hey! Hey! Yay! Yay! Rah! Rah! Go! Go!"—is the telltale song of that little all-blue wonder, the Indigo Bunting.

And finally a tidbit from birder Tim Bush: One day as I struggled to sum up the distinctive sound of the Prairie Warbler's song, describing it as going up a ladder or a scale— a buzzy "do re mi fa so la ti do"—Tim dropped a gem. "It sounds like a 1950s UFO taking off," he observed.

Nailed it.

I hear the burry *Breet! Breet! Breet!* and whooping whistle of a Great Crested Flycatcher from somewhere far away. I know this sound well from birding at a friend's place in the foothills of the Catskills, and for all the world in that moment I might as well be there, in a forest a hundred miles north, instead of in New York City. The throaty, almost creaking song of a Black-Throated Blue Warbler draws my attention to him, beloved for his tendency to stay at eye level and for his unique dapper look (tuxedo clad with a pocket square). I can almost imagine he's singing his initials: "B—T—B!"

It's still relatively early by normal human standards, but getting late enough in the morning that birding groups should start working their way through the Ramble. As if on cue, near the Azalea Pond I run into one led by Sarah Elliott, her frail form instantly recognizable from yards away by its crown of orange hair. She has paused her group long enough to retrieve a plastic ribbon she herself had tied around a tree only yesterday; in a clever innovation, she carries the ribbons in her bag so that if she finds a nightjar—oddly unbirdlike, nocturnal insect eaters that spend the day asleep on a tree branch, perfectly camouflaged—she can flag for others in which tree to search for the roosting bird. Yesterday's nightjar, a Common Nighthawk, has failed to return to the same roost today, so Sarah dutifully removes the ribbon so as not to mislead anyone.

Sarah lights up when she sees me, and while I'd like to think that's especially for me, I know better; that's just the kind of person she is. Simultaneously genteel and down to earth (a combination perfectly expressed in the nature newsletter she pens), Sarah seems to have come from an earlier age, when politeness was valued and lunching ladies banded together to save the Great Egret from extinction at the hands of milliners eager to add their plumes to their hats, an effort that led to the creation of the Audubon Society. Sarah spends as much time telling her group about the plants in the park as she does explaining about the birds; she is all about natural things. Well, except that hair color.

I start to tell her about the Hooded so she can take her group over there, when I see her eyes widen a bit behind the thick lenses of her eyeglasses. She spots something over my shoulder.

Sadly, it's not a bird. It's someone from one of the park's other three morning constituencies—a dog walker—and despite the park's rule that dogs must be leashed at all times, his Labrador retriever is bounding through the understory of the woods, uncontrolled.

"Oh no," Sarah says, no doubt as much concerned for the red columbine that will be trampled as for the possible Hooded Warblers, Northern Waterthrushes, and other ground-dwelling and near-the-ground birds that have been flushed and will have surely fled ahead of Rover's gleeful charge. "That dog should be on a leash."

She says it to me, and not loudly; scolding is not Sarah's mild-mannered style. But the dog walker hears it anyway and flips his middle finger at Sarah without breaking his or his dog's stride. It's not the first or the last time something like this will happen, even in just the span of this morning. Sarah is too classy to respond in kind. To my shame and regret, I say nothing.

Rover, his hands-off handler, Sarah and her group, and I all move on in our separate directions, and the Ramble's tranquility reasserts itself. I'm well past my needed initial half hour of solitude, and the flip side of enjoying a morning in the park—hanging out with other birders as crazy about all things feathered as I am—has been primed by Roger, Sarah, Marty, and Jack. Fortunately, a familiar figure approaches.

"Il n'y a pas d'oiseaux," I say to him. "There are no birds" is about all the French I can muster from my grade-school memories.

"That's not true!" Claude replies, and he and I both know it; this is just my standard greeting to him, since I know he's fluent, offered anytime we meet and there isn't a plethora of birds in the immediate vicinity. "I hear Roger Pasquier found a Hooded on Strawberry Fields."

I'm happy to see the Ramble Hotline has done its work and come full circle, though I'm not at all surprised.

"I remember a few years ago, I had perfect views of a beautiful Hooded over at the Swampy Pin Oak . . ." Claude has been birding the park a long time, though he's unbent despite his years. He has many such stories, but in that way he is like most birders: We have place memories, associating particular locations with particularly impressive sightings, as if the moment has imprinted on that spot and continues to echo there, even years later. Claude is reminiscing about that prior bird as if it were yesterday, when I cut him off with a cocked head and a sharp gesture.

Something has just bypassed our conversation, the singing of the robins, and the rumble of a passing maintenance truck to slip into my ear and drill into my brain. I wait to hear it again, to be sure.

"Blackburnian!"

The day's target bird is singing from somewhere in the oak above our heads. Claude's eyes light up as much as mine; he hasn't seen one yet this spring either. Age-related hearing loss means the Blackburnian Warbler's thin, incredibly high-pitched song is outside his range, but he trusts my ears, and I've heard the telltale last note: urgent, sliding even higher in pitch, as if the bird were being strangled. There's a Blackburnian here, all right; now we just have to find him.

"Motherfucker!" I blurt out in frustration as he pours himself into my ear, over and over again, but denies me so much as a glimpse of his glory. Claude and I work the tree, sifting through the other warblers feeding on the bugs in its catkins; we call them out as if to tag them to eliminate them from the search—"There's a Magnolia at three o'clock"; "Got something at six o'clock! Sorry, just a Yellow-Rump"—treating the crown of the tree as if it were a clock dial for easy directional purposes. It's not that these other warblers are not worthy; they're just not Blackburnians. And maddeningly, that species has a tendency to stay high in the trees. Warbler neck is real, people.

Just when our necks are about to give out, Claude catches a glimpse. He directs my gaze to the proper "time" . . . and then it comes out into the open.

I could describe a Blackburnian Warbler, informally dubbed the firethroat, but it would miss everything that's magic about the bird. How do you describe how the presence of a creature can take you outside yourself to a most exalted place?

For me, only myth can do that. So I made one up, after an extraordinary encounter with a Blackburnian that, against type, was at eye level, no more than an arm's length away, where it stayed for at least seven minutes on that same perch, throwing its head back and belting out its song, with not so much as a care that I was there. I was paralyzed. And when it was over, I had no other way to express what had happened than this:

> The sun, after a day looking down on the incredible array of life across the globe, arrived in the west so moved by all that it had seen that as it turned orange and sank toward the horizon it began to weep tears of joy. These flaming tears fell from the sky and briefly formed a lake of fire, and one small bird that had flown a vast distance to see the miraculous fire lake landed at its shore, exhausted. Overcome with thirst, it looked at the burning liquid of the lake and thought: "Such a gift should not go ignored." And the brave bird took a drink.
>
> From that moment on, the fiery liquid lodged in its throat, so that now it glows with the color of the setting sun. And when the firethroat sings, the last note slides high as the fire rises to try to return to the sky. And the joy of the sun at a world full of life is once more known to all those who look and listen.

If you've ever gotten a good look at one, you'll understand. That's what a Blackburnian Warbler *truly* is.

Claude and I bask in the bird for a while, and then it's gone where our eyes can't follow. I make a mental note to be sure to mention this bird and its vicinity to Dick Gershon and Mary Burchard—two pals with as much passion for the Blackburnian as I have—if I run into them later.

Claude and I would continue to bird together for a while, then coalesce with some other Central Park regulars into an impromptu posse, before I would check my watch in a panic and race to work before I was beyond the limits of tardiness decency. I would see more Blackburnians that season, though never so many as to be my fill. And each spring would bring new wonders to be witnessed in this little sacred patch of the earth, Central Park.

Over the years, I would learn more about my fellow Central Park regulars and their life beyond the park. Claude, it turns out, is fluent in French because he grew up in France, until his Jewish family was forced to flee across the Pyrenees to escape the Nazi occupation; Roger is an accomplished author. But these things only emerge gradually, because in the park we tend to have a singular focus. The measure of a person isn't that this guy is one of the wealthiest in the country (the CEO of Goldman Sachs) or that this woman is homeless (passing her time in the park, she had her curiosity piqued by all the folks running around with binoculars; she showed an interest in the birds, someone gave her their old pair, and she became one of us). These are things I would only learn about them much later, because I already knew what mattered: They are crazy like me about birds. That passion should be the only passport for entry.

The cast of characters would change. Birding tends to skew to an older population, so time robs us of our dear ones with greater than usual reach. Mary Burchard, Dick Gershon, Sarah Elliott, and Marty Sohmer are all gone; for Marty, we birders took up a collection that easily surpassed expectations so that we were able to secure a rather expensive official Central Park plaque on a bench in the Ramble in his name: "In Memory of Marty Sohmer—birder extraordinaire—friend, mentor, mensch."

But Roger and I continue our early morning banter, and Claude, now in his nineties, prowls on through the Ramble, still unbowed if a little unsteady on an incline. And a whole new crop of birders has cycled through the park, many of them sharp-eyed and quick-witted youngsters who'll be at it for decades, if they're lucky and smart enough to keep at it.

As for me, I would keep to my spring migration routine every year—days like this one that turn every morning into a treasure hunt—through plague and pandemic. And during the intervening years, for a brief time, I would find another happy place—one that would fulfill the nerd in me the way Central Park, ever and always, fulfills the birder.

6

Knocking Down Doors in
the House of Ideas

"YOU HAVE TO remember, we live in a liberal bubble. What's okay in New York is not okay in the rest of the country."

Terry Stewart, the relatively young, relatively likable president of Marvel Comics, looked uncomfortable as he laid down the law. The entire motley editorial staff, more accustomed to high-spirited hijinks than emergency meetings, was packed into the hallowed conference room one floor above our usual realm. Behind enormous, magnificent frosted-glass double doors etched with a spiderweb pattern in honor of our flagship hero, we convened in the office's most luxe space, and yet one still too small for our number; the room felt airless. But that can't have been the source of Terry's discomfort. It was me, and one other face in the room watching him as he delivered the edict, that made what he had to say so awkward. This was about me—not just about the epic PR disaster I'd been a part of, but about who I was: an openly gay person working at Marvel Comics.

Nobody outright said that my boss and I were on the hot seat; they didn't have to. And yet, as much as I should have been squirming in the glare, I couldn't have been happier that I was in that room, because it meant that what Terry said next, he had to say with my face right there among those of our colleagues.

"This can't happen again."

"This" was *Alpha Flight* #106, the 106th monthly installment of a comic-book series that my boss was in charge of, chronicling the adventures of a team of second-tier Canadian superheroes (sorry, Canada) called Alpha Flight. The issue would have remained unremarkable and largely forgotten, except for one small fact: It was the first time a Marvel superhero had come out of the closet. And for Marvel in 1992 that meant the sky was falling.

In the mainstream comics business, "heroic" could be male or female; white, black, brown, or green; from any nation or of any ethnicity; a multimillionaire or a kid from the streets; blind or wheelchair-bound; impossibly short or monstrously huge; heck, even from another species or planet. But the one thing "heroic" could not be was gay.

At the end of the meeting I walked out of that conference room terribly dispirited. For the first time, I was at odds with my beloved Marvel, by the very nature of being who I was. The feeling would last maybe a day, until I realized that, as the imaginary worlds I'd conjured since childhood had shown, I was congenitally incapable of not telling stories about who I was and the world as I knew it.

Can't happen again? I was just getting started.

I'd just have to be a bit surreptitious about it. And in that, I was part of a long tradition.

It started with a name change, the creation of a public alter ego to mask the Jewish identity of the creator. And even with that, in an era of rampant anti-Semitism, these creative geniuses were forced into the margins of publishing, into a sphere of the business that in the 1930s (and even today) was entirely too lowbrow for anyone to take seriously.

Yet from the pens and pencils of these geniuses, entire worlds took shape, populated by characters who themselves masked their identities to right the wrongs of society. Perhaps drawing on the history of persecution of their immigrant parents and grandparents in the old countries of Europe, these Jews came to New York City and unleashed American icons who fought for the little guy: Captain America (created by Joe Simon, né Hymie Simon, and Jack Kirby, né Jacob Kurtzberg) battled Nazis head-on in the pages of Timely Comics; meanwhile across town, at a rival publisher, Superman (created by Joe Shuster and Jerry Siegel) and Batman (created by Bob Kane, né Kahn, and Bill Finger, né Milton Finger) fought crime. The marginalized business became an industry.

Soon enough, Timely would get a name change of its own, and Stan Lee (né Lieber) would team up with Jack Kirby to create the Hulk, the Fantastic Four, Black Panther, and the X-Men, and with Steve Ditko (the rare non-Jew) to create Spider-Man. In this silver age of comics, heroes had foibles, problems, and ordinary human concerns; that approach proved immensely popular. And the juggernaut of Marvel Comics was born.

These larger-than-life archetypes, embodiments of ideals and powerful forces, would endure for decades. Their exploits, externalizing the conflicts and concerns of a society, would be chronicled by many storytellers, who would add to and reinterpret their legends, just as ancient storytellers passed around and embellished the tales of their gods. So in creating the superhero genre, these Jews inadvertently rescued mythmaking from obscurity (and, in the case of comic-book characters like Thor, drew directly from mythology for inspiration). In Western culture, where myth has atrophied, superhero comics became the last bastion of mythmaking. The unrecognized hunger for myth where so little remained would eventually catapult Marvel into the cinematic blockbuster stratosphere (along a similar trajectory to mythic Star Wars). But more important, Marvel would plant values and icons in the imaginations of millions, myself included.

When the nuptial bomb went off in the lives of my friends, when we were in our mid-twenties, I found myself slated for four weddings in the course of a single summer—a daunting itinerary of travel and gift giving on a magazine publishing salary, but one scrapes the cash together to support the ones we love. As everyone caught up with one another at the receptions, I found myself each time saying the same thing: "I'm copyediting for *Fame,* but what I really want to do is work in comics." And without fail, the response from everyone was, "Well, duh. We knew that freshman year. What took you so long to figure it out?" (The wink-nudge serialized superhero adventures I'd type up and post in the halls of our freshman dorm, cast from my roommates and the others living there, might have been a tip-off.)

Back in New York, a gym buddy came to my rescue. Kelly Corvese not only holds the title of Marvel's first openly gay editor but also can lay claim to being one of the nicest guys on the planet, which is no doubt why we ended up bonding over barbells at the Body Center. One day, as we sweated in that nearly all-gay basement gym—his mane of hair held in place by an Olivia Newton-John–style headband, me shod in *Flashdance*-like oversized yellow boot socks (hey, it was 1990)—he let me know when a job opened up and subsequently got my foot in the door for an interview.

I marched into the marbled lobby of 387 Park Avenue South armed with confidence that dropped with each floor the elevator rose as it closed on my destination. Yes, I had an in through Kelly, and I was certain they didn't get many Harvard grads applying—at least, not on the creative side. But I was beginning to fear that might be a problem, that I would be viewed as overeducated for the position. That fear compounded the pre-interview jitters and snowballed with nervous energy about my first time seeing the offices of Marvel Comics—

Marvel! It had held my fantasies in thrall since childhood. What if I were to witness the promised land, only to be denied entry?

As I was led through the halls, a vast space with rows of drafting tables opened up: the storied Marvel Bullpen, where the magic happened (or as close to it as any one place). Here a staff of a dozen or so pencilers, inkers, letterers, and colorists, all twentysomethings fresh out of art school, did touch-up work or last-minute jobs as they refined their craft in the hopes of landing a better gig. I didn't know any of them yet, of course, but I was struck by the casual energy: Bunche (né Steve Bunche), shod in high-tops, his burly backside crammed into cutoffs, and crowned with a 'fro ruled only by its own articles of self-determination, at any moment might be joking with Laz (né Ed Lazellari) or Murr (né Ed Murr); Stick (né Kevin Tinsley), his spare frame swimming in a black T-shirt, might be chatting with Pond Scum (né no one remembers, not even him), his impassive face framed by a waterfall of black hair. Amid this boisterous vibe, as they touched up a world shattering beneath Galactus or tweaked the perspective of a New York City careening behind a web-swinging Spidey, not a necktie could be found.

I was ushered past the bullpen into more hallways, where oversized framed posters—phenomenal art of my heroes in action—thrilled me at every turn. But something in their eyes added a touch of scorn, as if they were looking down on me to say, "You're not worthy."

As I faced my interviewers, my gaze scanned the clutter of a typical Marvel office: flat files piled on top of one another for storage of original artwork, their cool metal exterior offering not a hint of the unbridled imagination and dynamism they harbored inside; drool-worthy paraphernalia ranging from action figures to replicas of signature items like Thor's hammer or Cap's shield; more posters; and comics everywhere, an exuberant riot of color and character—as I would learn, not unlike the Marvel workplace itself.

For me, it might as well have been a crack den.

Buddha (né Bob Budiansky), the full editor in charge of this particular corner of Marvel, looked at my résumé, looked at me, and looked back at my résumé. The assistant editor position was entry level and would entail a one-third salary cut from the already meager scraps I was earning as a magazine copy editor. This particular assistant editor's job was in the Epic imprint/custom comics division—in other words, outside the Marvel mainstream. I didn't care. It was a start.

"Well, you're way overqualified for the job," Bob said, almost chuckling. This for the dry, laconic Buddha was almost an outburst. "The assistant editor's position is mostly xeroxing."

"I know; Kelly has filled me in. I'm okay with all of that."

I think the hunger must have shone in my eyes, and Bob took pity on me; the offer came shortly thereafter.

My only hesitation about taking the job was that if Marvel didn't work out, I would have derailed whatever career I might have had in magazines. In terms of circulation and buzzworthiness, I'd been slowly making my way up the magazine food chain. (Okay, *Fame* was more of a food fight.) Outside the comics world, Marvel in 1990 didn't carry much publishing prestige.

The hesitation was short-lived. I started at "the House of Ideas"—the informal nickname for Marvel—two weeks later.

That decision was not without family repercussions. To their credit, neither my mom nor my dad—long divorced at this point—said anything to my face about it. But the behind-the-scenes scuttlebutt was that this was not what the family Harvard grad was supposed to be destined for. Doctor or lawyer? Yes—the latter particularly in my grandmother's eyes. Born and raised in Guyana when it was still British Guiana, as the long-haired, light-skinned daughter of Georgetown's well-to-do Black dentist, she had an aristocratic streak and clear ideas of where her family was meant to be in society—even if we weren't there at the moment, and even though she herself had bucked her presumed societal roles any number of times in her life. I was her only grandson and her golden boy, overachieving both academically and on the debate circuit. (All that repressed gay energy had to go somewhere, so overachieve I did.) A career in law seemed a natural fit.

And so it seemed to me, for a brief while. In my Harvard admission interview, when asked what I wanted to do with my life, I flatly answered I wanted to practice law for most of it, then retire and go back to school for ornithology; the interviewer was taken aback, and no doubt rather amused by the certainty. As it turned out, my romanticized notion of lawyers couldn't bear even a few months' freshman-year scrutiny. Plus my budding acceptance of my queerness did not jibe with what in 1980 seemed to be an inherent part of any successful New York lawyer's career: a house in suburban Westchester with a wife and two and a half kids. That would not be happening.

So the law went by the wayside. Storytelling, on the other hand, was in my blood, so when the drift into magazine publishing turned into working in comics, I was over the moon. For me, Marvel was a dream come true. To most families—but especially to a Black family pinning its hopes of triumph over America's hardships on its Harvard star—Marvel was a dream derailed.

I was with my grandmother at a show when we ran into family friends in the audience before curtain. The Kurases were from my hometown on Long Island and had known me since their daughter and I had started high school together. They'd shared in the community's pride when I'd gone off to school.

"What are you doing now?" Mrs. Kuras asked.

"I'm working at Marvel Comics!"

My enthusiasm slammed against their slack-jawed expressions like a songbird that didn't see a window's pane of glass.

"But he's still smart!" my grandmother blurted out as we shuffled away in search of our seats.

If there was a job that was the dark armpit of Marvel, it was the sub-missions editor. Of the millions of (mostly male) imaginations fueled by Marvel, some of those imaginings turn to professional hopes, like mine; the vast majority of those are artistic and doomed for lack of talent. That didn't stop scores every week from sending in samples of their work unsolicited to the Marvel office, and the submissions editor was tasked with sorting through them and sending a polite, boiler-plate rejection letter in response. And as the most junior assistant edi-tor in the Epic/custom comics division, that job fell to me.

It was grim work, crushing others' heartfelt hopes that so closely mirrored my own. I would try to soften the blow by handwriting some encouraging words at the bottom of the form letter, if the aspi-rant showed a glimmer of promise. But there was no escaping that I had become, as I dubbed the role, the Shatterer of Dreams. I even had a rubber stamp made with a supervillain-style logo of that title— though I never actually used it on any of the return letters.

So the job was not without its comic relief. For years afterward I kept a file of samples that for one reason or another were so wildly off base that they merited archival preservation. There was the trio of art-ists who decided that they'd seem more legit if they packaged them-selves as a business; the name they chose for their corporate consortium was "Creativity Ltd." One misguided soul took an issue from the writer/artist Frank Miller's run on *Daredevil*—a groundbreaking syn-thesis of story and art—and scribbled over the entire thing, every inch of every page, with dense curlicues in ballpoint pen, to prove that he knew how to ink a comic. (To comics aficionados, this is the equiva-lent of graffitiing the *Mona Lisa* to prove that you can paint; my im-mediate boss and office mate, Rob Tokar, and I were aghast.) Special mention is reserved for the guy who took the trouble to write, draw, and actually print in finished form a sample issue of his original superhero creation, complete with cover art: It followed a teen burdened with fantastic powers and his pair of pals in a suburban high school, all of it unremarkable, until they're menaced in the wrong part of town by glowering thugs. The thugs, of course, were Black; the hero, his friends, in fact everyone else in the story, was white. I desperately wanted to attach a Polaroid of myself to the rejection letter, but I refrained.

The phone calls could prove particularly challenging.

"I work in a shoe store in Abilene, Texas," one gentleman drawled on the line, "and when I show my art to customers, they say, 'Damn, boy! You should work at Marvel Comics!' So can I work at Marvel Comics?"

"Well, sir, we'd have to see a sample of your artwork," I started to explain, but he was preoccupied with something else.

"How come you put all them little pictures on the same page?"

It took me a second. "You mean the panels?"

"Yeah! Yeah, the panels. Are you trying to mess with people's minds?"

WTF? "No, sir, I assure you, we're not trying to mess with people's minds—"

"'Cause artists throughout history have tried to mess with people's minds, like Vincent van Gogh!"

At this point, Rob was looking at me curiously as I turned blue from asphyxia trying to stifle my laughter, so I put Abilene Al Bundy on speakerphone. "That's sequential art," I explained, "so we can tell the story effectively."

"Because I look at all them little pictures on the same page, and I must tell you, *it fills me with a phobia.*"

That was it. I had to mute the phone's mic as Rob and I roared, and the caller went on to repeat that unique turn of phrase twice more. He sounded completely sincere, but if he was having some fun at our expense, more power to him.

Submissions tales like those pale in comparison to some of the dubious ideas that landed on our desks from within. Custom comics are the red-headed stepchild of any comics publisher; as opposed to the ongoing storytelling in the Marvel mainstream, the creation of a custom comic is a onetime affair outside continuity, bought and paid for by someone—usually a foundation with a noble purpose—who wants to reach kids through their favorite superhero. An invariably heavy-handed message results: Think *Spider-Man vs. the Asthma Monster.* ("That was too close! If not for Billy's inhaler, your friendly neighborhood Spider-Man would be spider-mush on the sole of the Asthma Monster's feet! Do *you* have your inhaler ready?" THE END.)

So imagine Rob's and my surprise when the then president of Marvel, an Orville Redenbacher–looking fellow named Jim Galton, came to us directly with the command to start developing a custom comic featuring Joe Camel, the mascot of Camel cigarettes.

Say what now? As in let's promote a cancer-causing nicotine habit in the youth of America?

We were handed already sketched-out images of Joe Camel as an icon of cool, a jet-setting James Bond of smooth seduction and endless adventure. Action Joe steering his sportscar with one hand while gunning down the bad guys with the other. Lazy Joe kicking back on a Mediterranean yacht with bikini-clad babes at the ready. And in every instance, a cigarette perched on his dromedary lips.

We howled our dismay and tried to point out that this was a public-relations nightmare for Marvel in the making. But since this was coming from the very top, there was no appeal except to Galton himself, and he seemed to have blinders on this. As luck would have it, Galton was soon gone—replaced by the much more approachable Terry Stewart—before Joe could literally get off the drawing board.

I was still submissions editor—in fact, I couldn't have been at Marvel more than a week—when the New York Yankees' second baseman forced me to make a decisive call on a curveball that came my way.

To be clear, I know as much about professional sports as I do about construction techniques with lumber and power tools (recall the bird feeder). But, also true to stereotype, the lesbian fact-checker at *Fame* was thoroughly locker room literate and a Yankees fan. Through her, I'd become familiar with their second baseman at the time, Steve Sax, strictly because he was damned hot, especially in that pin-striped uniform; so as a going-away gift when I left *Fame* for Marvel, she gave me an eight-by-ten glossy of Sax in action on the field.

Facing the naked wall in front of my desk when I arrived at Marvel, I put Steve in my personal decorations' starting lineup, as a bit of office-acceptable eye candy. And that caught the attention of Paul Becton.

Paul at over six feet tall is a big man and an imposing presence, with a rather easygoing nature that belies his size. He was one of Marvel's staff colorists, having mastered the percentages involved in the CMYK coding that specifies what shade will result using a four-color printing process. We met for the first time when he came to my and Rob's office to drop off some coloring markups, and there was an immediate basis for kinship, since we were both Black staff members. But the Steve Sax pinup was what really had Paul, a lifelong Yankees fan, anticipating a lasting camaraderie.

Rob introduced us, and I could see the light in Paul's eyes the moment he caught sight of the photo on my wall.

"Oh, so you're a Yankees fan!" he said.

When I thought about it, I had to be honest. "No, not really."

"What, you're just a homosexual with a thing for Steve Sax?" he said facetiously. In 1990, amid the straight-boy mindset that dominates the comic-book world, this suggestion was so impossible as to be a guaranteed laugh.

I grinned with a matter-of-fact shrug.

"Yes."

That thing you see people do on TV when they're supposed to be speechless, where their open mouth is moving as if it were trying to form words but nothing comes out? It's real.

"Oh . . . o-okay," Paul finally managed, as he made a quick exit from a situation he didn't know what to make of. It would take him a little time to sort it out, to realign his worldview—I think in particular

a brawny fellow Black guy being unabashedly gay was new to him—
but he'd be fine.

I, on the other hand, was less than fine when, as Rob's assistant
editor, this openly gay man had to work on an evangelical Christian
comic. Marvel, in seeking new audiences and sources of revenue, had
entered into an agreement with the Christian publishing powerhouse
Thomas Nelson. The result was Illuminator, a devout teen whose
superpowers increase with the deepening of his faith. ("Like a nuke
from heaven!" I still have no idea how Rob got that tagline through
to print.)

"Tom, what are we thinking?" I asked Marvel's editor in chief, Tom
DeFalco, when I cornered him in the hall one morning shortly after
learning of my and Rob's forced conversion. "You're putting *me,* of all
people, on a Bible-thumping comic?"

Tom, a stout guy with a voice that somehow always seemed conspiratorial, shrugged. "So you'll have to work outside your comfort
zone. It builds character."

We did our earnest best, but it wasn't good enough. After the first
issue, we in the editorial and creative team were summoned behind
the spider-webbed glass to placate our unhappy Thomas Nelson coun-
terparts, who had flown in all the way from Nashville to express their
dismay. We sat across the conference table from some very buttoned-
down professionals, while we unruly Marvel folks, all under thirty,
counterfeited a vague semblance of responsible adulthood.

How had we gone astray? Illuminator hadn't been depicted as sufficiently religious. This had us scratching our heads, because as our
partner company had instructed, all the guy did was pray, fight evil,
and pray some more. The depictions of him praying somehow missed
the mark, however. When we asked the Thomas Nelson reps to be
specific about what they were looking for, they answered almost in
unison: "His hands need to be palms pressed together, head bowed at
a forty-five-degree angle."

The ones who hadn't actually spoken nodded in agreement. We

Marvel folks also nodded, smiled, and shot disbelieving glances at each other. Apparently piety can be measured with a protractor.

Illuminator had an extremely truncated run, and happily my tenure in the custom comics cul-de-sac of Marvel was equally brief. The submissions editor job was something of a revolving door, so like my predecessors I spun out at the first exit, the moment an assistant editor's position opened up in another office.

Every Marvel office is a little fiefdom. An editor, supported by his assistant editor, controls a stable of characters and the various titles they appear in. (There's a Hulk office, a Spider-Man office, and so on.) The editor is responsible for setting a direction for the characters that maintains their integrity (or, perhaps, takes them into whole new territory), principally through the creative team—writer and artists— that the editor hires for the various comic-book series. And equally important, the editor serves as the nerve center coordinating the output of freelancers—the aforementioned writer and artists—who work off premises; so it's on the editor to crack the whip and get the team pulling together so that the issues come out on time. And nothing carries the stench of failure for an editor more than a book missing its ship date; it's arguably worse than sinking sales for his titles.

I say "his" because at Marvel in the early 1990s, the staff of a dozen or so editors, a roughly equal number of assistant editors, and a handful of associate editors consisted almost exclusively of men. And with the exception of myself, Karl Bollers, and Marcus McLaurin, those men were all white. The bullpen had a higher percentage of women (including the stern but protective "den mother" who ruled over that roost, Virginia Romita), and the pool of interns was distinctly more Black and brown, better reflecting Marvel's readership. But the editorial echelons were nearly all white guys.

The exceptions to the male rule when I landed at Marvel were Marie Javins, who would become an inveterate world traveler, a pillar of the comics industry, and eventually editor in chief at DC Comics; and Bobbie Chase. Bobbie (née Barbara) had a well-organized, no-

nonsense reputation as an editor, particularly about keeping her books on time. She hails from an old Hudson valley family that's as Yankee as they get—private about religion, outspokenly liberal about social issues, and a little bit patrician. I was all on board with the first two and used to the third from Harvard, but most important of all we liked that we were both smart. I interviewed with her when the assistant editor position became open in her office, and we hit it off immediately.

Though the move was technically lateral, it brought me into the Marvel mainstream: Bobbie held the reins on one of Marvel's classic properties, the Hulk—the big green rage monster—which was in the midst of the acclaimed run of the writer Peter David; and on the flaming-skulled "hell's angel" biker, Ghost Rider, who had jumped from obscurity to hot item (pardon the pun) with the writer Howard Mackie's reimagining of the character. Plus, since a licensed toy comic, *G.I. Joe,* was also under Bobbie's rubric, I got to spend time with its muse, the legendary Larry Hama—one of the few comics writers to pull off the holy grail of comics writers, a silent issue: a complete story told entirely visually, with no words on the page at all.

Now every day was Christmas: open a FedEx package to find the latest stunning pencil artwork depicting the twists and turns of Peter David's plot, knowing the readers will scream with what comes next; travel to Montreal to supervise the print run of *Ghost Rider* #25 with its crazy pop-up centerfold; get a surprise visit from Howard, who as a former editor himself would use his *Ghost Rider* duties as pretext to come home to hang with Bobbie and the gang.

"Hey, Howard!" I'd say cheerily, only to be met with a quizzical expression.

"Wait—are you talking to me? Because I'm just a guy from Brooklyn; I didn't go to [melodramatic pause] *Haaarvaaard.*"

I'd roll my eyes, and before long the whole afternoon was gone in relentless jibes about the educational provenance of Bobbie's assistant editor, musings on the biodegradable shelf life of Drake's Devil Dogs, and photo tableaux of the three of us striking poses as if from the old *Mod Squad* TV series. The work got done; it didn't mean we couldn't have a hell of a lot of fun doing it.

Not long after I joined Bobbie, a reshuffling of some flagging titles between offices left *Alpha Flight* in our lap. The wide independence that each Marvel office enjoys, combined with the fact that Bobbie isn't your average comic-book geek (that is, not male), had a lot to do with what happened next.

Bobbie tapped a then little-known writer named Scott Lobdell, an affable comics geek with a Jim Carrey plasticity of face and body, to take over the monthly writing chores for the book, giving Scott the first big break of his young career. Like most of Scott's writing, his proposal for *Alpha Flight* was half-brilliant, half-dubious; he could really shine with a good editor, and Bobbie was a great one. So we went to lunch at one of the local Marvel haunts to toast our new working relationship and to hash out the good story lines from the bad.

"And I want to bring Northstar out of the closet," Scott added, not long after Bobbie had shot down the idea that that character's unhinged superhero sister, Aurora, was actually a quadriplegic hidden by nuns in a basement somewhere. Talk about dubious!

"Agreed. It's time," Bobbie said, and I nodded vigorously.

In fact, it was long overdue. I was still at Harvard when *Alpha Flight* first hit the stands, and even after I read only the first few issues, my gaydar was blipping about Northstar; a superspeedster and Olympic ski champion, he had women throwing themselves at him, "but you never seemed to be interested; I guess you were focused on your sport," his team leader cluelessly observed. But to anyone paying attention, the clues were clear: *Alpha Flight*'s creator, John Byrne, had conceived of Northstar as gay from the get-go. By the time the writer Bill Mantlo took over the book, AIDS was ravaging the world, and he littered Northstar's dialogue with none-too-subtle coughing fits; happily, an editor nixed the death of Marvel's only gay character by HIV. Perhaps in a fit of pique, Mantlo instead added the eyebrow-raising twist that one of Northstar's mystery parents was actually a fairy (!), and the superhero's illness was caused by a half fairy's physiological incompatibility with our mortal plane. He wrote the character out of the story by having him beam himself to the Land of Fairies, where he could live in health among his people (!!!).

No, nothing gay to see here.

A subsequent writer would undo the fairy origins nonsense as a lie told to Northstar to trick him, and poof! Northstar was back. After that tortured history, having Northstar come out as just plain old gay seemed to us like a mercy to readers.

Perhaps if Bobbie had been a man who fit the comics-reader stereotype of the arrested-adolescent, sexually insecure fanboy, that Bobby would have been too uptight, grossed out, or spooked by the thought of an openly gay superhero to get behind Northstar coming out. But Bobbie is a good-looking, modern woman with commonsense Yankee values and a gay brother to boot (not to mention her gay assistant editor). This just made sense. With the broad latitude afforded to Marvel editors with their characters back then, if Bobbie was on board, there was no one to immediately say nay. Scott got his green light, and the die was cast.

In retrospect, maybe we shouldn't have been so naive.

"Is this correct? Is Northstar revealed as gay in *Alpha Flight* #106?"

The caller had seen the monthly solicitations—the description of the issues, usually with the cover art, that the comic-book stores use to gauge how many copies they want to order. I confirmed it for him, then turned to Bobbie.

"We just got our first phone call about *Alpha Flight* #106; is there anything we need to do?" I'd never fielded a phone call about any issues of any of our titles before; I figured there must be a standard procedure.

"When we get press inquiries, we just have to let Pam Rutt know,"

Bobbie replied. So I dutifully trotted downstairs to the office of Pam Rutt, Marvel's publicity director, a very nice woman whose week I was about to ruin.

I knocked on her open door, and we smiled at each other; we didn't often get a chance to interact, so this was a nice change of pace. I imagine the pace for her typically involved making sure the death of Captain Marvel got a little mainstream press attention, or that a boost in sales got a mention in the business pages.

"Hi, Pam! I just wanted to let you know that we got our first phone call about *Alpha Flight* #106."

"Oh? What happens in *Alpha Flight* #106?"

"Northstar comes out of the closet."

I watched the blood drain from her face.

"I need to see a copy of that issue right away," she managed to say as she started speed-dialing I-don't-know-who.

By the time I got back to my desk to grab that Xerox for her, my phone was already ringing. "I need seven more copies, right away!" Pam said before dropping the call to take another. And by the time I got back from the Xerox machine with the eight copies, my phone was ringing again. "I need another seven copies."

In the end, I was told that someone at the highest corporate levels tried to pull the issue from the printer. But it was too late; thankfully, it had already gone to press.

Mind you, it's not as if the issue featured exposed man flesh, suggestions of physical intimacy, or even a chaste same-sex kiss; nor was it any kind of gay manifesto. Rather predictably for the era, the plot couches its sexual orientation reveal in an AIDS context, and to make it extra palatable, even AIDS is viewed through the lens of an abandoned infant who's afflicted, whose protection Northstar takes upon himself. Enter misguided villain, bent on mayhem; punch-fest ensues; and between flying fists Northstar utters the three words "I am gay!"

That's it.

It was enough to ignite a media firestorm, even though our rivals at

DC Comics had already introduced at least two gay superheroes. But this was different; this was a main character in the series (albeit, since it's a team book, not the title character). And this was the top-selling comics publisher in America. This was Marvel.

In a boneheaded move, rather than capitalizing on all that media attention since the deed was done anyway, Marvel corporate shut down all further communication with the press. Bobbie and I were directed to route all further inquiries to Pam, effectively muzzling us; since Scott was freelance rather than staff, the corporate guys couldn't tell him what to do, but if he wanted a future at Marvel, he likely knew to keep mum. Even Pam was sent before the media with a mandate to say little more than "no comment." *Alpha Flight* #106 drew the kind of mainstream spotlight comics almost never get, the kind one gladly sacrifices one's firstborn to achieve, and Marvel just threw it away.

Despite that and the story's shortcomings, the issue sold out in a week and went into a second printing.

That did little to curtail the backlash from certain quarters. The reaction from fan mail was evenly split; an enraged comic-store owner in Texas wrote to berate us, because, he said, from now on he could only sell *Alpha Flight* in the adult section, covered in a brown paper wrapper. A woman wrote how she'd empathized with Northstar so much that she'd dreamed she was draped in the Canadian flag while being pelted with stones. In the subsequent emergency editorial meeting, Terry Stewart detailed some of the corporate-level fallout: Some advertisers such as Mars Incorporated, the purveyors of M&M's candies, pulled their ads; the Archdiocese of New York nearly issued a statement against us but gave us a pass—only because Marvel had published a Pope John Paul II comic ten years prior.

The antigay bias behind the negative reactions was cloaked in respectability thanks to something neither Bobbie, Scott, nor I had reckoned with. Two misconceptions that held sway in the 1990s (and that horrifically is resurging today) converged to fuel the animus: (1) Anything gay is inappropriate for youngsters; and (2) comics are strictly a juvenile medium. The first falls flat immediately when one considers that there are gay kids, as I had been; gay parents and relatives; and gay people and issues in the news, a constant feature in the era of AIDS. The mere existence of gay people could no longer be considered taboo, and the assumption that any mention of gay people requires discussion of explicit sexual content is patently false; *Alpha Flight* #106, with a story as sexually safe as a cloistered eunuch, is the perfect rebuttal. (Besides, nothing that moved the sexual-activity needle beyond the somewhat suggestive, regardless of the orientation involved, could get past the Comics Code Authority, a 1950s relic that reviewed all of Marvel's and DC's books at the time.) The second is a peculiarly American stance, since comics in Europe and Japan are just as likely to be read by adults, and even on U.S. shores the notion that only kids read comics is belied by the millions of comics fans over the age of twenty-one.

But in 1992 those two misconceptions could be put together to arrive at the conclusion that nothing gay should appear in comics. So Kelly Corvese and I, the two openly gay staffers, had to sit in that emergency meeting as Terry Stewart made that clear to our faces. I imagine this was how those Jews who started the comics business must have felt, identities hidden behind new names, cranking out special Christmas-themed issues, and nary an explicitly Jewish superhero in sight.

It was as if we had been told not to bother to exist.

At least I can say this: To the credit of those higher up the Marvel chain of command, neither Bobbie, Scott, nor I suffered any negative career repercussions as a result of our handling of *Alpha Flight*. In fact, Scott would go on to a lengthy and well-regarded run on the titan of comic-book franchises, the X-Men; he'd land that gig based largely on the strength of his *Alpha Flight* work. Both Bobbie and I would later be promoted.

And Marvel attempted to capitalize on the tremendous sales of *Alpha Flight* #106. The no-gay, no-way edict still held; corporate couldn't unring the bell with Northstar's coming-out, but they could silence its echoes so that no further mention or manifestation of Northstar's sexual orientation was to be found in the subsequent issues of *Alpha Flight,* effectively stuffing the character back in the closet. That didn't stop them from tasking my old boss, Rob Tokar, with creating a *Northstar* four-issue limited series, which wasn't allowed to address Northstar's gayness in any way. As anyone whose brain wasn't stuffed halfway up their ass could have told you, fans of every stripe rejected this as ridiculous. Poor Rob was left to preside over a total flop.

My romance with Marvel wasn't on the rocks for very long. In an unexpected turn of events, I landed my first-ever comic-book series of my own to write—a horror comic called *Darkhold: Pages from the Book of Sins*—and I was once more over the moon.

This had been my game plan from the beginning. While I loved being at Marvel—I'd found my natural habitat, as if a migrating shorebird crossing miles of ocean had finally landed on the perfect beach—I didn't necessarily want to be xeroxing the work of others for the rest of my life. The assistant editor's job was a means to an end; writing was where my ambitions lay.

The surest path in those days to become a writer was through the ranks of editorial; for example, both Howard Mackie (writer of *Ghost Rider*) and Larry Hama (writer of *G.I. Joe*) had been editors prior to their freelance writing careers. It makes sense, in that while a comics professional scouting for new talent can glance at a page of artwork and know pretty much instantly whether a penciler has the skills to draw comics, there's no quick and easy way to similarly evaluate writing samples. You'd have to read through an entire synopsis, and even that wouldn't tell you whether the writer can successfully pace the story across the pages, or furnish dialogue that does the quadruple duty of revealing character, providing exposition without seeming too expository, entertaining in its own right, and moving things along in a manner that fosters an appropriate tone, all while remaining as minimal as possible. Thus new writers needed to be known quantities, through personal relationships and a track record established in short works such as stories in anthology comics and backups to the main feature in annual issues, the types of stories that we lowly assistant editors typically had thrown our way. With New York's cost of living, the additional freelance work helped us upgrade our diet beyond the pizza basic food group.

Further, we assistant editors were inculcated with the best practices of comic-book storytelling in "Assistant Editor's School," a weekly hour-long meeting presided over by perhaps the most important and beloved writer-editor at Marvel besides Stan Lee: Gru (né Mark Gruenwald). Gru served as executive editor—second-in-command to the editor in chief, Tom DeFalco—for pretty much the whole time I was on staff at Marvel. But more important, Mark Gruenwald was to Marvel what Marty Sohmer was to Central Park birding; more than anyone else, he established the ethos that ruled the place and allowed all us lunatics thrown together to call it home. (In 2006, Mark would be declared "the Patron Saint of Marveldom.") Possessed of a dry wit, a receding hairline offset by a ponytail and mustache, and an unflappable poker face, he loved practical jokes (the more elaborate, the better), Captain America (whose comic book he wrote for many years), the Three Stooges (well, nobody's perfect), and the superhero genre. He made it his mission to make sure we new recruits to Marvel knew how to do the genre right, establishing a master class in storytelling through sequential art that was as thorough and well designed as any course at Harvard. Even during spring migration, on Tuesdays I would abruptly bolt from the park when I remembered that the 9:30 start time of Assistant Editor's School loomed—that's how valuable it was. Gru was determined to transmit the knowledge that would make us better editors and writers.

I was on the right editorial track for writing, but I wanted to jump-start the process. No one with my limited experience would be handed a regular monthly title, unless I myself generated an irresistible idea for a new monthly; so, surveying the landscape of the Marvel Universe, I noticed that despite a healthy previous history of horror comics such as *The Tomb of Dracula,* its roster of titles had long since been horror-free. Marvel's ultimate book of black magic—called *Darkhold* and dubbed "the Book of Sins"—had been dreamed up in the 1970s by the writer Gerry Conway as Marvel's version of H. P. Lovecraft's *Necronomicon.* It had "existed" according to the comics for millennia; but what if long-lost pages of the Darkhold, separated from the rest of the book, started turning up in the hands of the unwary, to tempt their souls to unleash their evil upon the world? What three brave, ordinary people would dare to step up to stop the madness?

For several days I stayed late, drafting the proposal for such a comic on my own time, using one of the two Wang computers the office had available; personal computers were not quite widespread back then. I didn't even notice the hours go by as the normally boisterous office emptied out and turned silent. I was onto something: a horror-based, non-superhero angle on Marvel yet wholly consistent with the rest of the Marvel Universe—I even built in a doozy of a plot twist—and I was certain that if I crafted the pitch just right, an editor would bite.

As it turned out, an editor at just that moment was planning an expansion of a line of supernatural superheroes, and that editor loved it. She happened to already be my boss.

It made for a more incestuous arrangement than usual, but only slightly so; in the Marvel of the 1990s, an editor in charge of a book often freelanced as the writer on another editor's book and so on in a web of freelance-staff relationships. Mine was unusual in that it was within the same office! But as I'd hoped, the proposal was irresistibly strong, and since Bobbie was planning to use the success of the rebooted *Ghost Rider* as a springboard to launch several interconnected titles, she rolled *Darkhold* into that line.

In retrospect, that proved to be a plus and a minus. When the Midnight Sons line launched in the early 1990s, with *Ghost Rider* as its flagship title, *Darkhold* debuted as a founding member, and that meant a huge boost in sales of the first few issues; no complaints on that! But it also yoked a story that was envisioned as true horror—and superhero-free—to the four other titles that were conventional superhero sagas, albeit with a supernatural veneer. It made *Darkhold* the odd duck of the mix. And it didn't help that its writer's inexperience sometimes showed.

But to be writing a regular book, adding to the lore and legends of the shared universe that had captured my imagination since childhood! The only greater pleasure came from the experience of watching something I'd made up in my head take shape professionally for the rest of the world to see, for what felt like the very first time. When all of us Midnight Sons writers went on brainstorming retreats, holed up for a day in a Manhattan hotel suite or an old Long Island manse, tossing around supernatural subplots from the bizarre to the biblical, the resulting output varied in quality, but the pure energy in the room always amazed.

I wrote what I know, which meant *Darkhold*'s three principal heroes reflected the diversity I live with daily: a feisty academic who was not only Black and a woman but—rare as a lead character in the comics—elderly (though far from infirm; she was loosely based on my "you should have been a lawyer" grandmother); a burly white guy (at least I made him Canadian); and the linchpin, a young Italian lesbi . . . uh, woman who lives with her very best woman friend. The closest I could come to saying it outright was when another character gets fresh with her and says, "So you're a d——," whereupon she grabs him by the collar as he exclaims, "Yikes!" But to anyone reading the book, with the two women sacrificing their well-being for each other, the romantic relationship is clear. Vicki Montesi was likely Marvel's first lesbian main character, though I can't say for sure. Pun intended.

Darkhold lasted only sixteen issues, but two stories stand out: a tragic tale steeped in Marvel history in issue #12 that earned kudos from Gru, and there is no higher praise; and "Skin," a *Darkhold* tale in the anthology quarterly *Midnight Sons Unlimited #2*. Writing in the immediate aftermath of the verdict in Los Angeles in the case involving Rodney King—the Black man brutally beaten on camera by white cops, who were nonetheless acquitted—I poured my rage onto the page. This *Twilight Zone*–style story, a Black Lives Matter comic before there was a Black Lives Matter movement, was incendiary enough that the original letterer hired for the job refused to set down the words when he saw the script, and a new one had to be hired. It offers its own twisted take on what lies beneath the skin.

Meanwhile, I'd been promoted to associate editor, which meant that while still working under Bobbie's aegis, I had my own books to control. One of the first titles I got, briefly, was *The Punisher*. A hypermacho tough guy, the Punisher murders those he perceives as criminals, ever since his family was gunned down in the crossfire of a mob war. I'd always hated that Marvel had elevated this character to the status of a hero, and his self-appointed role as judge, jury, and executioner was hardly consistent with my progressive values.

"Seriously, Tom?" I wailed, cornering Tom DeFalco again; I imagine he was bemused by how I took comics so personally. "You're putting anti-capital-punishment me on *The Punisher*?"

He shrugged. "Eh, it forces you to think outside the box."

So I hired John Ostrander, noted for his anti-capital-punishment themes in *The Spectre* over at DC, to write the book. He promptly sent the Punisher to the electric chair and had the anti-mob crusader join the mob. In that order.

But the most amusing mismatch of all was when Bobbie assigned me to edit *Marvel Swimsuit*. A stand-alone special published annually, *Marvel Swimsuit* was exactly what it sounds like: a *Sports Illustrated* swimsuit issue knockoff, which is to say, an excuse for Marvel's already super-endowed superheroines to show off their curves, for the titillation of adolescent males and adults developmentally adjacent to adolescent males. It was now in the hands of me, a gay man.

I was up-front with Bobbie, who couldn't have been especially en-amored with what *Marvel Swimsuit* peddled either. If I was going to do *Swimsuit,* I was doing it my way. No more Captain America in the distant background in frumpy board shorts, while Black Widow fills the page in little more than a thong; from now on, the guys and gals of the Marvel Universe would flaunt it on an equal footing, a fifty-fifty ratio. Not only did that better encompass the kinds of things I and presumably other readers like me wanted to see, but it would inocu-late Marvel from charges of sexism. Equal opportunity objectification.

It turns out that nobody objectifies better than a gay man. I rounded up some truly amazing comic-book artists and instructed them to take their cue from the most provocative images of the era: the Calvin Klein underwear ads and Herb Ritts and Bruce Weber photos, the pouty-lipped close-ups and the glorification of dramatically lit body parts. And with that, for two issues in a row, I turned the artists loose.

I don't think readers quite knew what hit them. As the comic-book writer Warren Ellis wrote in his newsletter, "That year's issue was the gayest thing you ever saw. Like, gaydar installations all over the North-ern Hemisphere just straight up burst into flames. Anyone who be-held that book from a distance of twenty feet became, by genetic testing, 3% gayer. It was so fucking funny, it was so not what Marvel did at the time, and it was so well played."

And for whatever reason, my second issue was the last time Marvel published *Marvel Swimsuit.*

The menace was insidious at first, yet it nearly destroyed Marvel's mightiest heroes. From the darkest, redolent depths of corporate America came the most perilous supervillain of all: Ronald O. Perel-man.

The perfume magnate had bought Marvel early in my tenure there; God only knows why. Shortly thereafter he took the company public, and the stock price soared. But like the world-devouring Galactus, whose hunger must be appeased with the consumption of entire planets, Perelman needed more, and so a small if storied comics company was suddenly managed with an eye toward the short-term stock price, rather than its long-term health. This was particularly problematic in comic-book publishing, which has always been a business of marginal profits and subject to boom-bust cycles. In Perelman's push for ever greater gross sales, key franchises like X-Men and Spider-Man put out more and more ill-conceived titles that stretched the quality of the artwork and ideas too thin, with meaningless crossovers (story lines that begin in one comic and then jump to another, forcing the reader to buy titles they'd never pick up otherwise just to stay on top of the tale) and endless stunts ("special foil-cover issue!") to move copies. This alienated readers, so when the bust came, it was deeper than anyone had experienced in ages.

The first round of layoffs left our normally lively office like a tomb. As in so many workplaces that get hit with "downsizing," we had to watch members of our family traipse out downtrodden, facing an uncertain future. But at Marvel, it felt as if a covenant had been broken. Old-timers like Jack Abel and the legendary and lovely Flo Steinberg had continued to have a home with us, both of them as proofreaders; Flo had been there from the beginning, as Stan Lee's secretary, and Jack had had a long inking career until a stroke affected his right hand. The deal seemed to be, "We won't pay you much, but you'll love what you do, and you'll be able to do it for as long as you can still clutch a pencil." The sobering fact was, that was no longer true.

When the next round of layoffs came, several months later, I had no illusions; the books I'd been assigned to were all new experiments and expendable. When my phone rang and I was summoned to the office of Bob Harras, the X-Men editor who by then was running the show, I knew what it was for. Bob clearly hated what he had to do, not just to me, but to a slew of others; I knew it wasn't anything personal. Although being laid off was a wholly new experience, for some reason

I was rather calm about it. Maybe I was trying so hard to be nonchalant that I actually convinced a part of myself that all would be well, even though I had no idea what I would do with myself next.

In the early days of 1996, I packed up my desk and went home, though the spider-webbed glass doors would open to me one more time. That summer, to everyone's horror, Mark Gruenwald died of a heart attack at the age of forty-three; it was as if the Marvel we had known died with him. By December of that year, as the company's fortunes continued to fade and its stock plummeted, Marvel entered bankruptcy protection.

It would take many years for Marvel and the entire comics industry to recover. It would be even later still before Marvel would strike on a winning formula for movies, bringing what was once the sole province of us geeks to the myth-starved masses. Profits from films of the Marvel Cinematic Universe now exceed all rival franchises, even Star Wars. (Sadly, the comics publishing division, from which all this storytelling stems, sees little of that revenue; in a bit of legal jujitsu, ownership of the characters was transferred to a different corporate entity in the 1990s, before the movies exploded—no doubt to keep as much money as possible in the hands of people who had the least to do with creating the intellectual property.)

And Northstar? He would be only the first of several openly queer superheroes fighting for love and justice in the Marvel Universe. He would join the X-Men, and later he married his African American boyfriend in the pages of *Astonishing X-Men* #51, published in June 2012. It was the first-ever same-sex wedding depicted in mainstream comics; indeed, it was splashed all over the cover of the issue, and inside the grooms share a passionate kiss at the altar. Marvel not only didn't muzzle the PR department this time; it went so far as to have the upcoming nuptials announced exclusively on the popular daytime talk show *The View* by the host Whoopi Goldberg.

Somewhere, Pam Rutt weeps.

7

Life Turned Upside Down

I HAVE NEVER SEEN so many stars in my life. It's as if someone has lowered the night sky so that a million distant pinpricks of light are now just out of reach, right in my face. Orion, with the three-star-studded belt, is the only constellation familiar to me; I'm back in the Southern Hemisphere, so these are not the stars of home. It doesn't matter. I am literally starstruck.

Clad in shorts and a T-shirt, I can enjoy the breeze, warm and dry—the latter being the very condition that offers such astonishing clarity. That, and the lack of light pollution: Uluru-Kata Tjuta National Park is in the middle of nowhere—"middle" being almost exactly geographically centered on the Australian continent, and "nowhere" being the sparsely populated outback—so there are no cities whose artificial lights dispel the dark of night. I look up and understand how so many cultures have seen destiny written in the stars, or envisioned their myths in the patterns of light above their heads. I can't look away.

That proves to be my undoing. I'm walking around with my head in the clouds (minus the clouds), paying no attention to where I'm going. Though I've stuck to the paved roads, I've still managed to get turned around; I must have missed an intersection or something. I've gone so far that only one path remains, lit for a few feet ahead by the lonely beam of my flashlight, with an open expanse of arid land covered in darkness on either side of me. I can't turn to my smartphone for directions; the issue goes far beyond lack of signal, to lack of smartphones. They don't exist yet; in 1996, mobile phones are bulky handsets, a novelty that's catching on with Australians ("call me on my muh'buyl," they would say, and it took me forever to figure out what that meant) but hardly anywhere else. Which means there's no way to call for help either. As far as I can tell, there's nobody around for miles, and since I'm traveling alone, no one knows where I am.

I'm well and truly lost, and somewhat terrified—a condition that echoes the general state of my life when I started this journey Down Under.

The music in my headphones—a song offering a mixed-bag assessment of ordinary life on an uncertain path—couldn't have been more apropos if I'd penned the lyrics myself. After overnighting in the Bay Area with my old college roomie Ken to break up the trip from New York, I'd embarked on an epic twenty-hour flight to Sydney; as I surfed the in-flight music options, I stumbled on "Hand in My Pocket," an Alanis Morissette song that was relatively new, one I'd never heard before. I settled into my economy seat and tried to get comfortable, not only with the lack of legroom for the long haul, but also with the uncertain journey my life had become.

Laid off from Marvel, in February 1996 I found myself in that rarest of situations: in possession of a wealth of both time and, momentarily thanks to the severance payout, money. "I'm going to Australia!" I announced to friends and family, a bit recklessly, since the Marvel payout had to last for who knew how long. But considering the expense and the fact that Australia is so distant that it merits more than a week or two if one is going to go at all, I couldn't imagine I'd find myself in a better position for such an adventure than right then. I'd be exploring all-new birding territory, and if I scrambled, I'd get there in time for Sydney Gay and Lesbian Mardi Gras, an international party that was the stuff of legend. Birds and boys: It seemed the perfect combination to distract me from the fact that my dream job was done and I was professionally adrift. And it didn't hurt that along with my dismal prospects I'd be leaving behind the dismal Northeast winter for the Southern Hemisphere's summer warmth and sun I'd learned to love in Buenos Aires.

I'd had the travel bug ever since my trip through Latin America. I think I inherited it from my grandmother, who after her divorce explored the globe—Hawaii, Egypt, China—every chance she could. The fact that she was a Black woman (albeit one who could "pass") alone never slowed her down. I, on the other hand, was J.R.R. Tolkien's Bilbo Baggins: a homebody, with little opportunity to venture very far and less interest in doing so. Then, just as Bilbo was dragged outside his comfort zone and into an odyssey, after which he longed for adventure, my Latin America trip triggered the latent travel gene from my grandmother; after that, I was always dreaming of where I'd go next.

Far-off Australia, full of endemic (that is, found nowhere else) species of birds and utterly strange mammals, jumped to the top of the list. At least in the short term, Australia provided an objective in life that I was otherwise sadly lacking. I had no idea what I was hunting for in the world at large to fulfill me—or even to bring in a paycheck—but I'd settle for what the island continent could give me for now. So I found myself on a transpacific flight with Alanis crooning in my ear about the everyday contradictions of a youthful existence, and when she told me that despite all of it I'd be fine, fine, fine, I tried to believe her.

Sydney struck me as completely alien, not because of its architecture, though the opera house, great sails in the wind on a shimmering bay, was a sight to behold, nor because of its people, predominantly white—been there, done that in the States. Sydney was alien in its soundscape. Not only were the birdsongs ones I didn't recognize, but they had a bizarre, otherworldly quality to my American ear. Currawongs, birds unique to Australia with voices worthy of *Jurassic Park,* in particular conjured a distant planet. The weird chorus made just walking down the street thrilling, and it underscored for me just how much my subconscious brain leaned on ambient sounds, and especially the vocalizations of birds, to give me a sense of place and time of year.

I hungered to know from whom all those strange sounds were coming, so birds were priority number one nearly from the moment I landed. Australia has kingfishers that don't fish (kookaburras), magpies that aren't really magpies, Superb Fairywrens that earn both descriptors, and parrots in such profusion they got new names: galah, rosella, corella, and so on. Both the budgerigar ("budgie") and the cockatiel, popular as caged birds, are native to Australia. But the big, distinctive parrots Down Under are the cockatoos, and the iconic species for me was the Sulphur-Crested Cockatoo. All white but for a yellow wash concentrated in its showy crest, this parrot achieved international stardom in the 1970s when one co-starred opposite Robert Blake in *Baretta,* a cheesy TV detective show. The fame proved detrimental to the species; it became prized as a pet, an unnatural fate for the individuals condemned to it and an invitation to poachers trafficking in exotic birds to target wild populations. Leave it to humankind to make a mess of things for our fellow creatures based solely on a made-for-TV fad.

I, too, was targeting the cockatoos, but not for exploitation. No captive birds for me; nothing in my view is more antithetical to the fundamental nature of a bird. To take a master of the air, a being born to roam the limitless sky, and sentence it to a lifetime in a cage or cripple it by clipping its wings, just so you can enjoy it from your armchair, amused? You might as well pluck the eyes from Picasso, or chop off a concert pianist's hands, solely to satisfy a passing fancy. The casualness of the cruelty is matched only by its callousness. I have to work not to flinch when someone learns I'm a birder and proceeds to gush about the birds they keep as pets.

Thanks to a quick consult with an ornithologist at the Australian Museum, I had a lead on where in Sydney to look for the cockatoos.

"You can find them in Centennial Park," he said in a tone somewhere between baffled and amused. So I girded my loins for the trek to Centennial Parklands and the painstaking search that lay ahead. I'd looked for parrots before, in Latin America, and past experience told me they could be insanely difficult to spot once perched among leaves. They don't move around like songbirds, so even an all-white one might prove difficult to find. This surely would be a case of the Fifth Pleasure of Birding:

Fifth Pleasure of Birding:
The Joy of Hunting, Without the Bloodshed

Take the Mourning Warbler: In the eastern United States, it's the last of the warblers to return in the spring, never in great numbers, and since it's a ground dweller, for its own protection it has evolved skulking habits that keep it buried in dense undergrowth. Finding one requires patience, luck, and a knowledge of one's quarry—the kind of scrubby patch to search, familiarity with its throaty, rolling song, full of vibrato (*Cheery-cheery-cheery-chory*), to alert you to the presence of a male you still can't see. Your ID skills have to be primed, too, lest you jump at every Common Yellowthroat, a warbler that also favors low-to-the-ground scrubby habitat. By late May in Central Park, the Mourning Warbler has become *the* bird to find, and you might spend hours revisiting the same stretches of overgrown ground, hoping . . .

. . . and then persistence pays off: You hear the song, you wait for the bird to emerge, and you take an indelible imprint of the moment with your mind (or more and more lately, with your camera and tele-photo lens for Instagram). No bird shot required.

. . . or there's nothing and you fail, but you live to try another day.

(In fact, when one year a Mourning Warbler obligingly spent nearly a week in the Ramble, constantly flaunting itself out in the open on an exposed wood chip path, we birders had our delight and amazement mingle with disappointment; that bird had ruined the hunt for that season.)

As I walked into Centennial Parklands, noting the unfamiliar trees—I didn't know much about the plants of home back then, but I knew these weird-looking things weren't them—I had the annual Central Park hunt for Mourning Warblers in mind. I couldn't be sure I'd get another chance at this hunt for the Sulphur-Crested Cockatoo, so failure was not an option; I had to scour the area, no matter how much time it took.

Not five minutes and fifty feet into the park, the avian equivalent of a white jumbo jet came squawking out of the sky. I hadn't expected they'd be so huge! The cockatoo landed in the open, feeding a few feet away from me on something on the lawn, and was rapidly joined by other white jumbo jets plummeting noisily into nearby trees, other parts of the lawn, the rim of a garbage can. I was thrilled to see these iconic birds for the first time, and so well; it was a classic case of the Seventh Pleasure, the "unicorn effect." But it hadn't been much of a hunt!

The ease of this sighting might have been pure luck, but the be-mused expression I recalled from the Australian Museum ornitholo-gist said otherwise. I finally understood that smile: At least in Centennial Parklands, Sulphur-Crested Cockatoos were about as elu-sive as a Manhattan pigeon, with a roughly equal propensity to turn into a nuisance. For the people of Sydney, these cockatoos had be-come *too* familiar, occupying something less than an exalted position. We tourists were just too green to know as much.

Sydney continued to defy expectations. I found it strange to be in the middle of a major English-speaking city and see parrots in street trees—in this case, gorgeous Rainbow Lorikeets. Stranger still was walking the waterfront, watching the Silver Gulls flying across Sydney Harbor in the day's last light, when something different caught my eye. Darker. Flying differently. Getting closer.

A bat, the size—actually, bigger—than the gulls. In the middle of Sydney.

I've spent my whole life enjoying natural wonders, but I draw the line at giant bats flying over downtown! Turning away with a shudder, I decided it was time to enjoy another kind of wildlife.

I'd heard of Sydney Gay and Lesbian Mardi Gras, but I anticipated I'd have a blasé response. I'd watched New York's massive Gay Pride Parade every year from start to finish, and I spent my weekends most of the rest of the year dancing until dawn (always with earplugs, to protect my high-range hearing for birding purposes) at the Roxy, a cavernous club that was wall-to-wall man flesh on a Saturday night. Sydney was shaping up to be a nice town, reminiscent of San Francisco in some respects as a city on a bay, but how could its annual gay gala hope to compare with New York's scene?

Coordinated choreography and matching outfits, that's how.

No ragtag collection of marchers, in the same T-shirt at best, as seen in gay pride parades stateside from coast to coast; Mardi Gras was a next-level procession. Participating groups trained for weeks on gyms' aerobics floors and in dance studios to make sure everyone had the moves down right, and when they finally got the chance to flaunt it down Oxford Street through the heart of gay Sydney, the hard-bodied Aussies sashayed forth in flesh-revealing costumes as perfectly synced as their dances. In an evening parade that lit up the town, a hundred-plus floats and thousands of dancers poured before the eyes of all of Sydney, or so it seemed, gathered to cheer on drag queens in sequins and handsome lads in not much of anything.

Even to a jaded New Yorker, it was fabulous. It was nothing compared with what came after.

That night I was back at Centennial Parklands hunting different game, at the post-parade party. The ticket was pricey; I was lucky to get one, because the party typically sold out months in advance. As I entered a building on the Sydney Showground, a part of the park with sprawling fields for cricket and other sports, and soaring exhibition spaces, I was curious what my ticket had bought me.

The pavilion was enormous, big enough to comfortably fit *three* of New York's cavernous Roxys inside it, and it was packed with people, queers of every stripe from all over the world, with their queer-friendly pals. The lights pulsed and swayed, and the crowd was doing the same to some pop anthem, when everything abruptly went dark and stopped.

> If you see a faded sign at the side of the road that says
> "Fifteen miles to the LOVE SHACK!"

The recorded voices of the B-52s belted out the opening lyrics of their hit song over the sound system as two costumed B-52s look-alikes took to the stage at the front of the pavilion and lip-synched. Mere moments into the tune, half a dozen impossibly lithe, half-naked guys popped out of nowhere from underneath the stage to join the lip-synching duo, striking a pose before breaking into a choreographed dance; a moment later, half a dozen equally lithe, equally semi-naked women popped up and did the same, and more taut-torsoed guys, and more long-legged gals, until the stage was flooded with dancers surrounding the performing pair in a deliriously queer Busby Berkeley–style extravaganza. At the climax of the Vegas-like spectacle, fireworks exploded from the stage to shower everyone in sparkling light.

The crowd roared its approval.

Grinning ear to ear, I turned to the stranger next to me. "That was amazing!"

"Oy, mate, it's a different show every hour in here, staggered with the shows in the other two pavilions."

My eyes widened. "*Other two* pavilions?!"

Including one that resurrected a bit of opulent excess from the height of the 1980s club scene in New York: a drag-queen-bedecked trapeze swing soaring over our heads. After that, as I moved from pavilion to pavilion, there was no holding back. I plunged into the pure giddiness of the revels with everyone else, some twenty thousand strong, and when "Love Is in the Air," the well-worn remix from the 1992 movie *Strictly Ballroom,* echoed through one of the halls, I was suddenly afflicted with dreaded HAWS (Homosexual Arm-Waving Syndrome), and my hands were swaying above my head just like everybody else's.

It went on like this for hours, the only indicator of the passage of time in that strobe-lit gay fantasyland being the mounting hunger in the pit of my stomach, suggesting that it had been a while since I'd fed. But I was far more concerned with my hunger for the sandy-haired muscle boy dressed only in provocatively skimpy shorts (in Australia, there is no such thing as shorts that are too short) who was gyrating next to me. In moments we'd synchronized pelvises and moved into close contact, bodies in gravitational lock.

"What's your name?"

"Arno. I live here in Sydney." I felt as if that information were volunteered to make it clear that, if I so chose, the gyrations could continue beyond the dance floor.

"Where are you from originally?" The accent wasn't Australian, yet the vowels and consonants fell against my ear in a way that tickled at some knowledge I didn't realize I had. Something similar would happen on a walk through the woods years later, when I'd think "There's a Black-Throated Green Warbler here" without knowing why, and sure enough, I'd spot the bird moments later; only upon reflection would I realize my subconscious had picked up a slight *chip* call and from previous repeat exposure had already learned it as the call note of the Black-Throated Green, even if my conscious brain had yet to catch up. Something about this guy's accent was ringing alarm bells—the kind that go off when my subconscious has sorted a particular bird's vocalizations from the ambient soundscape and is trying to alert the rest of my brain about a really, really important fact.

"South Africa."

Not just a white South African, but that strong "th" was pure Afrikaner. Apartheid had ended just a few years earlier, so memories of its horrors were raw; in the years leading up to its demise, I'd gone so far as to change banks so that my money was invested only with financial institutions that had divested from all things even remotely South African. And yet here I was in dance-floor foreplay with the enemy, and not only was I enjoying it, but the fact that he'd been revealed as forbidden fruit only made it hotter. God only knows what mating calculus was going through his head. In the next few seconds, I'd have to sort out my own: I'd either walk away on principle and hunt other game, or throw caution and history to the wind.

My feet kept moving, but not away from him.

We left together, emerging from the pavilions into the next day's dawn. We were greeted by austerely dressed Bible-thumpers handing out antigay screeds, in the hope that we queers would learn our error and repent; staking out the Mardi Gras party constituted an annual rite for them, apparently. I just rolled my eyes, but Arno was incensed, thrusting the leaflet back at the proselytizer with some sharp words. He'd endured that line of attack from his own family, he said; I suspected that might be part of the reason he'd left South Africa. A society designed for the oppression of one people rarely stops at the one.

Looking back, I'm neither proud nor embarrassed to have bedded an Afrikaner. I wasn't intimate with an entire population with its fucked-up mores and past crimes against Black humanity; I was with one person, Arno, who couldn't help the circumstances of his birth any more than I could mine and who to some extent either was still entangled in or had freed himself from the legacy of his people. Which and how much, I couldn't say, except that he'd broken free enough to spend a night with me. In the end, we were two young thirtysomething men who made a connection in a world fraught with reasons why we shouldn't. Though when we lay spent, I looked him in the eye and couldn't resist a quip:

"Your people fucked mine for so long, I figured I'd return the compliment."

My other Sydney hookup was much more alarming and revelatory. A few days after Arno, and after recovering from the sleep-depriving bacchanals of Mardi Gras, I met Robert in an Oxford Street bar and in short order was headed to his place. (Hey, no slut shaming!) Short dark hair topped his handsome face and well-built body, which Australia seems to manufacture in its men routinely. We had our fun, and pleasantly enough Robert invited me to spend the night.

The next day as he made coffee, he flipped on the TV, tuned to *Good Morning Australia* or some such morning show. The story was about a newly elected member of Parliament, Pauline Hanson, who was notorious for spewing racist bile, which her mouth proceeded to emit on cue like a fire hose. To my horror, so did Robert.

"The abos!" He actually used that word to refer to Aboriginal people, which in Strine (Australian dialect) is the equivalent of saying "nigger" for Black people. "The abos just take and take, and contribute nothing to Australia," he said, echoing Hanson as he nodded his approval. "And the Japanese buying up land in Australia must be stopped. *This is not a yellow country! This is not a yellow country!*"

I looked at him slack-jawed. What had I spent the night with? I felt soiled.

I can't recall my exact words, but my rebuke was swift and harsh, dismantling the ingrained racism against Aborigines and Asians that he took for granted and seemed to think I'd agree with too.

He blinked, rather stunned. "No one's ever spoken to me like that before!"

"Well, surprise! You took home a Black American," I thundered on my way out the door.

That he could get so far in life without having been dressed down for those sentiments is telling. Sorry to say, such attitudes were not uncommon in Australia, if usually not expressed as openly as Robert had; there's a reason Pauline Hanson had won her election and, thirty-five years later, continues to be a force in Australian politics. It's hard to throw stones as an American, from a country rife with racial prejudice, but I couldn't turn a blind eye either. I never experienced anti-Black racism while I was there; people of African descent are few and far between Down Under, since in Australian history there was no period during which Africans were brought to its shores enslaved. However, that history includes plenty of its own atrocities, most especially the treatment of the first Australians, the Aborigines. I wasn't going to become expert in that sorry past in my relatively short time in Australia, yet I could begin to grasp the present, in casual quips overheard and scenes mostly outside Sydney, of idle Aboriginal youths on street corners or of a drunken elder. Aborigines seem to occupy a position in Australian society that combines the worst of what African Americans and Native Americans are on the receiving end of in the States: In other words, there is no more downtrodden place on Earth.

And the resentment of Asians paralleled something I'd discerned in Argentina. There, as in Australia, Black people were rare, and being of African descent wasn't viewed as a detriment (in fact, quite the opposite in Buenos Aires). And yet, in a country with the third-largest population of Jews (after only the United States and Israel), the hostility to Jews was thinly veiled. The smattering of Nazis who took refuge on Argentine shores might account for a bit of that, but the better explanation is more universal.

People hate whom they have. In humankind's pathetic need to group identify by treating a different group as "other," we turn to what's in proximity for our villains. That may seem obvious, but having lived my life "othered" in my own country as an African American, only to see that denigration evaporate in a new setting while watching it applied to someone else, made it visceral.

It would seem to be a fundamental flaw in the human psyche. I can scarcely think of a place on Earth or an era of history when this hasn't been true. And one need not fixate on the most extreme examples— Nazi Germany, Bosnia, Rwanda, too many others—because that lets us off the hook for the petty ones in our own hearts that cause their own corrosive damage.

In Argentina the insidious menace is the Jews; in Australia, smack in the Pacific, it's Asians; in the United States traditionally the white man's burden is Black people, while in Australia it's their own black people; in Berlin years later I would catch the whiff of disdain for the people of Turkish descent who live among them. No matter where you go, it seems there's somebody who's somebody else's nigger.

I was ready to get out of Sydney for a while. I'd purchased a Qantas Airlines pass that let me take a series of domestic flights—the only way to get around the continent in a timely fashion—so I shipped myself to Cairns (pronounced "cans" in Strine), the gateway to the Great Barrier Reef. Having experienced the follies of humankind, I craved nature again, so I sought out what I'd heard is one of its great wonders.

"It's too bad you weren't 'ere yesterday," the cabdriver at Cairns airport said as we headed for the town proper. "The weather was a beaut!"

From the backseat I glanced at the ceiling of gray clouds and the bit of spit they'd just started to drop on the windshield.

"No worries," I said, adopting the phrase I'd heard Aussies use routinely. "It's only a little drizzle."

And with those words, I must have offended some obscure Australian sky god, because the last consonant had barely left my mouth when the clouds unburdened themselves of every conceivable drop of moisture in a nearly nonstop deluge *for the next four days.* The region experienced its worst flooding in forty years; bridges were washed out, and people in remote areas had to be airlifted to safety. So great was the sheer quantity of water that the silt it carried into the ocean rendered the Great Barrier Reef invisible. (To my everlasting regret, because since that time when I might have seen it in its splendor, half the corals of the Great Barrier Reef have died, due to the effects of global warming.)

On the fourth day, with everything I owned sopped like a sponge and myself soaked to the bone, I trudged bedraggled into the Qantas office. "Send me someplace dry. Anywhere. I don't care where!"

I took a brief detour to Darwin on Australia's northern coast. Despite being one of the hottest parts of the country, swimming is essentially forbidden, neither in its rivers and lakes nor in the ocean, because of the prevalence of saltwater crocodiles: Yes, these crocs are as likely to be found in marine environments as freshwater. The largest living reptile on the planet, the males grow to a length of twenty feet, every inch of which considers you lunch. On a cruise to see these beasts in their glory, the riverboat came equipped with boom arms dangling slabs of raw beef several feet high; within seconds, a scaly behemoth would lunge that distance above the water to claim its snack. Message received: Swim in these waters, and you, too, can become a blood-red part of the circle of life.

With the wet weather in Cairns not quite yet relegated to memory, I left Darwin for the driest part of Australia, the so-called Red Center of the outback, to see Uluru. Rising above the desert plain to more than a thousand feet high, this enormous rust-colored sandstone formation (dubbed Ayers Rock by English settlers) is the largest monolith in the world; because its composition differs from that of the surrounding landscape, erosion over eons exposed this single hunk of rock, more like a flattened mountain that stands alone. Perhaps the country's most iconic landmark after the Sydney Opera House, Uluru sits at the heart of Australia physically, emotionally, and, for its Aboriginal people, spiritually. I couldn't come all this way to Australia without experiencing something of Uluru, if only to watch it ignite a fiery red, if conditions were right, at sunset.

I didn't know that I'd be getting a nighttime sky show as well. Nor that I'd be so dazzled by the show that I would lose my way in the empty desert, alone, with no one knowing where I was, and with no means of communication. Nor that I was about to get a lesson of my own on presumptions about race and humanity.

Getting lost was not at all in character for me. I'd prowled a dozen kinds of unfamiliar wilderness on my own in search of birds, from California to Costa Rica, and a solid sense of direction combined with a habit of noting landmarks along the way had always let me trace my steps back. Just a few days earlier, when the Great Barrier Reef had been denied me, I'd struck out from Cairns during one of the few breaks in the downpours to explore the surrounding tropical rain forests; I'd stumbled upon an opening in the trees, fogged with humid morning air, where a trio of the giant flying fox bats I'd first seen in Sydney wove in and out of the mist on great swoops of their wings, as if pterodactyls still roamed the skies. Mist and awe not withstanding, I was able to find my way back.

This was different, partly because it was night, partly because the outback can be miles upon miles of emptiness. To ease my panic, I decided the only course was to keep walking along the road—I wasn't even sure which direction I was headed in anymore—until I found some sign of human life. When I saw a lone trailer in the distance, spotlighted by its porch lamp and with light coming from the inside—not residential; it looked to be an office of some kind—I knew it was my only salvation.

Any sense of relief dissipated quickly as I watched the lights inside the trailer go out and a white woman step outside and start locking up. My opportunity for rescue was about to get into her pickup and drive away, so I had to act now or remain lost. Further, this was shaping up to be a white woman's worst nightmare: alone, at night, miles from any civilization, in a vulnerable position fumbling with keys, and about to be approached unexpectedly in the darkness by a total stranger—a large Black male stranger. The only thing missing from this offensive Hollywood script was a hoodie pulled over my head and my hands menacingly in my pockets. And if this was a white woman's worst nightmare, that made it *my* worst nightmare, because in the States "I feared for my life" is the refrain of every white person who ever harmed an unarmed, innocent Black person and got away with it; the white "Get Out of Jail Free" card, played with reckless abandon. Here in the wild frontier of the outback, I couldn't imagine that this woman wasn't packing a pistol in the tote bag she carried. I had every confidence this could only turn out badly.

I had no choice. I tried to make myself as inoffensive seeming as possible and braced for trouble.

"Excuse me, ma'am, but I'm completely lost," I said in my most meek, nonthreatening voice as I stepped into the porch light where she could see me. "Could you tell me the way back into town?"

She paused, maybe out of surprise that someone else was there. Maybe as she considered the directions to town. Or her escape routes. The moment hovered, primed to go any of several ways.

"Sure, you go back down this road until you get to the crossroads, then you make a roit, and then . . . Oh, why don't ya just hop in my truck and I'll droive ya!"

Wait. What?

"Uh, o-okay. Thanks." Not what I was expecting. At all. She knew I was Black, right?

Rebecca, a middle-aged blonde, introduced herself as I clambered into the passenger seat. I felt nervous for her, and for me: What if I had been a lunatic? What if *she* is a lunatic—would I end up in a basement, handcuffed and hobbled by an outback Kathy Bates in an Aussie version of *Misery*? Not to mention the generations of African American survival instincts telling me that a Black man doesn't get into a car with a white woman he doesn't know.

"Where are ya from?"

"New York."

"Howdja end up 'ere?"

I started to explain how I'd been amazed by the stars to the point that I hadn't paid enough attention to where I was going, when I realized Rebecca probably meant how I'd come to be in Australia. But she lit up when I talked about the stars.

"My husband runs the observatory up the hill! He should be home any sec. I'll droive ya to my place; you can meet my teenage daughter and have a cuppa tea and some tucker until John gets home!"

Wait. What?

I'd claim to have good instincts about people, but my night with Robert proves otherwise. Yet somehow I ended up in Rebecca's home, an ordinary, well-tended house that would fit neatly in any suburb, having tea and snacks with her and her sixteen-year-old daughter. Then the father, tall and weathered, came home to find his wife and only child entertaining a Black male stranger, and I once again braced for trouble.

"I just locked up the observatory," John said after introductions and a bone-breaking handshake. "But what the hell, let's go up and see what we can see."

A short drive later, I was peering at nebulae and globular clusters, things I'd only seen in photographs, now live before my eyes. The observatory was no Mount Palomar; it consisted of a small collection of high-end telescopes for the amateur astronomer, gazing up from their tripods into the southern sky. With such optics, even with the pristine viewing conditions at Uluru, the celestial objects I saw could only appear as tiny flecks in space, barely discernible as the clouds of gas, dust, and light from which the universe is made. But to me, witnessing their grandeur for the first time, they were remarkable, as breathtaking as the generosity of the people who had defied my expectations, carried like luggage from a different place with a history of different woes, to give me the stars.

Sometimes it pays to get lost.

At John's recommendation, I joined his tour of Uluru the next day. I had planned to climb the rock, in a nod to the iconic gay film *Priscilla, Queen of the Desert,* which culminates in its three queer heroes summiting in full regalia. ("A cock in a frock on a rock," the actor Terence Stamp, nearly unrecognizable inhabiting his transgender character, Bernadette, quips of the plan.) But then I learned from John that the Aborigines who steward the land ask visitors not to climb Uluru; it's considered disrespectful of their most sacred site, akin to zip-lining through the Vatican. (In 2019, the climb was officially closed permanently.) So instead I opted for the base tour, a two- to three-hour walk around Uluru's perimeter that John led in the early morning, before the desert summer heat would make it impossible.

It proved to be one of my better choices. I knew that the monolith was central to Aboriginal spirituality, but I didn't understand until that tour that that spirituality was written in the rock, not by human hands and not in words or images, but in the natural features of the stone. Each protrusion and fissure, every rockfall and sheared-off cliff face, was tied to some myth of Australia: the trail left by a legendary lizard, the shattered spot where two great beings clashed. As viscerally as the pictorials in stained glass in the windows of a cathedral, Uluru tells the stories of Australia to those who know how to read it. But these constitute more than just images of sacred tales; the myths live in the rock, the spirituality integral to the land itself.

I was moved by Uluru to consider my own spirituality. I'd been raised without any organized religion, something I considered a boon when I saw the long suffering so many of the queer faithful endured when their sexuality seemed to come in conflict with their faith and its religious authorities. As a child I'd vacillated between atheist and agnostic, not fully understanding either or feeling that they really fit me. My spiritual impulses resided in a summer breeze and a blade of grass, and eventually birding was the principal lens through which I connected with the natural world that nourished me. While a deep connection to nature can be a part of the spiritual experience in many religions, it's a hallmark of the nature-based pagan. My penchant for myth, imaginative creativity, and metaphorical thinking also made a pagan path (note: there are many!) a no-brainer. Now I like to self-deprecatingly call myself a tree-hugging pagan, but back then I resisted the pagan label; I was already a Black, gay, nerd birder, so the last thing I needed was something else to make me even more of an oddity.

At Uluru, without trying to co-opt the sacredness of the site for the native Australians, I was inspired to examine some neopagan ideas I'd been mulling but that, until that moment, I'd hesitated to embrace. That living myth could be found inhabiting the land reminded me of the neopagan concept of Earth as immanent goddess, not as a deity in a spiritual realm removed from the mundane, but in the flesh, integral to the hoof and bone and stone of the world, right here, right now. I grew increasingly comfortable holding several seemingly contradictory notions in my head at the same time: that there could be a truth in the poetic anthropomorphizing of Earth and moon and stars, and yet an understanding that an immanent deity such as a living Earth could never be fully understood or contained in limited human terms. We can call Earth "she," and any fluffy New Age vision of a (usually white) woman in a diaphanous gown with flowers in her hair was perhaps a useful convention for some, but hopelessly inadequate. And all these musings, I realized, were me being full of shit, making things up to make the universe more relatable and manageable. But after all, isn't that what religion is all about?

One big advantage of an immanent goddess is that you can actually meet your deity, face to face. So at Uluru, the idea came to me to embark on a quest to know that goddess. It became a pagan pilgrimage I would revisit on four more journeys.

As the heat began to take hold and the base tour wrapped up, I had an epiphany. Over the dry plain of the desert, near the far edge of Uluru, I spotted a falcon, an Australian Kestrel hovering in midair as it searched for prey. It was so distant it was little more than a small silhouette; I watched it hang in the crystalline sky, its tapered wings carving elegant, invisible script in the blue. "Earth is speaking to me," I thought with sudden force. "I have no idea what she's saying, but I know enough to listen."

It might have just been a heat-inspired delusion. I hadn't come to Australia seeking revelation, but, delusion or not, this is what I'd been given, and at a moment when the path ahead for me was unclear. I'd carry that epiphany home with me to the States and do a lot more listening.

"Hello, Christian!"

"Bobbie!" I'd know that voice anywhere. "What a nice surprise!"

"How was Australia?"

I wasn't back more than a week or two, so I gave her the bullet points, minus some of the more salacious bits. Not that she couldn't read between the lines; I didn't have many secrets from Bobbie. But a download on my trip wasn't the only reason she was calling.

"I have some news. Marvel just got the license from Paramount to create four series of Star Trek comics, and I've been assigned to edit them. Do you know any writers who might be interested in submitting a proposal?" I could hear her smirking through the phone line.

Do fucking cockatoos have wings?

All she'd been given were the titles of the four: two to be based on the series airing on TV at the time, *Deep Space Nine* and *Voyager* (not interested; the comics writer's hands would be tied); *Early Voyages*, about the adventures of the starship *Enterprise* before Captain Kirk (intriguing); and *Starfleet Academy*.

"*Starfleet Academy!*" I said without hesitation; just hearing the title,

I'd already formulated the broad outlines of what I'd do with it. I couldn't help myself; I was too versed in Trek lore for my thinking not to flash to the cadet squadron in the well-crafted *Next Generation* episode "The First Duty," set at Starfleet Academy. And with that template to work from, I was already populating the five-member team with archetypes, a diversity of species, and a traitorous mole. My proposal followed shortly thereafter, consisting of character descriptions and a timeline: brief plot summaries for each of the first year's twelve issues, to convey the story arc and its escalating adventures. It became the only one of the four comics Paramount approved out of the box.

Not only was I back in the Marvel fold, but it was on the terms I had always wanted in the first place: as a writer, a freelancer like Howard Mackie and Larry Hama. And writing Star Trek comics, no less.

So began the happiest professional period of my life. Everything aligned: I was working with Bobbie again, and she hired the perfect art team for the project, the penciler Chris Renaud and the inker Andy Lanning (with the team of John Royle and Tom Wegrzyn filling in periodically, to keep us on schedule so that we'd never miss shipping. Because Bobbie was still Bobbie). Not only was Chris Renaud insanely talented, but he knew Star Trek as well as I did. At times it seemed as if we were in a Vulcan mind meld together: There would be things I saw in my head that I didn't make explicit in the plot write-up that got sent to Chris, yet when the artwork came back from him, those things would be there on the page. Not to mention that he was an easygoing joy of a human being and a pleasure to work with.

And we were telling great stories. *Starfleet Academy* and *Early Voyages* were widely regarded as the most popular and successful of Marvel's Star Trek books. I'd learned from my mistakes on *Darkhold;* for example, this time I highlighted the mystery of the plot twist in the very first issue, as the cliff-hanger, rather than burying it. The most delicious fun would come when I'd deliberately write myself into a corner and have to come up with a creative way to get the story out of it. But that's a lie; even more fun was seeing Chris Renaud's pencils bringing that great escape to life. When we introduced the Klingons into our story in a tale that straddled timelines, Chris turned the story's climax into a breathtaking double-page spread that literally straddled timelines. I got to play with other Star Trek "toys" besides the Klingons, too, elements that had been neglected since the original series, most notably the blue-skinned, white-haired, antennaed Andorians, a visual tailor-made for the comics. (A few years later, *Star Trek: Enterprise* would hit TV screens and make extensive use of Andorians. We got there first.)

Even the weather aligned with the team effort. I recall that first summer working on the book as unusually comfortable: highs in New York in the low eighties with low humidity the entire time, so that I spent the summer sitting outdoors in the park on my laptop writing Star Trek comics and getting paid for it. I stopped myself every once in a while to take in the moment and recognize how good I had it.

Two issues of *Starfleet Academy* stand out as little bits of Star Trek history. In #18, when we brought back the Klingons, I had a crazy idea: Star Trek is one of only two fantastical universes with a working created language (the other being the elvish tongues of Tolkien's Middle-earth); so let's do an issue entirely in Klingon! It meant the story had to be told purely visually as much as possible; it would be my attempt at a silent issue. (It doesn't actually rise to that level of strict visual storytelling, sadly, but it was exciting to try.) I didn't have the Klingon-language chops to translate the dialogue on my own (though in the course of the issue I did invent the Klingon word for "wench") . . . but enter the Klingon Language Institute! Yes, there really is such a thing. Having translated everything from the Bible to Shakespeare into Klingon, the KLI found our little project to be mere *mangHom qaD*! *SFA* #18 was also a clever marketing ploy; we got to sell the same issue twice. When the English-language edition was released two weeks later, all we'd had to do was strip out the Klingon word balloons and replace them with English. It was the first time ever that a comic had been published entirely in Klingon. (A decade later, the comics publisher IDW would have the Star Trek license and would release an all-Klingon-language issue and trumpet it as the first of its kind. Nope. We got there first.)

In the issue preceding that one, I got to reveal Star Trek's first gay human character: the supporting player Yoshi Mishima—Japanese to honor the openly gay *Star Trek* actor George Takei, and named as a nod to the gay Japanese author Yukio Mishima. I'd originally intended one of the main characters to be the gay reveal (in addition to Yoshi, who would have been his lover), but Paramount didn't want to break that much ground in the comics. But since Paramount had the final say, and not Marvel, the blanket edict against gay characters didn't apply. Yoshi could just be Yoshi, and I was glad to do my part to finally include LGBTQ people in humanity's utopian future where we hitherto had not been seen. (Happily, the latest film reboots have made George Takei's character, Mr. Sulu, gay, and queer characters are now integral to the casts of the latest Star Trek series, *Discovery* and *Picard*. We got there first.)

Not everything was roses working on *SFA*. As the Yoshi episode suggests, Paramount approval could be a thorn in my side. But that comes with the territory with licensed comics, and as licensors go, Paramount was actually a good partner, letting me push boundaries and boldly go where no one had gone before more than I expected.

Part of that might have been because our point of contact at Paramount was himself openly gay. So when he and the rest of the Paramount team came to New York for several days of meetings with us Marvel folks, it fell to me to make sure Darren was taken out on the town.

"I want to go to a strip club!" Darren gushed with his slight southern twang, like a gay country boy finally landing in the big city.

Since it was a Tuesday night, there weren't a lot of options. So we ended up at King, an unremarkable gay bar on Sixth Avenue in Chelsea, where there happened to be strippers that night as well as an amateur strip contest. Darren and I bought each other rounds and cheered on the strippers with gusto and dollar bills; since the rest of the bar was somnambulant on a Tuesday night, the guys onstage were appreciative. Meanwhile, Darren and I were increasingly drunk.

"You should enter the amateur strip contest," Darren prodded for the third or fourth time.

"No way," I repeated. As a gym rat, I kept myself in shape, but parading around in public in my underwear was not my thing.

"Come on!"

"No."

"Please?"

"And don't forget to sign up for our strip contest," the emcee announced over the sound system, "with a cash prize of two hundred dollars!!!"

"Well . . . maybe . . ."

What can I say. I was drunk. And we freelancers are a hungry lot.

That's all Darren had to hear, and next thing I know he's signed me up under the name of one of the *Starfleet Academy* characters (the one Paramount wouldn't let me make gay, ironically enough). Having joined at the last minute, I was last in the lineup, and the guy right before me was a massively built steroid boy.

"I can't compete with that."

"Get up there!" And Darren pushed me onstage.

I did my thing, working my assets and taking it off down to my briefs. And because we'd lavished so much attention on the real strippers earlier, they cheered me on wildly, and I won.

"You have to be in my next film when I shoot in New York," the contest judge and porn impresario Chi Chi LaRue, a drag queen with a voice two octaves lower than Harvey Fierstein, cooed afterward.

"I'm flattered, Chi Chi, but I don't think so."

"Well, if you change your mind," she said and handed me her card.

The two hundred dollars, enough to renew my membership at my cheap-ass gym for another year, would be well spent. And Darren would be forewarned.

"Not a word of this to anyone. Ever. You understand?"

"I swear," Darren said as solemnly as inebriation would allow.

I woke up with a hangover and in a panic the next morning, since I'd overslept and now was certain to be late for the first big meeting with the Paramount team. I raced to the Marvel office and rushed through the glass spider-webbed doors of the conference room to see everyone already there—Bobbie, Darren, and the rest of the Paramount folks. I started to fumble an apology as they all stared at me coolly.

And then in unison, they all pulled out dollar bills and rushed toward me.

I nearly died of laughter and mortification, except first I would have had to kill Darren, and that would have been bad for *SFA*'s future approvals. It was nice to see something of the old Marvel still lived on.

So everything in fact was pretty much roses with *Starfleet Academy,* until somebody chopped down the rosebush. When it came time to negotiate renewal of the Star Trek license, corporate at Marvel and Paramount couldn't come to terms. So the plug was abruptly pulled on all of Marvel's Star Trek comics, and *SFA* ended abruptly after nineteen issues.

That would not be before a young teen reader would send us a letter of admiration for our work, expressing a passion for our wild, Amazon-like Andorian character, though perhaps Yoshi Mishima being gay is what really moved her. It moved her so much that in her adulthood, now a successful writer herself breaking barriers as a trans woman comics creator pushing for inclusion on the page and behind the page, Mags Visaggio would cite *Starfleet Academy* as one of her influences. Nothing could make me prouder.

I can't say that we had an impact on the broader Star Trek universe. Nothing that happens in the comics is considered canon, which is to say, the TV series and movies ignore the comics and go their own way. I consider it a victory that nothing we did in the comics was directly contradicted by what came later in the shows, a small indicator that we integrated our tales well into the established Trekverse. Indeed, some of our moves within the comic were later echoed by similar aspects on the shows. And at least one character from *Starfleet Academy* lived on in the work of other writers, who included the wild Andorian in non-canon Star Trek novels—perhaps the nicest validation.

But regardless of the place our efforts hold in Trek lore, I like to think our storytelling made an impression on readers, as it did with Mags. From the introduction of human queerness in Trek, to a principal cast that for a time was majority women, to a Black man in that cast from an established Trek alien species that until then had been all white—thus continuing to reverse the whitewashing of aliens in the original *Star Trek* TV series—we did our best to live up to Gene Roddenberry's vision of a better, more inclusive humanity, a humanity that has finally evolved past the need to "other" its neighbors.

The series' main artist, Chris Renaud, would resurface in Hollywood years later, working on animated films. Eventually he would co-direct a feature film called *Despicable Me* and give the world those yellow lozenges beloved by youngsters everywhere, the Minions. Go, Chris!

Kicked out of Eden again, I returned to the oath I swore when I got laid off from my Marvel staff job: Having worked at a job I loved, I couldn't fathom taking another full-time job until I found something else I loved just as much. So I earned my living freelance copyediting, drifting into the pharmaceutical arena where the pay is far better than in magazines.

In the meantime, with the penciler John Dennis I started my own series, *Queer Nation: The Online Gay Comic,* with some help from other artists, all of whom very kindly worked for the pittance I could pay them. The internet was still young, but the idea of reaching LGBTQ folks directly in their homes, without their having to buy the comic in a shop if they were closeted or in a remote area, and without the expense of printing, should have made the logistics of a queer comic on a big scale finally doable.

And I had a big scale in mind, not just for the audience I wanted to reach, but for the story itself: an over-the-top, tongue-firmly-planted-in-cheek satire/drama about the rise of an LGBTQ nation when a right-wing maniac takes over the presidency of the United States. (Not that that could ever happen in real life.) It all begins when a mysterious comet passes too close to Earth, the debris from its tail falling to the surface as "fairy dust" containing unique lambda rays that trigger the development of superpowers in queers the world over.

We managed to publish about two years of stories, a few pages every other week, and built up a strong following for the adventures of violent bad boy Lucifyr; drag queen Miss Thang, who can change her outfit with a snap of her fingers; pistol-packing Outlaw, the Last Lesbian on Earth; and a host of other heroes fighting the fascistic forces of President Pat.

In the end, the heroes of *Queer Nation* were defeated not by Pat but by economics. I wanted to keep the comic free for all to view, but I never figured out how then to make money to keep it going. So when the chance to buy a great, affordably priced Manhattan condo—a lifelong dream—fell into my lap, I no longer had the little bit of spare cash available each month for the comic, and I had to suspend it. My oath also fell by the wayside; if I was going to make a mortgage payment every month, I had better get a real job. So in May 2001, I took a full-time gig with a pharma-related medical education company.

My closing on the condo was supposed to be set for the third week of September.

Then 9/11 happened.

8

Elegy

I GASPED THE FIRST time I saw it. It was akin to looking upon a pair of beautiful, mournful ghosts of what once had been.

Every year, in remembrance of the 2,763 people who died when the twin towers of the World Trade Center fell, the New York City skyline is pierced by two beacons shooting up as if from their footprint. For several days around the anniversary of the attacks, the columns of light ascend, visible for miles in any direction on a clear night.

The Tribute in Light was originally planned as a onetime memorial. But its shining, ethereal presence moved so many that it became an annual occurrence, a cry from the heart of New York.

But it had an unexpected downside: It became a potential death trap for birds making the long journey south before winter takes hold. Most songbirds migrate at night, to keep cool during their marathon of exertion and to reduce their exposure to predators; they navigate in part by the stars, and they can be drawn to an intense light source, like the eighty-eight xenon spotlights of the Tribute in Light. So on some nights, confused flocks wheeled in ceaseless spirals around the beacons, risking death from either exhaustion or collision with the surrounding skyscrapers. From an ecological standpoint, the timing couldn't be worse: Those days in September are typically the height of fall migration activity in New York City. Something meant to exalt the dead seemed destined to become an annual killing machine of its own.

New York City Audubon, dedicated to protecting the area's birds, and the producers of the Tribute in Light art installation seemed headed for a collision of their own. But instead of engaging in a costly and protracted fight over this, they chose to cooperate. Volunteers from NYC Audubon stay up all night for every night of the Tribute, staring up at the sky from the foot of the site, and count how many birds they see in twenty minutes; the count thus monitors the density of birds, and when too many have been snared by the beams, the lights are temporarily turned off, long enough for the flocks to regain their bearings and disperse. In this way, thousands of avian lives are spared. And the Tribute in Light, in addition to eulogizing those we lost on September 11, 2001, becomes a tribute to what we can accomplish when we pull together with mutual respect to solve a problem.

Not much else good came out of that day.

I bolted awake at about 5:30 a.m., wakened by a dream about a gyrfalcon. Capable of bringing down other birds the size of a small goose, the gyrfalcon is the largest falcon in the world, prowling the skies of circumpolar regions in search of its prey. Having never been that far north, I'd never seen one—neither the dark or gray-colored varieties nor the rare white color morph—though I longed to. In the dream a white gyrfalcon had been flying in circles around my head, making me increasingly nervous. I wasn't sure why the dream had rattled me so, and now that I was up, the sense of urgency and unease faded. Since I was awake early and since the dream that had roused me was about a bird, I took it as a sign and decided to go birding in Central Park.

This was unusual for me for the fall. Though I'm a regular all through the spring, I don't bird the park much in the fall. For one thing, the birds aren't singing, and as an ear birder I both cherish those unique sound signatures and use them to help lead me to the most interesting finds. For another, adult males in breeding plumage—those spectacular specimens in bold patterns and colors—are far less common in the fall migration, when birds have molted out of their spring finery and drabber females and young birds predominate. But mostly, I barely hit the park in the fall because if I were to abandon my social obligations the way I do in the spring to devote myself to birding, I doubt I'd have any friends left. ("Get better friends!" the late Starr Saphir, a Central Park birding legend, once quipped to me in response.)

But I knew conditions were right for a bonanza day; when I'd gone to bed, the forecast was for a cold front to slide down from the north overnight, bringing northwest winds that would likely push a wave of birds heading south right to us. So I grabbed my binoculars, stopped by my polling place to vote in the mayoral primary (too many Black folk paid in blood for the right to vote for me to ever skip an election), and went to the Ramble.

The morning unfolded in spectacular fashion: a crystal clear blue sky, comfortable temperatures, the park in its full leafy glory; Great Crested Flycatchers whooping and swooping through the branches, Chestnut-Sided Warblers in their distinctive emerald-with-eye-ring autumn attire, American Redstarts fanning their tails and flitting through the air, alive with the faint trill of crickets.

It kept getting better and better, and though I'd arrived solo, as so often happens, a bunch of us regulars gradually fell in with one another to form a small group birding together through the Ramble. "You could almost forget you're in the middle of Manhattan," I said, and then had to add "except for the sirens." The urgent howl of emergency vehicles is a regular feature of the soundscape in a city as densely populated as this one, so none of us thought anything of it, even as we heard more. And more.

We continued through the Ramble. A stranger rushed up to us. "Have you heard? A plane crashed into the World Trade Center!" And just as quickly she rushed away. In New York, strangers don't randomly approach you to volunteer information, or if they do, it's because they suffer from mental illness, and it's best to steer clear. Moreover, everything around us—the profusion of great birds, the perfect pastoral setting of the park, the easy camaraderie among us birders—was at odds with her urgent pronouncement. Who was that strange woman, I thought, and what was she talking about? I imagined a little two-seat propeller plane sticking out incongruously from the side of one of the towers and tried to dismiss the vision.

We saw two park maintenance workers on the other side of a small clearing. Instead of working, they were huddled close around their motorized cart, listening intently to a radio. Something was going on.

Our group broke up to head our separate ways out of the park—all but one. One friend made the conscious decision to remain in the tranquility of the park.

"You're staying?" I asked, a bit breathless as I picked up my pace to exit.

"I'm going to sit here and read my book," she said with calm resolve as she found the nearest bench and pulled the book out of her bag. She seemed determined to hold off whatever darkness the world had in store a little while longer.

Hers was the most intriguing response I saw that day, so much so that I would ask her, years later, what book she had been so determined to read: the Bible.

Stepping out of the park onto Fifth Avenue and Seventy-second Street was akin to stepping out of an idyllic garden and into a nightmare.

From a car parked on the corner, its doors open so that the people gathered around it could hear its radio, I heard the news anchor Peter Jennings's voice: "It's official. Both towers of the World Trade Center are now gone."

I blinked. Gone?

I looked toward downtown, following down Fifth Avenue with the benefit of my binoculars, but at a certain point all I could see was a wall of smoke in the distance. That, and the people—well heeled and downtrodden alike, trudging in the middle of streets devoid of their usual traffic, all moving in the same direction: uptown, away from that wall. My mind flashed to the absurd sight of people fleeing in panic in Godzilla movies, but this was real.

A young woman in a smart black dress, making the uptown trek in pumps, passed me just as her cellphone started ringing. She answered and listened to whatever it was she was being told; then she staggered to the curb and sank to her knees, sobbing.

Yes, this was very real.

With all subways, buses, and cars halted, to get home to Twenty-second Street, I had no choice but to walk in the opposite direction of everyone else, swimming upstream for fifty blocks. Before I went home to bunker in my tiny studio apartment, I stopped at my workplace, also on Twenty-second, to find it abandoned, inhabited only by the glow and sound of a TV, recounting the tragedy with no one left to witness it.

For the next few days New York was locked down. Offices and most shops were closed, and to venture into the streets was to run a gauntlet of armed soldiers, military vehicles, and fighter jet flyovers. (This last was the most unnerving; I think a part of every New Yorker flinched at the sound of a low-flying jet. I still do.) South of Fourteenth Street was completely closed off to all but residents. But even where I was on Twenty-second, the acrid smell of the smoldering ruin in lower Manhattan wouldn't let up. We New Yorkers stayed indoors, but not only because of the dubious air quality.

Our streets were now haunted. Those whose loved ones were still unaccounted for in the reckoning of the dead had plastered the town with hastily photocopied "Missing" flyers, in the desperate hope that somehow they had survived the towers' destruction and were incapacitated somewhere and that someone might know their where-abouts. Because of a hastily arranged info center for victims' relatives housed in an armory building only a few blocks away, my neighbor-hood was inundated with these flyers. Invariably the photo on them was taken in some happy moment—a birthday, a wedding, a joking snapshot—and now that moment was preserved as testament, faces smiling from every lamppost and shopwindow. If you stopped to read the descriptions, you saw they came from every walk of life, from janitors and busboys at Windows on the World restaurant to titans of finance at Cantor Fitzgerald; their names were a polyglot tour of the globe, their smiling faces of every complexion; and near the end were always to be found the fateful words "worked on the 103rd floor" or a similar lofty level. And you knew they were gone.

So we stayed home, cooped up in tiny apartments with nothing to do and nowhere to go, riveted to the news on our TV screens. As I watched the towers burn time and again, a scene of human horror and falling bodies, I fixated on something in the foreground: a gull passing by on serene wings, pristine in white and gray. The juxtaposition of those images jarred my sensibilities; they were too incongruous to rec-oncile. I was reminded that for all the madness we people inflict on one another, the grandeur of nature endures. I thought of the achingly blue sky of the past few days, of the grace and wonder of being in the park that morning; that even with that cataclysm the migration goes on, the great cycles of nature continue. I found comfort in a larger world resilient despite our worst.

After two days of nonstop news—the local all-news cable channel, NY1, was keeping the whole town informed on what was happening in our wounded city in the aftermath—the reporting took a new turn. A triage center had been set up in the sprawling Chelsea Piers sports complex that starts at Twenty-third Street along the Hudson, on the West Side, a NY1 reporter told us; now they'd put out a call for supplies like ice, personal toiletries, and clean T-shirts. "Finally!" I thought. "Something I can do to help." So I grabbed a box, bought out the local supermarket of all their ice, and since I lived about as far east as you could go before falling into the East River, I waited for the crosstown bus—at least some of the buses were running again—to carry me to the opposite side of Manhattan to Chelsea Piers.

While I stood at the bus stop, another guy walked up with his own boxful of the requested items. "You saw the NY1 story too, eh?" I said to him, and we shared a moment until we boarded the nearly empty bus once it arrived. Not empty for long; as the bus continued west, at each stop more and more people climbed on carrying boxes, until the bus was packed with New Yorkers and their armloads.

As we neared the West Side Highway, the afternoon sun washed the streets with gold. I was awed by the spectacle; not the gorgeous light itself, but rather the face of New York it illuminated. For looking out the bus window, I saw a thing as beautiful as any tanager or warbler I would ever see: a river of humanity flowing west, like that stunned mass walking uptown on the morning of the attack, but this time twice as dense, this time purposeful—pulling wagons and pushing laundry carts and balancing boxes overflowing with the things we'd been asked to bring if we could, and we did, by foot, bus, and taxicab, in numbers that the wide-eyed volunteers at the triage center had to scramble to accommodate.

By the time I got back home, the same NY1 reporter was on the air again. "Stop! Stop! They have enough!"

I have never been more in love with my city than on that afternoon.

On Friday that week it finally rained, in a steady, all-day gloom. The streak of perfect weather, which had seemed so wrong in the aftermath of all that had happened, at last gave way to a city's grief.

And grief, not rage, was very much the sentiment in town: grief for the dead, of course, but also grief for our wounded city and for that so very New York sense that anything is possible. Over the months that followed, I would listen to U2's plaintive "All I Want Is You" many times over, in yearning for the lost souls and a metropolis still whole that I wanted back. But that bright, untouched metropolis was never coming back, if it had ever really existed. It turns out that anything was indeed possible in New York and the possibilities were darker than we had imagined.

In other parts of the country, I think the cry for vengeance ran stronger than any other impulse. But in New York, while American flags appeared everywhere in a display of unity, that patriotism wasn't sharpened into a weapon of retribution, much as such feelings were justified. At least in what I experienced and saw around me, the patriotic fervor manifested itself as an outpouring of welcome and thanks to the many who had traveled to New York from other parts of the country to help put our city back together; the patriotism informed a fervent desire to heal.

New Yorkers, a famously brusque lot, for a little while were actually kind and patient with one another, in semiconscious recognition that we all needed to mend. Everyone in town had been touched somehow by what had happened; this once, every New Yorker—from those who ride the subway to those who tool around in limousines, from swells in Park Avenue penthouses to people living on the streets—had something in common.

So on that rainy Friday, the first day that my office was open again after the attack, I stepped outside at lunchtime with no plan other than to clear my head. I ended up doing what we generally don't do in New York under normal, non-hookup circumstances: I chatted with a total stranger.

He looked to be about my age, standing on the same Flatiron District street corner: a guy seeing something in the rain, or behind the rain, as I was. I don't remember his name; I don't remember how the conversation started. I only know we spontaneously decided to have lunch together, this total stranger and I, in the old-school diner right behind us, Eisenberg's. We told each other our stories as I allowed myself the comfort of a grilled cheese sandwich, the gray of the world washing against the windows while we stayed warm and dry inside. When we were done, we ventured back into the rain and went our separate ways, never to cross paths again.

I had tried mightily to convince myself I wasn't emotionally affected. Maybe it was my long-standing attempt at Vulcan-like mental discipline; maybe it was a determination to "not let the terrorists win" by admitting I'd been derailed in any way. I tried to play it off to friends and family that everything in my world, beyond the obvious disruptions, was business as usual. I am sometimes a fool.

I was relieved when I reached Sean in the days after 9/11. Though we'd been friends for years, I didn't know what part of town he worked in, and I feared that his large financial institution might have been headquartered at Ground Zero. I was counting my blessings that my immediate social circle had gone unscathed; Rob Deraney was just about the only other person I knew in finance, and he didn't work anywhere near the towers. Rob and I had just started testing the waters of romance; I was still figuring out how much of a spark there might be between me and this smart, handsome man. Both about the same age, we'd met at an LGBTQ Ivy League alumni mixer, where I was struck by his ebullience, enough that we'd gone on a couple of dates afterward. We were due for another, so after things had settled a bit after the disaster, I gave him a call at the vacation rental he shared at the shore with a few friends.

One of those friends answered, and when I asked for Rob, there was an intake of breath and a silent pause.

No, Rob didn't work in the twin towers. Some lucky few who did, maybe they missed their usual train that day and so were running late, or they partied too much the night before and woke up so hungover they took a sick day, and that twist of fate saved their lives. Rob had the opposite kind of luck. He just happened to have had a breakfast meeting with his clients at Windows on the World, on the morning of

September 11, on the lofty 106th level of the North Tower. It turns out one of those faces preserved by a snapshot in an eternal smile was known to me. I had counted my blessings too soon.

Robert J. Deraney played the piano he kept in his Upper West Side "classic six" apartment that he dreamed of owning one day if the building ever went co-op. He was forty-three years old.

Years later, settling into a seat on the Long Island Rail Road on the way to visit family, I pulled out my book to pass the time during the ride. My wanderlust had reasserted itself, this time with a longing to trek the Himalaya; so to get a flavor of what that part of the world is like, I was reading Jon Krakauer's *Into Thin Air,* the chronicle of a disastrous attempt to summit Mount Everest. I was eager to get back to it, since I was nearing the end, and in those final pages I found a poem that hit me like an arctic blast and swept me back to the morning of 9/11, before the planes and the 2,763 lives lost, to a predawn dream about a gyrfalcon that whether by coincidence or portent was urgent enough to wake me up. I'd read the poem a long time before but forgotten it. By William Butler Yeats, "The Second Coming" begins,

> Turning and turning in the widening gyre
> The falcon cannot hear the falconer;
> Things fall apart; the centre cannot hold;
> Mere anarchy is loosed upon the world,
> The blood-dimmed tide is loosed, and everywhere
> The ceremony of innocence is drowned;
> The best lack all conviction, while the worst
> Are full of passionate intensity.

9

On Top
of the World

PURGATORY IS REAL. Just go to Nepal and cross the threshold
into the domestic terminal of Kathmandu's only airport.

The overall impression is of a place lost in time: a cavernous, disorganized space whose antiquated signage and well-worn plastic seats hark back to a bygone era. Airline check-in stations are
movable stands; vending machines dispensing soda and snacks serve as
the nearest thing to a food court. Giant electric fans drone on, as does
the constant, polyglot buzz from the masses of people; but like those
people, the air the fans are meant to move doesn't seem to go anywhere. Here, amid chaos, confusion, and luggage stacked higher than
the heads of the ubiquitous groups of Germans visiting this small
mountain-spined country, tourists and locals alike mill about clinging
to the same slender hope: that today might be the day they get out.

When I had arrived in Kathmandu three days earlier, in the beginning of October 2010, I had passed swiftly through the international
terminal and took little notice of the airport. I was far too excited at
being one step closer to a long-held dream, about to embark on the
adventure of a lifetime: trekking the Himalayan mountains. The ulti-

mate goal: the foot of the tallest point on the planet, dubbed Mount Everest by British imperialists but known either as Sagarmatha (as the Nepalese call it; "Head in the Sky" or "Peak of Heaven," among other possible translations) or for centuries as Chomolungma ("Mother Goddess of the World" in Tibetan). Because the mountain sits right on the border between Nepal and Tibet, I'd chosen to approach the "Mother Goddess" from the Nepalese side—the political situation in Tibet, under Chinese occupation, being too fraught. (I still persist in using the Tibetan name, because the people on both sides of the mountain, the Sherpa, are ethnically and linguistically related to Tibetans.) But for this trip, unlike so many others, I wouldn't be traveling alone.

Scott, my on-again, off-again boyfriend, was already waiting in our Kathmandu hotel when I arrived. Tall and taciturn, Scott was a graphic designer back then, a man with an amazing eye in need of some recognition of that talent. We had little in common: White, West Coast born and bred, Scott had next to no interest in birding or the nerd culture I metabolized as an essential part of a healthy diet. Our relationship should not have worked, and in fact with each passing year that we'd lived crammed together in my small New York one-bedroom apartment, the silences between us had become more pronounced. Eventually Scott relocated to the West in a friendly split. But after the better part of a year, as he struggled to put his career together, he'd wanted to come back. And I wasn't one to say no to a handsome, broad-shouldered guy who offered the comfort of familiarity and seemed to have a good heart, if a restlessness about who, what, and where would make that heart happy.

Scott had dreamed of visiting the Himalaya even longer than I had, so now, in a test of our reconciliation, we'd decided to do it together. (The Sanskrit word "Himalaya" translates literally as "Abode of Snow" and is the term for the entire mountain range; so strictly speaking it's incorrect to make it plural and say "the Himalayas.") Without direct flights from New York to Kathmandu, I'd chosen a stopover in Bang-

kok, where I could take an extra day to visit an old friend; Scott left
New York City later, with only a brief connection in India, and arrived
in Kathmandu sooner. Reunited in the Nepalese capital, we were eager
for the real start of our adventure—though Scott was unaware that I
had two hidden agendas for the trip.

Our plan was straightforward: We had zero intention to attempt to
summit Chomolungma. Neither of us had any technical climbing experience, and only fools bent on getting themselves and others killed
try to conquer the mountain's challenges—whiplash weather, extreme
cold, treacherous precipices, and want of anything to breathe—
without it. Instead, we would fly with our guide from Kathmandu to
the small village of Lukla, the gateway to the Everest Trail. From
Lukla, nestled in the lower altitudes (2,860 meters, or 9,380 feet) of
the range, Scott and I would trek: Over the course of several days and
aided by a porter to carry our bags, we would walk the forty miles and
the steep climb in elevation to Everest South Base Camp (5,364 meters, or 17,598 feet), and then back.

But so far, instead of walking, we'd only been sitting, for hours—
when we could find a place in the Kathmandu airport to sit at all.
We'd spent the day before doing exactly the same thing: sitting and
waiting. We were not alone in this; scores of Nepalese, who looked as
if they were just trying to get from point A to point B to visit family,
were stranded as well. An equal number of Westerners, would-be trekkers like ourselves, were in the same holding pattern, stymied by
weather that looked like mostly clear skies to us but that somehow
precluded flights to the mountains. Some tourists perched atop the
piles of duffel bags, others stretched out on the floor, but all of us wore
the same forlorn look. When air traffic supposedly resumed, but still
hardly anyone was moving, word filtered out that a crash (nonfatal,
happily) at Lukla had shut things down again, until the debris could
be completely cleared. This news gave all us trekkers pause; apparently,
there was more to flying into Lukla than mostly clear skies would sug-
gest. Now we were not only waiting but unnerved.

It was maddening, after months of planning, to be so tantalizingly close to walking among the clouds, only to find oneself stuck on the ground. While idling the day before, I'd already reread the first of only three books I'd packed for the trek. (Our duffel bags had to weigh strictly fifteen kilos or less.) So I pulled out the second, my journal for this trip, and began to catch up on my entries. It wasn't long before Scott nudged me.

"I'm not sure," he said, "but the Nepalese seem fascinated by what you're doing."

My face buried in my scribbling, I looked up to catch more than a few of them staring. That's nothing new; from Argentina to Thailand, in the far-flung places I've traveled where they rarely if ever see Black people, I've been stared at. (The most annoying was a punk kid who shouted to his friends, "¡Mira! ¡El hermano de Michael Jackson!" in Mexico. The most amusing was in Buenos Aires, when the only tickets left for that week's opera performance were the most expensive—after the exchange rate, about the same price as the cheap seats back home at the Met. So I ended up in the magnificent Teatro Colón in a box seat like some visiting sovereign, with all of Argentine high society seated in the orchestra looking up wondering who I was; I simply smiled serenely, as any good visiting sovereign would.) I suppose I know how a rare Kirtland's Warbler feels when it finds itself in Central Park with us birders lining up to ogle it.

But this was different. I got the impression that it wasn't so much me they were staring at as what I was doing. I wouldn't think writing in longhand for hours would be perceived as unusual, but apparently it was.

Having noted every detail of every dream I'd had for the last two nights—we had that much time on our hands—I was done journaling anyway. Out came the third book, my field guide to the birds of Nepal, so I could at least be productive and bone up on the species of the Himalaya. My work highlighting which species in the guide are found at altitude attracted the attention of two children, ages about ten or eleven, who no doubt were bored out of their skulls, too, just like everyone else. Of course I was delighted to show them the guide; whenever anyone evinces an interest in birds, but especially youngsters as I was when I started with South Shore Audubon, I get effusive. The pair wandered off eventually, but soon returned with a token of appreciation for me for showing them the birds: a small wafer with something chocolate-like from the vending machine. The processed confection would have been hard to swallow but for its sweet source, which rendered it irresistible; the kids were parting with a precious treat to gift it to me. And, coming up on eight hours without any real food, I was starving anyway.

An hour more of tedium, and the day was done. Several groups of trekkers had made it out near the day's end, but not us. There would be no further flights to Lukla this day, we were told. After a second entire day parked in the airport, Scott and I were sent back to our hotel once more, dejected and no closer to the heavens. We wolfed down a long-delayed proper meal and collapsed in our room; we had to be ready to rise early the next day so that we could start the wait for a flight all over again. Exploring more of Kathmandu that night was out of the question.

Kathmandu! The syllables alone conjure exoticism to the Western ear, a suggestion of Shangri-La. In reality, Kathmandu constantly jostles against itself, past and present: Ornate sixteenth-century brick palaces vie for the sky with massive temples, while the streets are an ongoing traffic apocalypse. On dusty roads just wide enough for a minivan, scooters zoom in both directions past passersby on either side, while a donkey pulling a wagon loaded with a giant block of ice forces said minivan to crawl behind at its plodding pace. The major thoroughfares are a source of speeding terror and incessant din, and the boulevards in and around Durbar Square, the heart of the old city, can turn into clogged pedestrian mosh pits—"pedestrian," that is, until a car tries to push through the crowd. In a walk through that historic district, during a day Scott and I spent touring the city when

I first arrived, we ended up packed in the midst of a mob that couldn't move; I grew worried that any sudden surge would leave us crushed, and Scott, who's uncomfortable in crowds to begin with, was on the verge of a panic attack.

After long, tense minutes extricating ourselves, we retreated to an upstairs outdoor café for lunch, and Kathmandu transformed. Forgotten below were the crowds and the insane traffic, replaced by the calm of a warm breeze and a sky dappled with fair-weather clouds. The neighborhood's redbrick buildings spread before us, only now revealing a mosaic of rooftop gardens, lush with herbs, vines, and flowers, obviously well tended. Kites drifted on the breeze, tethered to a few of the gardeners, and Black Kites, the ubiquitous feathered kind that seem to have spread their wings to every corner of the Old World, soared alongside.

That evening, strolling the formal and foreign beauty of the Garden of Dreams and wandering the maze of narrow alleys and lively shops of Thamel, Kathmandu's tourist district (my mind happily imagining a cutthroat around every bend), or watching a trio of young Hindu women, covered completely from the neck down in flowing, colorful fabric that nonetheless couldn't hide the swing of their hips as they sauntered by, I finally surrendered. Let me be jostled between the frenetic energy of the streets and the serenity of the rooftops, between donkey-drawn ice carts and bicycle rickshaws and motorbike drivers hurtling ahead with passengers clinging for dear life behind. I had left Bangkok with a sense that, outside its glorious temple district, it was a teeming and tawdry metropolis; Kathmandu, by contrast, left me smitten.

Not so smitten, however, that Scott and I weren't ready to leave.

Waking at 6:30 in the morning on Airport Day 3 and ready to vacate the premises on a moment's notice, we waited in our hotel room for word that we might get out. This was our tour company's concession after yesterday, when the impatient New Yorker in me took charge upon seeing others take flight while we were left behind.

I'd gotten stern with Ngima, our guide/translator/facilitator/constant companion from the tour company. (Being hangry hadn't helped my mood.) A small, slightly built Sherpa with sun-wrinkled skin that made his age impossible to guess, Ngima had the gentlest soul and a somewhat passive disposition; passivity was not going to get us on the next plane. With two days already lost—time we could only make up by sacrificing crucial rest days needed to acclimatize to the increasing altitude—any further delay would pretty much guarantee that we wouldn't be able to make it to Chomolungma. And I hadn't come all this way to be denied. To ease my agitation, the tour company had agreed that we should wait in the relative comfort of our hotel for as long as possible—something they should have thought of at least a day earlier.

At 7:30 a.m., the call came through: Be ready in forty-five minutes to get to the airport, and then, once we were there, more waiting. Another eight hours of it, watching other Westerners depart. The flights to Lukla were going to end for the day soon, and Scott and I would be back at the hotel. I was ready to scream.

Then, suddenly, Ngima had procured boarding passes! I felt like Charlie holding the golden ticket to Willy Wonka's chocolate factory; when we were ushered into the boarding gate waiting area, it was akin to entering the promised land.

We crossed the tarmac to a tiny propeller plane, where they seated Scott, Ngima, me, and the handful of other passengers so as to most evenly distribute the weight. My adrenaline surged; we were actually doing this!

The flight attendant handed each of us a pair of cotton balls; I turned them over in my hands quizzically, until she motioned toward her ears. Simple but effective noise cancellation in place, the propellers roared and we zoomed at last into the sky and were greeted by our first good look at the Himalaya. They're the tallest mountains on the planet for a reason: They're the youngest, formed only about forty-five million years ago (a short season in geologic time) when the Indian subcontinent slammed into the rest of Eurasia; the Himalaya are the crinkled-up impact margin. Because they're so young, erosion hasn't had time to grind them down and soften the sharp edges. So the mountains out the plane window were all hard angles, striking fractals of stone in sharp relief, adorned with jagged peaks.

One of those peaks was coming right at us.

Our short flight was about to end at Lukla, and with the speed we were hurtling toward the wall of rock, it seemed it would end tragically. Suddenly I understood why flying to Lukla was such a difficult transit; buffeted by Himalayan crosswinds, puny propeller planes had to touch down on a ledge carved into the side of a mountain and then immediately execute a ninety-degree right turn, or else become a permanent part of the landscape. ("Fender bender" crashes like the one we'd heard about the day before are almost routine. Lukla airport is regularly ranked the most dangerous in the world, although I didn't know that at the time, which is probably a good thing.)

I could feel the other passengers holding their breath, too, their eyes bugging out just like mine in the split second before landing as the mountain rushed forward to claim us. The moment the wheels were on the ground, the pilot slammed on the brakes and, thankfully, managed the hairpin turn with neat precision.

It made for one hell of a rush as a welcome into the Himalaya, and as we stepped off the plane, there was no doubt that we were in a different locale altogether. The balmy warmth of the Kathmandu valley had given way to crisp autumn air and the scent of burning firewood. We'd arrived at a cluster of mostly stone buildings, one or two stories high, with blue roofs against a backdrop of snowy peaks: Lukla, the gateway to the Everest Trail and Chomolungma.

At long last, our real journey had begun. But one of the two things I hadn't shared with Scott was that for me the journey had started years earlier, and this was more than just a trek. I was about to embark on what I considered the most important trip of a multipart spiritual pilgrimage. I was on the final leg of the Five-Way Road.

. . .

As a "tree-hugging" pagan (the term "pagan" is so broad, encompassing so many divergent belief systems, that there are more brands of paganism out there than feathers on a swan), I find the divine in the natural world, here and now, through which I connect my inner spirituality to the larger universe. Though I resisted the label for a while, my queer experience had taught me that denying the truth about oneself rarely leads anywhere good. As the Borg say on *Star Trek*: Resistance is futile.

I'm also an old-school northeasterner in that I consider religion a very private, personal affair; it shouldn't matter to anyone except the person doing the praying/meditating/speaking in tongues/whatever or nothing at all. It's bad form to throw one's own religion in other people's faces, and worse to throw a spotlight on somebody else's.

Further, because religious beliefs encompass the irrational, they invariably have elements that seem ridiculous to nonbelievers. Religion is poetry, trading in metaphors that convey truth that isn't literal but remains deeply meaningful to those to whom it speaks. To everyone else, it's gibberish. It can be worse than pointless to yammer away at each other in our different religious "languages."

All of which is to say, I don't usually take a personal approach to discussing spiritual beliefs, my own included. But there are two things to know, beliefs that are common to many nature-based pagans, to put this pilgrimage to the Himalaya in context:

1. There is no heaven or hell; the divine doesn't exist in a separate, perfect realm, but rather is an integral part of the material world we inhabit, and Earth itself can be seen as a living, breathing mother goddess.

2. The classical elements—earth, air, fire, and water—each associated with a cardinal compass direction (among other

correspondences), while scientifically discredited as the constituents of all things, remain a useful mental tool; they can serve as a lens to focus understanding, attention, and connection.

The first puts us tree-hugging pagans in the unique position of being able to know our deity physically, intimately, in a tangible face-to-face way. One would merely have to become wholly familiar with life in every part of the globe to know her completely! That of course would be impossible, even in a thousand lifetimes. But maybe I could know her, at least in essence, in one.

The idea dawned on me about a dozen years earlier, while I was in Australia in 1996, in the morning light of the walking tour I took around the base of Uluru. Before me stood this magnificent natural wonder that already had me thinking about myth made manifest, about an immanent goddess. But more, Uluru epitomized the South, which for many of us pagans is associated with the element of fire and the human will, the drive to get things done. Located in the heart of Australia in the Southern Hemisphere, here stood an enormous red monolith in a sun-scorched desert, in a habitat shaped by wildfires— all the South in one package. Most important, I could *feel* the sacred nature of the spot. Maybe I was attracted by the same ineffable qualities that make Uluru sacred to the Aborigines, or maybe it was sacred to me by association, taking on that quality in my eyes only because I knew it has that quality in theirs. But even that was valid, Uluru giving insight into our mother Earth by offering insight into one of her peoples.

At that moment, I conjectured: What if one were to extend the concept, taking an elemental approach to knowing our mother Earth—identifying four other natural wonders of the world (for West, North, East, and Center) that epitomize their respective elements? It wouldn't be the same as getting to know every inch of the planet, but it had the potential to introduce me to mother Earth on a grand, global scale, as seen through a very pagan lens. Thus the idea for a multipart, far-flung pagan pilgrimage was born, which I would eventually dub the Five-Way Road.

At first it was just an idea, nothing more than the intellectual exercise of figuring out where these sacred sites might be. They had to be natural; I didn't want human constructs like Stonehenge or Angkor Wat, because even though I prized insight into a local culture as part of these possible journeys, I didn't want someone else's interpretation to mediate between me and getting in touch with my goddess. The sites had to lie roughly in accordance with their compass direction, relative to a conventional geographic understanding of the globe; they had to inspire a sense of the numinous; and of course, they had to thoroughly represent their element, as Uluru had done for fire/the South. Bonus points for adding diversity to the habitats and cultures encompassed by the five. I mulled over candidates, never anticipating that I'd ever actually be able to visit more than one, if any.

But over the years, with that idea lodged in the back of my brain, I gradually found my way to one site, then another. On a return trip to South America to write about Rio for an LGBTQ travel publication, I tacked on a visit to the falls of Iguazú. Carving a huge crescent into a jungle river, this gigantic system of cascades on the Brazil-Argentina border boggles the mind; Iguazú awed me, thrilled me as our Zodiac was drenched beneath the falls, lifted my heart with its rainbows and butterflies shooting all over the place, and left me melancholy when a day of rain merged the sky with the gray mist from the falls. It couldn't help but feel sacred and serve as the epitome of the West, associated with the element of water and with emotion.

Two trips to Iceland were less successful. At the farthest edge of Europe and just below the Arctic Circle, this island is one of the most geologically active places on the planet. And since the Vikings who populated the island chopped down all the trees there for fuel and timber more than a thousand years ago, the lack of forest cover means one is keenly aware of the land and its every contour. Yet I never found that single spot, like Uluru or Iguazú, that called out to me as the epitome of the North and the element of earth. I still can't shake the feeling the site is there, somewhere I haven't found yet—appropriately, since North is also associated with hidden things. Perhaps it's a mysterious cavern underground, buried in Iceland's restless earth.

Then came Africa.

I'd been saving my pennies and accumulating vacation time for quite a while, with the goal of an East African safari in December 2005/January 2006. It would be a chance to see all the iconic wildlife and a whole new faunal region of birds (I had made certain to book a birding-inclusive safari). It would be a *Roots* experience; although my lineage almost certainly originated in West Africa, in setting foot anywhere on the continent, I would be the first in my family to return since our ancestors had been taken away in chains. And it would get me to the Great Rift Valley, a geological rupture stretching for four thousand miles that over the last six million years served as the birthplace of humankind. Somewhere in that vast expanse, only a fraction of which I would visit, I hoped to stumble upon the epitome of the Center—associated with the fifth element (transcendent "ether") and spirit.

I came home with indelible birding memories: bee-eaters launching themselves high into the air from a parapet wall on the island of Lamu, their carmine bodies flaming in the light of the setting sun; a glimpse of a ribbon dancing through the leaves, expecting to find a child playing with a strip of cloth and instead discovering an African Paradise Flycatcher chasing bugs, its long tail plumes streaming behind; a Tawny Eagle up close and on the ground atop its kill, as regal and deadly as any lion, leopard, or cheetah we saw stalking the savanna; a whopping 275 new bird species in all.

I also came home with a certainty of who I was. I'd left for the trip shortly after Christmas, and to help keep me fed on the twenty-six-hour multi-flight odyssey, I'd brought some of my dad's dinner rolls left over from the family feast. Impulsively I saved the last bite of the last one, and when I first set foot on African soil, I reached in my pocket and crumbled the roll to the earth. I felt awkward and a bit foolish, and it also felt right. I don't know why, but I'd felt compelled as the first to return to give the bread of my father to the land. Yet I had no illusions about "returning to the motherland," that I as an African American would somehow suddenly feel at home on a continent that was as foreign to me, and I to Africans, as any *Mayflower* descendant. Actually experiencing that disjunction, the cultural gulf between Black peoples separated by an ocean of time and tears, brought something home as no words could: We African Americans are profoundly American, and nothing and no one can diminish that.

I came home altered by one location in particular. My driver/guide and I were crossing a hot, dry plain in Tanzania in a rickety old van; an inescapable layer of red dust clung to the sweat on my skin. I was only a few days but already a gazillion zebras into the two-week safari, prompting a dry, dusty thought: "The lions aren't doing their job."

Then the van's engine began to labor as we ascended an escarpment via a series of switchbacks in the road, and things changed: The heat broke; the open windows now brought cool relief. The once Mars-like landscape grew green and lush. I perked up, curious what might lie ahead. The van topped a rise, turned a bend, and stopped. My guide jumped out.

"Come, come," he said, gesturing for me to exit too.

I stepped out to a newly revealed vista and gasped. Reaching out in both directions stood a perfect circle of mountains, and spread below us, cradled on their slopes, was Africa in microcosm: forests and savannas, rivers, lakes, and swamps. We'd reached Ngorongoro, which had been an enormous volcano until it erupted so forcefully two and a half million years ago that its cone collapsed in on itself, forming one of the world's largest intact calderas. The volcano is long since dead, but the remnant crater is anything but; Ngorongoro is packed with life, as I would soon learn firsthand in encounters with an abundance of Africa's legendary beasts. It was akin to stumbling into Arthur Conan Doyle's Lost World.

Only in Africa does the megafauna we were born alongside still roam free, and Ngorongoro's rich resources and crater boundary concentrate that megafauna into a density unmatched anywhere else. Rhinos like muscled tanks graze easily; a full-grown elephant lumbers past the tents of your campsite. The effect is of a land untouched by the ravages of human civilization. Watching the orange-red rays of the rising sun splinter over the crater's rim, one can be forgiven for mistaking it for the dawn of time.

In a literal sense, the dawn of humankind rests in this soil. Close to the crater in the greater Ngorongoro area sits Olduvai Gorge, where the famed paleoanthropologist family, the Leakeys, exhumed crucial fossils of our prehistoric kin. Only researchers are allowed to enter the small canyon, leaving the rest of us to peer over the rim at the walls of striated red rock where our secrets are buried and to wonder. In the neighboring Serengeti—"the Sea of Grass"—the nearly treeless expanse allows a steady wind to blow through Olduvai; as I stood at the precipice, I thought how the same Serengeti wind must have blown a million years ago, felt by the ancestors of every human being on the planet, just as I was feeling it now. I let my imagination listen for their voices still carried by that wind.

It turns out I had dispensed with notions of returning to the motherland too soon; here was the motherland for all humankind. And in Ngorongoro, I have no question that I found the Center, the epitome of Earth's spirit.

With the search for the North/earth tabled, that left only one part of the Five-Way Road unexplored. I'd saved it for last, not only because it would be the most arduous, but because it embodied everything I identified with: the East, associated with the mind and intellect, with the element of air, and therefore of course with birds. As far as I was concerned, the place to go was obvious.

. . .

Ngima, Scott, and I set off immediately on the Everest Trail for what little was left of the day after landing in Lukla, having met our porter there. At twenty-six years old, Subass had a strikingly handsome face and the lean build of nearly everyone in the Himalaya, his rich brown skin somewhat darker from the sun than that of most of his Tamang people. We would learn, in the course of the trek, that he was studying for his master's degree in public health at a university in Nepal's hill country, but he worked the peak of the trekking season in the Himalaya to earn enough for tuition—for a semester, the equivalent of a hundred dollars in U.S. currency. Subass's further education, the key to his future, hinged on a sum inconceivably out of reach to his parents with their five other children, yet amounted to what I'd spend on a nice dinner out in New York. As startling a reset in economic understanding as that was, the hard realities were made far more immediate as soon as we started to trek. In a pattern that would repeat daily, Subass hoisted *both* Scott's fifteen-kilo bag and my own on his back and soon disappeared ahead, moving at a fast clip—in flip-flops. Led by Ngima, Scott and I followed at a gentler pace, wearing the hiking boots we'd carefully broken in before leaving the States, boots we'd bought specifically for the trek at a price that exceeded a semester's tuition for Subass.

We didn't go far, because dusk settled onto slopes dotted with conifer trees and isolated cottages; yet we went far enough to know we were in a different world. Trains of the yak-cow hybrid called *jopkyo* passed, burdened with supplies, the gentle jangling of cowbells heralding their approach from a distance. The path, skirting around occasionally steep drop-offs, was narrow and so well worn it was just shy of seeming paved; this and even more difficult passes are the highways of the Himalaya. No roads, no vehicles, none of the infrastructure I took for granted. With few exceptions, the only way to move anything— groceries, drink, fuel, construction material, toilet paper—in or out of this area, the Solukhumbu, is by jopkyo or on foot in baskets carried on the backs of porters. People like Subass were as essential here as the tide is to a beach.

Life here is set at the pace of your own two feet. We fell into the rhythm.

After only an hour, we stopped for the night at a lodge in the tiny village of Cheplung (elevation 2,700 meters). One has to put the word "lodge" in Himalayan terms: Erect an uninsulated structure with no hot water, where only the dining area is heated (by a central stove) and where guests share restroom facilities—pit toilets down the hall—and you begin to grasp the basic level of accommodations. I'd read what to expect, yet confronting the chill of our room made for another reset in Western expectations. We surely could have gotten a somewhat better roof over our heads in larger Lukla, but Scott and I rolled with it and slept with our sweaters on.

Scott and I had traveled well together on previous trips, to Paris, Belize, and Las Vegas; the latter in particular had been a joy of Scott's making. He'd surprised me with a trip for my birthday to a place that I imagined to be patently absurd, and he'd planned it so that once we got there we reveled in the absurdity: the Star Trek Experience theme ride (loved it!), the Liberace Museum (an ode to the piano performer's kitsch flamboyance, situated in a deserted strip mall), and accommodations in the tragically faux Frenchness of the Paris Hotel and Casino, in a winking callback to our romantic visit to the real thing. Vegas is everything that's tacky about the States xeroxed up to a thousand times normal size, and we were so busy ogling its folly that we never even gambled. In this and our other travels, Scott and I had proven how much fun we could have together on the road. But as we shivered in our first Himalayan lodge, it came as a relief that we could handle a more challenging environment and its hardships without falling apart as a couple. In charting a renewed relationship, it seemed a good sign.

But still I didn't feel I could share my personal, peculiar spiritual dimension of the trek with Scott. He was definitely in the camp that finds paganism to be gibberish; he'd made that plain enough in his disdain for my modest traditions for celebrating the winter solstice (the longest night of the year, for which I'd stay awake from dusk until dawn) and the summer solstice (the longest day of the year, for which I'd stay outdoors from dawn until dusk). He'd make it clear again in a few days, when during a stop in the Himalayan crossroads town of Namche Bazaar, I'd commission a local artist to paint a mandala (a geometric design of symbolic and meditational value) rather than buy one of the gorgeous existing ones he had for sale. I wanted a mandala that incorporated symbols I find important.

"You should get one of the real ones," Scott chided and said no more, but I understood. His preference was rooted in aesthetics and authenticity, to which meaningfulness to me and my odd approach to spirituality took a decidedly back seat.

What's more, my own uncertainty made it difficult to communicate the spirituality of the trip. The Five-Way Road gave me a conceptual framework for the journey, but now that I was actually here in the Himalaya, I didn't know what that meant in practice. On the other legs of the pilgrimage that I'd deemed successes, I'd been guided by intuition, by what I'd felt: heat and wonder at Uluru, emotions and awe at Iguazú, time peeled back to human origins at Ngorongoro. This was different: I would not arrive at a destination to immediately experience it, but rather would have to walk there over several days; and because this was meant as a journey of the rational mind, intuition should be secondary at best. I had no idea what sort of epiphany I was hoping for, beyond the rush I'd felt that night, when the crescent moon had swung into a gap in the clouds to shine over the steep valley.

As we started the next day's trek on a cool and cloudy morning, I was too exhilarated to give any of that much thought; our first real day of trekking lay ahead. As we made our way up the Dudh Koshi river valley, within two hours the clouds were gone, bringing shirtsleeves warmth and light spilling into the valley. We wound our way along lush gorges, sliced by ribbons of gushing water plunging down their sides to join the river far below, its rapids jade green with glacial melt. Then we crossed the gorge, with only a rickety steel-and-cable bridge between us and a plunge of our own. Such bridges are typical of the region. No doubt these unsteady, flimsy spans—the guides, like Ngima, make sure that not too many travelers pile on them at once—have conveyed countless trekkers and residents alike across safely for years. No doubt . . .

My nerves survived such crossings and were later soothed with tea. Milk tea, lemon tea, black tea, ginger tea, mint tea—tea is a thing in the Himalaya, so even this non–tea drinker got into the act. It goes down easy with the vistas we drank in: the peak of Khumbila (at a "mere" 5,500 meters not even one of the Himalayan titans), a mountain sacred to the Sherpas, erupting through clouds to rule gracefully over the Dudh Koshi valley. We'd reached the Monju entrance of Sagarmatha National Park, Nepal's protected area for the tallest point on the planet. Chomolungma was still days away, but we got our first glimpse: no more than its long flank in the distance, beckoning to us.

We weren't the only ones eager to get there. We ended up in something of a trekker traffic jam at the entrance, with a dozen parties heading up and an equal number coming down the same trail all at once, plus trains of jopkyos bearing wide loads. I finally appreciated Ngima's wisdom in having us trek a little ways when we'd first landed in Lukla, rather than staying there for comfier accommodations: He'd made a valiant effort to space us out from the crowd. After days of pent-up passengers in Kathmandu with no flights, we'd all arrived at once, at the peak of trekking season; so Ngima had put some distance between us, right at the outset. His plan had worked, at least until now.

The congestion meant that at least for a while we had to pause periodically and step aside to let others pass. I wasn't complaining; the last two or three hours of that day's trek was nonstop ascent, and despite being aerobically fit, I was gasping for air. Even the brief pauses were welcome! By the time we'd gone from Monju to Namche Bazaar (elevation approximately 3,400 meters), we were 600 meters higher than where we'd started. Both Scott and I were feeling it.

No sooner had we arrived in Namche Bazaar than the mountain weather once again turned on a dime, and it started to pour. Fortunately, Namche Bazaar, the biggest community in the Solukhumbu, has only grown as it has catered to trekkers; so there was comfortable refuge from the rain readily available. (A basic hotel including a private bathroom and a hot shower!)

My mood wasn't so easily comforted. Scott and I had picked October for our journey because it was the warmer of the two trekking seasons (the other being in spring), with clear skies typically prevailing. But the dense cloud cover and off-and-on rain that had greeted us on our arrival at Namche Bazaar continued into the next day, and the next, and the next. Chomolungma and the other high Himalayan peaks, our objective on this trek, were hidden behind a veil of gloom.

I felt as I had in Kathmandu airport: frustrated to journey all this way, only to be denied. That feeling only deepened my malaise, for after all I was supposed to be on a spiritual quest; apparently my spirituality was so shallow that it washed away with a little rain, couldn't survive if I were deprived of the visual crutch of some mountaintops. I didn't dismiss the spectacular sights of the lower elevations, but I'd hoped for something more profound than just sightseeing. Once again I was left floundering about what insight I'd expected, and at least in terms of my pagan pilgrimage I questioned what I was even doing in the Himalaya.

Further compounding my frustration, I couldn't pursue birds as I normally would. I knew that would be the case going into the trek with non-birding Scott.

Besides, while trekking, the focus has to be on covering a certain amount of ground each day, leaving precious little room to dally or divert to track down a great species. The result was that I was traversing what to me was virgin birding territory, replete with life birds, and I had to limit myself to the ones that threw themselves at me on the trail. I thought I was prepared for that reality, but as we walked through rhododendron stands and little forests with tree limbs festooned in moss, echoing with bird sounds I'd never heard before and couldn't chase to discover their remarkable source, it chafed. A lot.

Birding Tip

Avoid trying to bird in the presence of non-birders. As you wait patiently for half an hour for that Marsh Wren to give you that definitive glimpse, you'll just piss off all your friends and relatives for holding them back.

The Large-Billed Crows, ubiquitous all-black sentinels at all the elevations we'd reached so far, presented themselves readily, most dramatically around the sweeping moors beyond Namche Bazaar, slopes carpeted in lichens and shrouded in mist, so that the crows seemed like props to complete a horror movie set. I'd been thrilled by my first White-Capped Water Redstart, a jaunty bird of rushing streams loosely resembling a small robin that's gone bald. But I'd had to let so many other sightings slip through my fingers.

The Himalayan Monal relieved that angst, at least for a little while.

Imagine a creature splattered with the rainbow iridescence of a hummingbird—aqua on the face, scarlet on the neck, golden green on the back, electric blue on the wings, copper on the tail—set off by continuous jet black underneath. Now feed it growth hormone so that the "hummingbird" has the robust stature of a game bird, and top it off with cocky plumes launching up from its head. The pheasants of Asia are notoriously stunning, and of course in my field guide I'd seen renderings of this one, the national bird of Nepal. But when we spotted our first male strolling slowly on a wooded slope, I could hardly breathe, and for once it wasn't because of the altitude. Even Scott was impressed!

The monal helped bring me out of my malaise; how could it not? Moreover, some part of my mind unclenched, the part that had been so desperately trying to find meaning in a mountain. Now I was content to let the trip be whatever it was going to be; to accept the gloomy weather along with the monal and whatever else I might find, even if it meant missing Chomolungma and the other titans, because metaphysically what I was after wasn't clear skies but clarity of thought. The elements around me were beyond my control, but the forces within me—most especially my own thoughts—were mine to master. This pilgrimage more than the others was about the journey, not the destination, and that journey was an interior one. I was here to learn whatever the Himalaya had to offer.

As if on cue, we arrived in Tengboche (elevation 3,867 meters), the most important center of Tibetan Buddhism in the region. We'd been immersed in a Buddhist context throughout the Himalaya (unlike Kathmandu and lowland Nepal, where Hinduism predominates). Since the moment we'd arrived in Lukla, we were greeted by Tibetan prayer wheels, giant rotating cylinders inscribed with mantras invoked when the wheel is turned. And the iconography of Buddhism, from auspicious symbols to images of the concept-embodying goddess Tara, met us everywhere. In the great *gompa,* or monastery, of Tengboche, I would get a taste of the most essential Buddhist practice— meditation—Tibetan style.

Meditation has long been part of my pagan practice; indeed, while a pagan awareness can color all sorts of otherwise mundane things I do, from birding to making French toast, meditation is the only regular, defined activity associated distinctly with my paganism. I don't pray. I don't go to a church, beyond the one found everywhere, under the vaulted canopy of a magnificent stand of trees or a sky strewn with stars. I meditate, and since Buddhists are the unquestioned masters of meditation, I could stand to learn from them, about altering states of consciousness, mindfulness, focus, mental control.

Tourists, provided they abide by a simple set of rules (no photos!), are welcome to observe the monks of Tengboche in their daily meditation ceremony. So along with two dozen or so other travelers, I entered the gompa that evening, with no idea what to expect. (Scott declined to come; the ascent to Tengboche had taken a particularly heavy toll on him, leaving his heart pounding with each step. More than anything, he wanted to rest. It was most certainly not the right time to reveal the second thing that I'd been keeping from him.)

The interior of the monastery's main hall is decorated in gorgeously elaborate fashion, with a scarlet color scheme that complements the maroon and saffron robes of the shaved-headed monks. A giant Buddha dominates the altar at the front of the temple area, flanked by statues of two spear-carrying helpers; the ceiling, covered in dozens of mandalas, draws the gaze to their intricate patterns, absorbing one's attention even without a Buddhist's understanding of the deep symbolism conveyed in their imagery. In an atmosphere thick with incense, some twenty-five monks sat on four parallel benches, with the *Rinpoche*—the head monk—seated on a throne in front of the altar.

Epic horns, so long their ends rested on the ground, bellowed to start the ceremony, reverberating through the hall and our bodies. The monks chanted words I naturally couldn't understand; every so often the Rinpoche rang a bell, and in response all the other monks would do the same, creating a wonderful cascade of sound. Chanting, bells, chanting, bells, sporadically punctuated by a cacophonous explosion, a riot of crashing cymbals, big drums pounding, and horns large and small blaring. It was the polar opposite of any New Age tranquilizing soundscape, and I couldn't help but wonder if the sound explosions were designed to make sure none of the monks fell asleep.

Then, after all the monks were served tea, the ceremony shifted to low sonics: sustained, om-like monosyllables. I shut my eyes and found myself carried by the sound of the monks' voices, drifting for an eternity that was really twenty to thirty minutes. The effect was all the more transporting in its contrast to the cycles of sound that had come before.

The cycles of sound returned, this time with more ceremonial complexity. Buddhist symbols like a miniature white conch were chanted over, then touched to the top of the head; the Rinpoche was successively draped by novice monks in ever increasing layers of ornamentation, from a shoulder-wide collar to a multi-tiered cap and, finally, a wraparound crown with side panels, before it was all removed and bundled away by more novices wearing huge cockscomb-like crests. This time the sound cycles went on for much longer, and eventually I had to leave before the ceremony's end or risk missing dinner entirely. I exited with a bit of a headache—incense generally doesn't agree with me—but with a new appreciation for meditation and its many forms.

And just like that, the skies cleared. By the middle of the next day's trek, the air was cold and impossibly crystalline, as if new lenses on a pair of eyeglasses had brought the entire world into sharp focus. We'd reached the high Himalaya: Trees had disappeared, and the once ubiquitous Large-Billed Crows were fewer, replaced in part by a corvid of higher altitude, the Yellow-Billed Chough. The land was bare and stony, and the titans had at last begun to show themselves: The twin peaks of Ama Dablam were among any number of snowy, jagged summits that jutted like fangs into the sky. I'd never seen anything like it.

"If there were a place where gods dwell, this would absolutely be it," I said to Scott, and he didn't disagree. Mount Olympus had been displaced for sure by these younger, rough-hewn peaks.

But apparently the gods don't need oxygen, because it was in short supply. I was okay on any level transit, but the moment we had to ascend, I was taking baby steps, and even those left me gasping. At the top of one particularly steep slope, we passed a memorial to climbers who had died attempting to summit Chomolungma: a stone pillar surrounded by the names of the dead and by the red, blue, white, green, and yellow of Tibetan prayer flags. As difficult as merely trekking was at this altitude, the monument served as a reminder of why we rank amateurs would not be attempting an actual climb.

During that night in a lodge in Dingboche (elevation 4,240 meters), I was restless. Since I popped awake at 4:00 a.m., and knowing that the moon had set by that hour, I wandered out (softly so as not to wake Scott) to revel in the stars—in that crystal clear air, the best I'd seen since Uluru. I stayed up for the sunrise, which was blocked by the massive presence of Ama Dablam; instead, splinters of the lightening sky shot from behind the mountain, gold edged the surrounding peaks, and slowly slid down their white slopes, and gray-purple clouds on the horizon turned volcanic crimson on their undersides, until the colors mellowed and faded away. Some might see the hand of God; for me, it contained the sacred in and of itself.

We spent the next night in the tiny farming village of Lobuche (elevation 4,900 meters), in the shadow of double-peaked Ama Dablam. It was easily the second worst night of sleeping in my life; I woke twice at awful hours with an urgent need to urinate, which involved the wretched experience of traipsing down the hall to a pit toilet in twenty-degree Fahrenheit temperatures. Afterward, I couldn't get back to sleep; I'd been warned that sleeping at extreme altitude could prove difficult, but I'd assumed that with my ability to nod off nearly instantaneously, I'd be immune. Wrong.

Sleep-deprived, and with both Scott and me suffering from the beginnings of sinus issues, we made the big push on the morning of the eighth day of our trek to Gorak Shep (elevation 5,140 meters), a last, tiny outpost before Everest Base Camp. As we rested in the common area of the lodge, the toll of the altitude was written in the dazed, zombielike expression of every trekker. No one said a word; the constant wheezing, coughs, and sniffles, the slumped body language and shoulders hunched against the cold, and the general immobility said it all.

But then we stepped outside and saw, for the first time in our trek, the broad pyramidal peak of the titan of titans, Chomolungma. Ngima led us that very afternoon over sharply rocky terrain to Everest Base Camp (elevation 5,364 meters), our ultimate goal; though there's not much to the site, truth be told. A few tents of climbers lay scattered about, and a boulder was informally marked to identify the site, surrounded by lines of fluttering prayer flags and far too much refuse. Too many trekkers carry in too many plastic water bottles, with no intention of bringing the empties down with them, and there's no municipal trash pickup, no way for the junk to get out except by those who brought it in.

Still, the unimpressive site couldn't in the least diminish my and Scott's sense of accomplishment. We'd made it to the foot of the top of the planet! I briefly considered sharing the second thing I'd kept hidden from Scott there and then, but decided against it. I looked at the peak of the Mother Goddess of the World, lit in the last rosy rays of the sun, and felt something of the numinous. But even more, it was an intellectual thrill, knowing that I was gazing upon the point where the crust of Earth ended—this high, and no higher—and the outer reaches stretching to everything else began.

It had been a risk to arrive at Base Camp in the afternoon, because now we had to make our way back to Gorak Shep over the same sharp rocks as darkness gathered. We picked up our pace as much as we safely could, but nonetheless I paused to take a glance back: The moon had risen over Nuptse, the titan in the foreground of Chomolungma, throwing moon shadows through the entire valley.

Things went downhill from there, literally and figuratively.

We both awoke the next morning in the frigid confines of our unheated plywood shack of a room, to discover dense fog and a fresh dusting of snow outside; we could see this even through the half-inch layer of ice that had condensed on the *inside* of our window, from the water vapor we'd exhaled in our sleep.

Worse, we both woke with headaches, a sign of altitude sickness;

mine was mild, but Scott, despite a regimen of anti-altitude sickness medication, felt throbbing centered on his forehead—a red flag. We were paying the price for having had only one acclimatization day (a day without increasing altitude, to allow the body to adjust); we'd lost the others waiting in Kathmandu airport, so all that had been left to us was a single extra day to spend acclimatizing in Namche Bazaar.

We'd gone to bed planning a morning attempt at Kala Pattar—a storied overlook that gives sweeping views of all the titans at once, but achieved only through an entirely uphill hike from Gorak Shep in this thinnest of air. With snow on the ground to make the hike harder, and fog that might not lift to reveal the view, Kala Pattar was looking dim; with Scott's condition, it was out of the question. When altitude sickness kicks in, the only thing to do is go down.

It wasn't a pleasant descent. In addition to the headaches, our sinuses were now in full rebellion, with either a head cold or some other irritation. And on the other end we'd both developed intestinal issues that left us trying to restrain our bowels as we hiked. Add the inclement weather—the fog had become a frigid, penetrating drizzle—and by the time we got back to Lobuche, we were pooped.

The next morning, between bathroom runs, I decided to finally have that talk with Scott, about what I'd been concealing from him the whole way.

"Scott, do you think we travel together well?"

"Sure," he said, maybe a bit surprised by the question.

I reached into my backpack and pulled out the small blue box I'd had hidden there during our entire journey.

"Would you travel with me through life for the rest of our days?"

Inside was the simple ring I'd procured in his size from Tiffany & Co. before we'd left New York; I'd figured that I'd never get a chance like this, to propose to him at the top of the world, ever again. At the moment we were both physical wrecks; we looked bad and smelled worse after days going unshorn and unwashed. But if we could love each other like this, didn't that say something? So in a little farming village in the Himalaya, in sight of the two peaks of Ama Dablam that will always stand together, I popped the question.

Scott was shocked, but gave me his answer.

My journal entry for that day begins:

Q: What did you get today?

A: Head cold. Diarrhea. Engaged.

"Cooper! What happened to you? You got scrawny!"

Back at my editing desk in New York, the company CEO—an unfiltered woman with a big heart and a keen eye for guys who work out—took one look at me, her first since I got back from my Himalayan trek, and her jaw dropped.

She wasn't wrong: I'd shed one-quarter of my body mass from before the trek. Muscles burn fuel even when they're at rest, and to burn it, they demand oxygen; starved of that at altitude, my body said, "Nope! If you're not using it, it's got to go!" and ditched the upper body musculature in particular. Also, the Buddhists of the Himalaya are overwhelmingly vegetarian, so the multi-meal, high-protein diet I was accustomed to for maintaining muscle mass was unavailable. (I kept wishing they would go ahead and kill one of their chickens—just one!—so I could eat it.) The results were predictable: Cooper got scrawny.

There were other signs of the physical stress my body had undergone. I noticed a horizontal crease in my thumbnail but couldn't remember having slammed a door on it; on further inspection, I found that *all* my fingernails had such a crease. I looked up the rate of fingernail growth, and sure enough, the affected area calculated back to the time of the trek. My nails were showing the duress of the trek like a stunted growth ring in a tree.

Neither of these conditions proved permanent: The nails grew out, and with a return to sea-level oxygen availability and to my fitness and diet regimen, the muscle rebounded rather quickly.

Sadly, Scott and I weren't permanent either. I had asked Scott that we marry only in my home state of New York, and since same-sex marriage had yet to be legalized there, I figured that would give me a nice long engagement, to be sure that our reconciliation was indeed working. But the then governor, Andrew Cuomo, pushed same-sex marriage through the legislature mere months later, and Scott and I were wed one year to the day after our moment in Lobuche. Whether more time would have conferred more wisdom or given either of us cause to call things off, I can't say. Our union eventually unraveled under the same strains as it had the first time, and Scott and I, who'd traveled side by side to the top of the world and back, went our separate ways.

Other things, however, are still with me: memories of a unique place, its challenges and revelations, and the things I began to explore about myself along the way. I've grown much more comfortable in my own pagan skin; my spiritual longings still seek order and meaning in the chaos life throws at us, but as I learned to do during the vagaries of the trek, I'm much better at unclenching and just letting things be. Sometimes I can muster a fraction of the mental discipline of a Buddhist in meditation and crack a door open to a deeper awareness of the world. At my best I can take the 17,500-foot view of life, assessing with the cold clarity of distant Himalayan air. And other times I can feel as if I were full of shit and yet still keep moving forward, step by labored step.

When I need to know the deity on a grand scale, I can fill my lungs with her breath and be connected by air to her every summit. I can call on memories of the trek and the other journeys, pinned to syllables that are just gibberish to most but that paint a picture of a living world for me: Uluru . . . Iguazú . . . Ngorongoro . . .

Chomolungma.

10

Family Matters

IN ALL THE animal kingdom, there are no more devoted fathers than male Emperor Penguins. The female, upon laying a single egg as the Antarctic grows dark and frigid, leaves the egg with her mate and heads out to sea for several weeks to feast on fish. The males meanwhile spend the depths of the Antarctic winter huddled together for warmth in minus-thirty-degree temperatures and merciless winds, in an unbroken night that lasts for months, without any food the whole time, all for a single purpose: to protect that precious egg. They carefully balance it on top of their feet to keep it off the ice, and keep it warm under a fold of skin and the insulation of their feathers, waiting for it to hatch.

As they stand tall and immobile in a barren expanse blanketed in blue white, lit by the stars wheeling above and the ghostly glow of the aurora australis, one wonders what dreams they have during their long vigil. Do their empty bellies prompt visions of schools of fish aplenty? Do they imagine the face of their progeny soon to hatch out at their feet, a fluffy, downy ball of hope for the future?

When the females return to take up the child-care duties, the famished males finally head to sea for their turn to eat. They'll be back to help feed the young—young for whom the only source of warmth and protection to that point has been their champion dad.

None of which in any way describes my father.

Francis Cooper was many things—a science teacher raised in Brooklyn, a Korean War veteran, and an activist particularly around African American civil rights—but warm and protective toward his young children didn't come close to making that list. Quite the opposite: As far back as I can remember, as a kid I lived in abject terror of my father; the whole family did. He wasn't physically abusive; the onslaught was brutally emotional.

Nor was it constant. Always ready for a camping trip, which is when he was usually happiest, my dad packed me into our VW camper in the summer of 1972 and drove us on a guys-only trip to Nova Scotia to see a total solar eclipse. We watched the sky together in awe, a nine-year-old side by side with his dad, as day turned momentarily to night and a ring of fire carved a black circle into the heavens. A pair of science nerds was never happier.

Which only made it harder to take, when the man who you dared to hope loved you and who had so recently shown you the sun and moon (literally, and in conjunction) would fall into a darkness of his own for days and turn his family—but never outsiders—into the outlet for his ire. For long stretches a black cloud would descend, along with the secondhand smoke from his pack-a-day habit, on our small two-story Cape Cod on Long Island; at those times he would become uncommunicative, except when he was snarling or yelling, and the slightest thing could bring that on. It was hard to know which were worse: the mean outbursts or the prolonged, glowering silences. We learned to live with an air of menace much of the time, radiating from one man. I might have spent my youth in rooms bedecked with that signature of the 1970s, wood paneling, but the flooring was all egg-shells, which my mother, sister, and I trod upon carefully so as not to incur his wrath.

"Goddamn it," he muttered thickly one day in my preteen years when I'd broken a drinking glass while washing the dishes; we had no dishwashing machine, just the hands of my sister, Melody, and me, on alternating evenings. "BE MORE CAREFUL!"

He had a booming voice that had sung in a few choruses, and naturally the high-decibel reprimand only flustered me and made it more likely I'd break another. I had no perspective back then, was unable to reason through that while our family was lower-middle class scraping by on two schoolteachers' salaries, we weren't so poor that the accidental loss of a drinking glass should prompt such rage.

His overly sensitive, secretly gay child was no match for that. I was already internalizing the world's disgust with homosexuality and building my own reserve of self-loathing with it. Now I could add that there must be something wrong about me, to make me such a source of rage to him, such a disappointment. I wondered if it was my gayness itself, somehow apparent to him despite my best efforts to hide it.

My disgrace and humiliation in his eyes would reach a periodic low point in the semiannual presentation of a severed animal limb, a debacle that played out with ritualized consistency. I would dread its coming all afternoon, could detect its fetid presence wafting through the house as it boiled in a pot. When at last the family sat down to dinner, there it was on my plate: the foot of a pig, hoof and all.

"I can't eat this," my childhood self would say.

"You'll eat what I tell you to eat," he replied. To him, through some culinary tradition passed down from forgotten forebears in the Old South, pig's feet and its side of black-eyed peas was a delicacy, an occasional treat he'd labored to prepare. To me it was revolting.

"But I really can't eat this."

"*You'll eat every goddamn thing on your plate!*" he snarled.

"But I'll throw up."

"Just try," my mom would intervene. She and my sister didn't have a problem ingesting the amputated chunk of pig.

So I'd pick up the gray, sticky foot and bite. My teeth would sink through a thick layer of what presumably was skin; I'd laboriously chew the mouthful with its rubbery consistency, and a substance like glue would coat my mouth and the back of my throat. That, most of all, I literally couldn't swallow. I'd gag, and the whole mess would end up back on my plate. Perceiving it as a contest of wills, my father would send me to my room, when in reality it was a contest against my esophagus that he was never going to win.

When my parents divorced when I was fourteen, there was no question as to whom I wanted to live with. The split was acrimonious, and afterward my mother, Margaret, did her best to keep us from seeing my father at all; I can't say I fought her on that. I drew the line at changing my last name, however, as she would sometimes urge.

So my father largely exited my life during my high school and college years. The exception was when I was home on Long Island during spring break of my freshman year at Harvard, when I asked to see him to share some important news.

"I thought you should know: I'm gay," I said as we sat in his car. I was nervous but not fearful; now that he was relegated to the margins of my existence, his hold over my emotional well-being was diminished. When I'd told my mother, who had always been my safe harbor, the result was the emotional outburst one would expect from a liberal, nonreligious mom circa 1981: tears; "it's just a phase"; more tears; "why do you have to label yourself?"; and "what did I do wrong?" As a seventeen-year-old trying to hold my own mooring in these new waters in which I'd found myself, I had little patience for any of that.

My father's response, on the other hand, was in line with the constipated communication I'd known from him throughout my childhood.

"Oh." His affect was flat, as gray and opaque as the sky that day. "Do you want to see somebody about that?"

"No, I'm good with it." A psychiatrist was neither desired nor required.

"Oh."

And that was the last that was said of it, and all I saw of him, for many years.

When Francis and Margaret first crossed paths at City College of New York, he was older than most of the other undergrads; he'd enrolled after his stint in the air force. He and his buddy Vincent, having actually served, derided what they viewed as the cluelessness of the ROTC undergrads, including one Colin Powell. (Powell would unfortunately remain clueless at key moments throughout his career: first as chairman of the Joint Chiefs of Staff, when as the first African American to hold that post he would shamefully oppose allowing lesbians and gays to serve in the military openly, as if exactly the same arguments against their inclusion hadn't been deployed decades earlier against Black service members like himself; and later as U.S. secretary of state under George W. Bush, when he would shamelessly promote a lie of weapons of mass destruction before the United Nations, to justify a war against Iraq that would leave hundreds of thousands dead and the region in ruins.)

During his stint in the air force, Francis had never flown—his uncorrected eyesight was too poor—but he had longed to. He idolized the Tuskegee Airmen, the African American pilots who overcame bigotry to distinguish themselves in World War II, earning the hawk-inspired nickname "Red Tails" after the color they painted their planes' rudder. Now at CCNY, instead of his wings Francis pursued science courses and Margaret, a beauty born in Trinidad but raised in the States since the age of twelve. He was a trim former serviceman, with a red-haired beard if he let it grow in and skin light enough to "pass" if he had ever chosen to. But he prided himself on his African American heritage and cultivated something of a Malcolm X look. She had chocolate-brown skin and long, relatively straight hair she had inherited down the maternal line. They married, and my sister and I were soon born.

While all this is accurate, it suffers from some key omissions, the kind that families don't readily talk about, that became known to me only over time.

For example, "soon" for the first of the two births was a lot sooner than nine months later. Holding the proverbial shotgun was Elaine, my devoutly Catholic grandmother on my mother's side and, more important, a force of nature few earthly powers could withstand. At the age of six she contracted the 1918 flu and yet fought it off, where millions of others died. Raised strictly with British values in what was then British Guiana by her prominent, autocratic father, she nonetheless defied him to elope to Trinidad with a piano player. After subsequently relocating with her husband and daughter halfway across the globe to New York, she grew weary of his gambling and womanizing and took the unprecedented step for the era (let alone for a Catholic) of divorcing him. Before the split, conscious of the gambling debts he'd accumulated, Elaine did the unthinkable for a married woman, and a Black woman at that: She purchased a house in Queens and kept the title in her name only. She paid off the mortgage from her salary as a neuroscience nurse while raising Margaret alone. She was as formidable as she would later prove devoted to her grandson, and me to her. (She would lovingly refer to me as "the Boy," as if as her sole male descendant that were all the information one should need about me.)

I can only imagine the conversation, Francis summoned to Elaine's neat little row house upon her learning from her daughter of certain impending facts. She no doubt sat him down at the kitchen table, light streaming in from the small backyard, for a good talking-to.

"What were you two think*ing*? Going at it like *wild animals* without protec*tion*?" I can hear her voice saying with its hybrid Guyanese-British inflections; she might have been Catholic, but she also was a nurse and eminently pragmatic. "You have made this situation together with your *reckless* behavior, and now that there is another life involved, this is what you're both going to do . . ."

Against such a force, poor Francis never stood a chance, whether he wanted to marry Margaret or not.

Francis's biological mother, on the other hand, had abandoned my dad and his three sisters when they were young. We knew little about Thelma Burke beyond her name; we theorized, based on the very light skin of all the siblings, that she might have been white. Only the family lore about her endured; the tale was quite specific.

One day, she left the two eldest, Aleta and Audrey, at home and said she'd be right back while taking the two youngest, including Francis, with her. The real plan was to run off with another man; but at the last minute she changed her mind—not about running off, but about keeping the two youngest. Francis and his sister were found at the train station with a sign hanging on them: YOU CAN KEEP YOUR NIGGER BABIES.

Needless to say, the name Thelma Burke was rarely uttered among us, and only with disgust; she was persona non grata in our family. Francis's hatred for the mother he couldn't remember would be one of his defining features.

Thelma's departure had the consequence of leaving young Francis entirely at the mercy of his father, Henry, at least for a time. Thus Francis was molded under the austerity of the Great Depression and the tyranny of Henry, which by all reports made the oppressive atmosphere in which I grew up seem like a picnic. Memories of my grandfather are limited to dim recollections of visiting a dark man in a dark, joyless basement apartment, where none of us felt comfortable, least of all my father.

How much of this history weighed down Francis's relationships with my mother, my sister, and me, I can't say. I only know he entered the 1980s alone, bitterly divorced, and estranged from his two children. It wouldn't be until Francis met Miriam that things for him would begin to change.

. . .

"Your dad would like to see you," my cousin Donna, the only child of my beloved aunt Aleta, said in a phone call not long after I started working at *Fame* magazine in the late 1980s. Donna and I had always been pals, even though she was nearly a decade older, so she was a natural messenger. I was skeptical; why would I invite my father's negativity back into my life?

But the outreach had also come at a time when I was reevaluating. My warm bond with my mother had cooled a bit. We had always had opposite temperaments: me distrustful of emotions and keeping them on a short leash, she giving in to the passions of the moment. But with the eyes of an adult, my beautiful, sainted mother, my safe harbor as a child from my dad's glowering storms, was revealed as something more complex: a human being. One with her own flaws, in that she was subject to flights of fancy untethered to the here and now. Her push for Melody and me to change our last name gave an early indication; as difficult as my dad had been, he hadn't been revealed as a mass murderer to merit such absolute negation. But in our mother's desired world, we sprang as if by virgin birth from her womb. And commensurate with her fanciful desires, Margaret had a fungible relationship to the truth, I was learning. My sister and I were trying to lead our own responsible adult lives when Mom called Melody from Trinidad and Tobago, near the end of an idyllic trip Mom took back to her native land; she asked Melody to lie to Mom's boss so that Mom could extend her stay. ("Tell him that my father died," she instructed, although my maternal grandfather had passed away many years before. This, my grandmother would let slip, was nothing new for her; in her undergrad days, faced with a final exam she didn't want to take, according to Elaine, she'd sent an anonymous telegram to the professor the night before stating that his mother had died, so that the exam would be canceled. With Margaret's ruse eventually exposed, I can't imagine what mountains my grandmother had had to move to keep my mom from being expelled.)

"Just come out to Long Island and hear him out," Donna said. "I'll be there too." That safety valve made it less daunting, and my curiosity was piqued. It was enough to get me on the train out of Manhattan— that and the promise of a good home-cooked meal. Broke as I was, I was never one to pass up a free dinner, especially when the chef, my father's romantic partner of a few years whom I had never met, was reputed by Donna to have the skills of a kitchen wizard.

Though perhaps more than anything else, I was curious about that romantic partner. Who in their right mind would willingly live with my dad?

When I arrived, Miriam welcomed me into their immaculate home, a two-story house on a quiet, leafy block—more upscale than the one I'd grown up in and in a better neighborhood. Her short pepper-gray hair offset her medium brown skin and suited her small, lean frame, full of energy. And whatever she was cooking, it smelled delicious.

I hugged my father awkwardly. Dad was on his best behavior that night; he was actually *talking*. About the details of my high school and college graduations: It turns out he'd surreptitiously attended both, at the margins of the ceremonies, as best he could. About how he wanted to spend time with me going forward. Only one moment betrayed any bitterness, when I asked if he'd considered getting another dog.

"No," he said without hesitation. "I don't want to get attached to another animal, only to never see it again." Spanky, the family dog, had stayed with us after the divorce.

Other than that, my father was almost pleasant. And he had quit smoking! What miracle had this Miriam wrought? Still, I was wary.

When I poked my head in the kitchen, drawn by the burgeoning aromas, Miriam took the opportunity for some words of her own. "I'm not trying to replace your mother, who, judging by how her children turned out, did a fine job," she said. This (a) was good news, because the mother I already had was proving handful enough; and (b) spoke well of her, because my dad surely had vented to her about the bitter split and his exile from his children's lives, yet she was nothing but gracious to a woman she'd never met.

"Give your dad a chance."

I didn't see how I couldn't. If my father had maintained a relationship with a woman of this caliber, maybe he had indeed changed.

At least two things, fundamental to his identity, had *not* changed about the man. For one, he was still a fire-breathing activist, a stubborn pit bull of determination when it came to confronting society's failings. One of my earliest photos shows me at a civil rights protest— an infant in a stroller, pushed through the streets of Jersey City by my mother as she held my sister with the other hand, my dad leading the way. Whether it was fighting racial injustice side by side with their friend the firebrand Episcopal priest the Reverend Robert Castle when our family briefly lived in Jersey City, or later fighting school segregation leading a chapter of the Congress of Racial Equality when we settled on Long Island, both my parents marched, organized, and protested to effect change. It was simply a given growing up in our household, without it ever needing to be explicitly stated: If you see something wrong in the world, it's your personal responsibility to do something to try to fix it. "But what can someone like me possibly do that would make a difference?" didn't wash; you write letters to your elected representatives (the ones demanding environmental action from nine-year-old me were priceless and, sadly, lost to antiquity). You band together in civic groups with others who share your cause. You put your body on the line in acts of peaceful civil disobedience. (My father got arrested as a younger man in the civil rights era more than once.) Or you could deploy one of my father's favorite tactics and haul a transgressor through the system; "sue" was practically his middle name.

And Francis being Francis, he could not let something go.

"I have a case against the owner of a movie theater in Baldwin," my dad explained over dinner in a restaurant with Miriam, Melody, and me, not long after my first meeting with him in a potential rapprochement. The white theater owner had been disrespectful to the almost all-Black patrons waiting in a long line for admittance. "When the young couple ahead of me complained to the owner, he snatched their tickets from them, tore them up, and threw them in their faces! Like hell was I going to stand for that. I not only demanded my money back; I filed a complaint with the local authorities."

"So what happened?" Melody asked.

"It's been two years, but the case is still working its way through the bureaucracy," Dad said, as if that were the end of the story for now.

The whole time Dad had been talking, Miriam had sat silently with a Cheshire cat grin.

"Tell them the rest, Francis."

Dad shot Miriam an irritated look.

"The theater owner died a year ago, from a heart attack," my dad admitted grudgingly. "But that doesn't matter! It's the principle of the thing!"

The other unchanged part of him was his longing to fly. He'd begun addressing that way back when I was young; the family took a trip to upstate New York, where he enrolled in a course to learn to fly gliders, the albatross-winged, engineless sailplanes that, in the right conditions, can stay aloft for hours. He'd worked hard to develop the skills and accumulate the knowledge needed to pass his certification and finally, after being rooted to the ground the whole time he was in the air force, Francis got to fly.

He took me up with him once in a two-seater when I was a kid; my mom was terrified something would happen the whole time. But my dad knew his stuff: He caught a thermal—a bubble of warm, rising air—and used it to gain altitude. The world drifted below in new perspective, as one might see out the window of a commercial flight, but this felt freer, with only a thin layer of clear plastic between us and the sky, and with no sound beyond the whistle of the wind through the fuselage. A Red-Tailed Hawk drifted close out of curiosity, then moved off. I was thrilled to see a red-tail this way, up close in mid-flight. My dad, meanwhile, envied the hawk; by simply holding out its "arms," it could do effortlessly what he needed aileron and rudder, cockpit and canopy, to pull off. Still, flying a glider was the closest he could come to being a bird. We came to an appreciation for flying things from somewhat different angles, but in that moment our respective passions joined in midair, soaring high together.

The hold that flying had on his imagination, and the link to it and African American pride he felt through the Red Tails, had only deepened with time. He had become the only Black member of the Long Island Soaring Association and in retirement trekked once or twice a week out to the eastern end of the island to spend hours at the airfield, putting in his maintenance time tinkering with the planes, when he wasn't up in the air. As we renewed our relationship, he offered to take Melody and me soaring with him, as adults. Melody took him up on it and said the experience was incredible. To this day I'm not sure why I dithered about it; perhaps a stale inertia kept me from moving outside my comfort zone (because as an adult, hurtling through the air in a motorless mechanism definitely gave me pause). I made a mental note to do as Melody had done, thinking that I would get around to it eventually. I had plenty of time.

As I dipped a toe in the waters of reconciliation, I was on the alert for one of my father's dark moods. They were such a fundamental part of the experience of growing up with him that I couldn't accept that they were gone for good. So I held a part of myself back, waiting for a return of his mean, bullying side. Instead, I got sustained outreach.

He was awkward about it at first, taking big swings with things like a lavish check as a birthday gift. I accepted it but did not accept that he could buy his way back into my life. And besides, he'd been AWOL for the entire expense of my Harvard education; that had been all Mom and my student loans. Despite Harvard's robust financial aid policy thanks to its massive endowment, paying for college had left me in debt—not to mention the embarrassment from the several times I had handed the bursar's office the check for the semester on registration day, only to discover that my mom had postdated it. That hurt. I didn't stop to consider what struggles my mother was going through to make that check happen at all.

"You had to pay for Harvard?" my dad said when, at a tentative dinner together, I must have mentioned my loan payments in passing.

I looked at him quizzically. "How else do you think I got through four years of college?"

"I thought you were on full scholarship." His voice, soft as I'd never heard from him, was tinged with self-reproach.

"Harvard doesn't do that." They didn't back then, anyway; financial aid resulted from a needs-based calculation that pushed family budgets to the brink. He really didn't know.

What was more remarkable: We were talking about it. *He* was talking; this much more communicative Francis Cooper wasn't a onetime aberration from our first meeting. He continued to be present and engaged in subsequent outings. Not that he'd suddenly become a chatterbox; not that he wasn't still opinionated, stubborn, and a pit bull about something when he felt he'd been wronged by someone; but he was interesting to talk to. And I noticed something else. At the end of each meeting, he made a point of hugging me, and my previously uncommunicative father always had the same parting words: "I love you, son."

Things had been going well with Dad. Our get-togethers became progressively less fraught, and we began enjoying each other's company. Once Mom decided to retire early and move to Tobago, he became my only parent in proximity, just a short trip on the Long Island Rail

Road from my Manhattan home, although he would rarely let me take the train back, insisting on driving me into the city. Anytime I was flying somewhere, he was adamant about coming into town and driving me to the airport; and when I cleared the gate after my return flight, regardless of what plans for the subway, a taxi, or a car service home I had intended, there he was, waiting to drive me. At first I thought he was overcompensating for the years of exile, and maybe that was part of it. But I got a stronger sense of dedication: This was simply the extra mile one goes to for family in his world.

I looked back on my childhood, recognizing as an adult what I'd taken for granted as a kid: He'd gone the extra mile for me for most of my life. My formative Sunday morning bird walks with South Shore Audubon didn't happen by themselves, for one thing. After a long week of one of the most draining jobs on the planet—teaching schoolchildren—my father had roused himself early with a drag of his wake-up cigarette on his Sunday off, when he no doubt would have been happy to sleep in, solely so that his bird-crazy son could go on the walk. It was dedication to me, but also enjoyment for him; while not a birder himself, as a nature enthusiast he cherished the time spent outdoors with his son—even if he wasn't equipped back then to express that. Elliott Kutner was my birding mentor for all those years, but Francis Cooper was my dad.

He had some Emperor Penguin in him after all. But he couldn't articulate the caring, and my child's eyes couldn't see it through the near-constant storms of his temperament.

He would soon articulate it, though, in a way that was profoundly meaningful.

Not long before I started at Marvel, I became the co-chair of the board of directors of the Gay and Lesbian Alliance Against Defamation, a position that sounds far more exalted than it actually was. Back then in the late 1980s, GLAAD was a relatively new, grassroots, New York–based media watchdog organization, yet to evolve into the national giant best known for its media awards gala. It was an era before

Ellen and Anderson, before any openly LGBTQ celebrities or ongoing characters on TV. Quite the opposite: With the AIDS crisis at its height, queer people were often vilified in the press and the subject of degrading stereotypes and outright antigay bias on-screen. GLAAD had formed to combat that, and as so often seems to happen when passionate queer activists come together, we spent way too much of our energy fighting one another. I'd become active in GLAAD (with that Cooper DNA–driven determination to do something to make a difference) at a time when its board of directors had polarized into two warring camps; seen as neutral to both, I was tapped as the male co-chair to keep the peace.

When, on a summer night during my tenure, a male couple was gay bashed in upper Manhattan, GLAAD hosted an antiviolence rally near the scene of the crime. It was a bit outside our wheelhouse, since it was less about media representation than safety on our streets, but we had the resources and the outrage motivating us, so we stepped up. I found myself as co-chair on a hastily erected outdoor stage, introducing speakers and rousing the crowd to action, perhaps a bit too effectively: Whereas we GLAAD folks exhorted everyone to contact their representatives and demand justice for the LGBTQ community, a contingent took to the streets after the rally and blocked traffic to demand the same. That wasn't what we'd planned, yet there I was on the sidelines of a protest grown out of what we'd started, watching other people risk arrest to make our point. I was scared of being arrested, of what ramifications it might have; I'd been a Goody Two-shoes my whole life, my closest run-in with the law being the swordplay incident in the subway when I was seventeen. But as a leader of the organizing group, I didn't feel I could just watch. So I took a deep breath, stepped off the sidelines, and sat down with the contingent in the middle of the street. And for the first time in my life, I got arrested.

It turns out that in that era getting arrested in New York City for an act of civil disobedience was no big deal. The cops were blasé about it,

I got processed in a few hours, and I left the precinct with a desk appearance ticket for the future disposal of my case and went home.

It was late by the time I reached my apartment. The answering machine was flashing with a message; playback brought the familiar resonant voice, tempered from its boom.

"Hi, Chris, it's your dad. I saw on the news that there was a gay protest in the city and that some folks got arrested, so I just wanted to call in case you'd been there and make sure you're okay."

I think my mouth hung open a little bit. I had never discussed my GLAAD activities with my father; in fact, this was the first time the subject of my being gay had been broached by either of us since I'd come out to him years earlier. Things were still tentative with him, and since I had no inkling of how he felt about my queerness (but feared that Mr. Rage at Me as a Child hated that about me most of all), I treated it as a no-fly zone between us. Yet here he was, reaching out on that very basis. But not just that; reaching out about an experience he too had shared in his youth and prided himself on—getting arrested fighting the good fight. Almost as if he were proud to call me his son.

It has since become a family saying, only half a joke, that you're not a Cooper until you've been arrested at a protest.

After that, I stopped editing out the gay aspects of my existence from my dad's view. Because he was a Black authoritarian father, I had assumed the worst, when in fact he would prove time and again to be something not every queer person is lucky enough to have: an accepting parent. One time, too accepting: Trying to consolidate my Long Island trips, I'd dovetailed a Saturday with him opposite a hookup that night with a friend who lived in a nearby town. I'd expected to dash out to my date's car when he arrived at my dad's house to pick me up, but my father insisted on having him in and meeting him, the first time ever he'd met any of my romantic entanglements or confronted the fact of my queerness manifested in the living flesh. He and Miriam were warm and gracious, of course, and my date presented himself impeccably. But during that brief eternity I was desperate as a cornered quail, ready to flush and fly as far away as possible. I have never squirmed so much in my life—like a schoolgirl getting picked up on prom night, minus the corsage.

"Are you sure? I think you're out of your mind!" Melody said when I told her that Dad and I were planning a trip to Costa Rica together.

Now a few years into the reconciliation, Melody and I had been spending Thanksgiving and Christmas dinners with the extended, blended family: Miriam and her two grown children and their spouses and kids, me and Melody and her husband and kids, Aunt Aleta and Donna, and my maternal grandmother, Elaine, whom my dad considered every bit one of us. The holiday meals were boisterous affairs, with salty opinions seasoning the mouthfuls of turkey and ham, Miriam's macaroni and cheese and candied yams, Dad's dinner rolls chased down with my homemade eggnog (spiked Caribbean style with rum), and finished off with my father's specialty: his light, sumptuous, melt-in-your-mouth sweet potato pie that I'd never forgotten from childhood. Inevitably politics would come up, someone would mention the name Clarence Thomas, and the room would erupt into curses and shouts of fury. (Someone at the table once branded his role on the Supreme Court bench as "the silent, pliant cushion beneath Scalia's ass, upholstered in rich brown but stuffed with substanceless white fluff for its master's maximum comfort and support.") At Christmas, the evening would end in the living room in a blizzard of torn wrapping paper and an orgy of gifts, principally bestowed in multiplicity by my dad and Miriam. After one such holiday night, as he drove me back to the city at his insistence, we'd struck on the possibility of a trip together.

More important, Dad and I had struck up the beginnings of a friendship. I would trek out to his place to lend a hand around the house, particularly as he got older and when seasonal projects required hauling big objects. Francis was insanely handy with a drill, circular saw, and pile of lumber; I remained as hardware inept as ever, but I could at least put my gym-spawned muscles to use for the heavy lifting. Afterward we'd reward ourselves with a trip to the multiplex; Miriam, lacking the Cooper gene for science fiction, refused to watch such films, so I became my dad's genre-movie-going buddy. Sometimes, like a pair of truant boys, we'd take in two flicks back to back and cackle with glee when some horror-film jump scare drew an involuntary scream from the back row.

But a matinee double creature feature or a holiday feast was a completely different animal from overseas travel, with all its stresses, and being stuck in each other's continuous company for several days. And both Melody and I knew it.

"You're sure you're ready for ten days with Dad in Costa Rica?" she reiterated. And the truth was, I wasn't sure. The other half of the truth was, after a first, wonderful, solo trip to that ecotourist paradise a few years prior—where 850 species of birds are crammed into a country the size of the state of Maryland—I was eager to get back. But now that I was working at Marvel, I was more broke than ever, and Dad had offered to pay for most of the trip. We'd selected the remotest section of Costa Rica for our destination: the virgin jungles of the Osa Peninsula, where allegedly jaguars still prowl and arguably the world's most powerful bird of prey, the Harpy Eagle, still flies. This trip promised to only deepen my love of tropical American birding. But would it deepen my burgeoning love for my dad—or break it?

A six-hour commercial flight, a propeller plane ride, a van ride, a boat ride, and a four-wheel-drive trip over unpaved roads later, and we were well on our way to finding out, and that's just what it took to get to our lodge in Osa. Through it all Francis remained even-keeled and even impressed with my ability to manage in Spanish—not fluently, but after my long Latin American journeys I remained conversant enough that to someone like my dad who spoke only English, I seemed like a polyglot prodigy. Almost someone to be proud of.

Far more impressive was Osa, where the rain forest green is split by rhythmic flashes of electric blue—blue morpho butterflies on the wing, so huge I would glimpse the motion and spring into full alert mode to chase down what bird it might be. A Red-Capped Manakin, a jet-black little ball of feathers with signature crimson headgear, perched obligingly close and still, only for Francis to discover that the battery pack on the video camera he'd toted all morning for just such a moment was out of juice. (Rather than emotionally decompensating, he rolled with it.) Scarlet Macaws streaked overhead in raucous parrot clusters of red, blue, and green; a White Hawk drifted by on unblemished wings; Rufous-Tailed Hummingbirds made certain their long blood-red bills were everywhere that something bloomed. After a rainstorm, in a motorboat ferrying us to a distant trail, the driver paused the boat in the Pacific coastal waters; the school of fish passing beneath was invisible to us, but not the frantic gulls, the dolphins leaping around our boat, and the rainbow shooting up into the sky as if to geotag this treasure. One evening, a flock of Chestnut-Mandibled Toucans took to a distant treetop and bade farewell to the setting sun, "*¡Dios te dé! ¡Dios te dé!*," as we watched them toss back their oversized beaks with each cry, articulating the ineffable in the last light of day. We never saw a jaguar or a harpy. We didn't even notice.

In Costa Rica, as is so often the case in the Americas, identifying the flycatchers proved to be a bit of a hurdle. That's where the sixth of the Seven Pleasures of Birding kicks in:

Sixth Pleasure of Birding:
The Joy of Puzzle Solving

If you're the kind who waits eagerly for midnight for the new day's Wordle to drop, if you tune in dutifully each evening to see if you can outdo the contestants as they spin the wheel and Vanna turns the letters, if you pray for a rainy Sunday to keep you indoors so you can puzzle out where those last few jigsaw pieces fit, then imagine the challenge in trying to figure out what you've got when the mystery is a living thing that can fly! To wit: Central America has three flycatchers that are superficially nearly identical; the Boat-Billed Flycatcher, Social Flycatcher, and Great Kiskadee all are brown above and solid yellow below, topped with "bicycle helmet" head stripes of black and white. While at first they might seem impossible to tease apart, key differences quickly emerge: Boat-Bills have a giant schnoz, Socials are diminutive, and they have a completely different voice from the strident *Kis-ka-DEE! Kis-ka-DEE!* from which the third flycatcher takes its name. (Far more difficult was the Bran-Colored Flycatcher I spent an hour chasing and observing in Buenos Aires before I finally figured out what it was. The triumph I felt when I finally nailed the ID for that lifer is what the sixth pleasure of birding is all about.)

In short order, despite limited experience with the three species, I could separate them in a snap. Dad seemed impressed.

Birding Tip

Know your families! These groups of related birds typically share characteristics, such as general shape and behavior, and should become familiar to you with a little experience. If at a glance you can sort woodpeckers from pigeons and doves, flycatchers from warblers, then you can concentrate on the field marks—details of color, pattern, size, and sound—that let you zero in on the precise species within the family.

The nearest Francis came to a dark moment during the trip was at the start of a morning hike. The guide paused the group to point out a tree that had evolved long, razor-sharp spines completely encircling its trunk, to ward off damage from herbivores.

"Can I touch them?" a blond fellow hiker asked, reaching toward the spines tentatively.

"Yes, just be careful—"

The guide had barely finished the words when the woman slipped in the mud and, to keep from falling, instinctively hugged the tree.

The scream she uttered, as the spines embedded in her chest and arms, was so visceral it not only resonated through the members of our group but no doubt was understood by every other primate for miles around. The guide spent the next twenty minutes gingerly pulling the spikes out of her flesh as we could only watch, wince, and wait.

"How can they not carry a first-aid kit?" Francis muttered angrily to me; we were far from the lodge, with no immediate means to get her any proper attention. He was right, of course, but then he did something remarkable for him: He let it go.

We ended that day the same way we passed every evening in Osa: sitting together in the rockers on the porch of our cabin, looking over the bay. A buoy bell chimed in the distance. The cocktails you could purchase from the lodge must have been ordinary at best, but we savored every sip as the twilight failed and, in that place removed from the glow and flow of civilization, watched the stars splatter the sky.

The trip was so successful that when my dad invited me on a camping trip a year later to the Canadian Maritimes, I didn't hesitate. If we could handle Osa, and handle it so well, Canada would be a piece of cake.

Or so I thought. But the puzzle of Francis and my relationship to him would prove deeper and more complicated to solve.

II

The Tragedy
of Francis

W HEN THE VEHICLE ferry deposited me and my father on
Grand Manan, an island in the Bay of Fundy in the Canadian maritime province of New Brunswick, we were
struck by its unspoiled rustic charm. A regular visitor there described
it to us as "Martha's Vineyard before it was overrun"—an assessment
that I can neither confirm nor deny, having never been to the Vineyard. I can only say that from the iconic Swallowtail Lighthouse in the
north to the cliffs overlooking the Atlantic in the south, it beckoned
as the perfect summer getaway.

The timing also seemed perfect. Manhattan had been baking for
days in 90-plus-degree heat and 90-plus-percent humidity, the kinds
of conditions where all you have to do is look sideways to get drenched
from exertion. We couldn't get out of town fast enough when Francis
picked me up to start the northward trek: I was eager to be anywhere
cooler than New York City; he was eager to test out his new camper, a
Rialta RV. Still compact as RVs go, the Rialta was a definite step up
from the Volkswagen Westfalia that had carried the family across the
continent when I was a kid. Now, for our first camping trip together

in my adult years, we planned a swing through the Bay of Fundy's natural attractions, culminating in birding, hiking, and whale watching around Grand Manan.

Mother Nature had other plans.

The afternoon we arrived on the island, it was aglow in late evening sunlight that cast its meadows and evergreen forests, framed by the ocean backdrop, in cinematic relief. But by the next morning, the very same bubble of stagnant heat and humidity that had driven us from New York had slid far enough northward to slam into the cooler Canadian air; the result was an impenetrable fog. It settled on Grand Manan and refused to budge or burn off; visibility was so bad that I had to presume the huge, maybe white-headed, maybe white-tailed thing that landed atop a tree a few yards away was, maybe, a coveted Bald Eagle. So that killed birding. Whale watching was similarly out. Hiking was still a go—if you didn't mind a complete lack of vistas.

This proved a disappointment, to be sure. But as a seasoned traveler at this point, I knew the success of any trip, no matter how well planned, was a crapshoot dependent on variables beyond anyone's control—most especially the weather. You accept the vicissitudes and make the best of it, or if you can't, you shouldn't bother going at all.

Francis Cooper had not gotten the memo.

I knew right away that something was off with him. The loud but often affable father I'd become reacquainted with was nowhere to be found that morning. Instead, I was met with a scowl and a series of grunts as responses to simple inquiries: a sullen demeanor that was all too familiar from my youth.

"This fog sucks," I said, hoping an open acknowledgment of our predicament might bring him out of it.

Silence.

"Maybe they give tours of the lighthouse; that's something we might still be able to do," I added, grasping for a helpful suggestion.

He kept on with the routine of closing up the bedding in the RV.

"Uh," I said, "maybe they give tours—"

"*I heard you the first time!*" he snapped in a loud voice.

"Okay, well, if you'd just—"

"You can't see anything from a lighthouse in the fog; that's why they put foghorns in lighthouses." *You fucking idiot.* He didn't have to say it; his disgusted tone said it all.

He stalked out of the Rialta to detach the vehicle from the campsite's power and sewer hookups, slamming the door behind him.

"I meant the inside of the lighthouse," I mumbled to no one but myself.

Next, I suggested, and we booked for the following day, two spots on a boat trip to a nearby breeding colony of seabirds; that at least was still possible in the fog, and I figured it would give him something to look forward to. The new plan did nothing to improve his disposition, and as the day wore on, his glowering silence was broken only long enough for him to snap impatiently as he became increasingly short with me. Eventually I said nothing at all, so as not to somehow provoke him.

He cooked dinner for us in the camper that night. His dark mood in those close quarters was particularly oppressive, so I just kept my head down and chewed. The clatter of cheap travel cutlery on plastic dishware was unbroken by any conversation. Afterward, under the camper's sallow interior lighting, I started washing the dishes.

"No, no, *NO!* Not like *that!*" he shouted in his worst boom. The RV's small storage tank offered a very limited supply of water; conservation being key, Francis had a minimalist dishwashing method that I apparently wasn't adhering to closely enough. "Like *this!*"

He snatched the sponge from me and demonstrated, then tossed the sponge back in the sink in disgust. "*What the fuck is wrong with you?*"

Cowed, I picked up the sponge and tried again. I scrubbed a cup with just the little bit of water already inside it, turning it in my hands to get it clean.

Those hands were shaking.

I looked at them, astonished at their betrayal. Here I was, a grown man of some thirty years, and yet my hands had reverted to those of a terrified nine-year-old. I'd been reduced by his bullying into a child again.

This would not stand; I would not allow it. The grown man reasserted himself and decided, then and there, that he had something to say about it.

"What the fuck is wrong with *you*? You've been an asshole all day, treating me like a piece of shit when you speak to me at all, and for what? Because some weather derailed our trip? That's cause to be a fucking jerk to me? I don't know what damage has gone on in that brain of yours, that you can't deal with your foul mood without turning the nearest person into a punching bag, but understand this: I do not have to put up with it! I put up with it my whole childhood, but guess what? Those days are done. I have a wallet full of credit cards that will get me on the first bus back to New York if you don't check yourself, and I'll leave your tired ass here alone. You don't get to do this to me anymore. I've said it, and I'm glad I said it."

Birding Tip

There are no penguins north of the equator! Penguins are strictly Southern Hemisphere birds and are never found in the Arctic. (Conversely, polar bears are only in the arctic north; so any silly Coca-Cola ad that shows animated versions of the two together is peddling more than one false premise.) In the north, penguins are replaced by alcids like puffins, which fill the same marine fish-catching ecological niche—except that unlike penguins, alcids can still fly.

I think, right there, that camping trip saved me a couple thousand dollars in therapy.

My outburst gave Francis pause, and he reined himself in for the rest of the night; not that he wasn't still miserable to be around, but at least he wasn't going at me. That lasted through the following morning as we left with about a dozen others on our excursion to the breeding seabird colony.

There, from a blind set inside a berm of earth among the open rocks where the birds nest, we had in-your-face views of two lifers for me: Razorbills and Atlantic Puffins, the clown-billed "penguins" of northern seas. We were thrilled.

And just like that, Francis snapped back to normal. It must have been the excitement of such amazing views of amazing birds. The black cloud had lifted even if the fog had not, and he was literally and figuratively a happy camper for the rest of the trip.

It was both a relief and a revelation for me. The source of his upset was obviously the weather disruption of our trip, and yet even though he knew that, he was incapable of preventing himself from venting on the nearest person. I looked back on what as a child I'd assumed was a rage born of his finding me wanting, and realized it had little or nothing to do with me; his semipermanent foul mood was more than likely the product of finding himself trapped in a marriage that neither of my parents really belonged in.

But that wasn't quite right either, because Francis was indeed capable of curbing himself so as not to unleash his dark moods on others; he'd done it my whole life with people outside the family, and he did it on this camping trip. In casual encounters with strangers, he was pleasant, even after the fog had triggered his downward plunge, and even when a moment before he had been a monster to me. From talking with Miriam, I already knew his black moods weren't entirely a thing of the past; she still periodically endured them, even while Dad was on his best behavior with Melody and me—until that camping trip. The tragedy of Francis was that wherever that rage came from, he'd displace it only onto the people he held dearest.

His behavior on Grand Manan meant that he finally felt close enough with me since our reconciliation to be a beast to me. What a broken way to go through life.

Strangely enough, after that trip—after I'd left Marvel and through the late 1990s, leading up to the upheaval of police injustice New York City was to experience—we grew closer. Maybe because I finally understood the broken dynamic of the man; maybe because on that trip I'd put him on notice that if he stepped out of line, I was more than capable of fighting back, or even dumping him, until he came to his senses. In that weird way of bullies who are finally confronted, I think he respected me for that; he certainly told the story of our dishwater clash to Miriam, who later adopted my closing line as her coda whenever she clapped back against one of his vicious episodes: "I've said it, and I'm glad I said it!"

"Mom, I'm going to college!" Amadou Diallo, a twenty-three-year-old immigrant to New York City from West Africa, said over the long-distance line to his mom back home; after about two years in the United States, he had saved nine thousand dollars from his long hours selling socks, gloves, and videos on Fourteenth Street. I might have passed him a dozen times, considering I live downtown and regularly use Fourteenth Street as my pedestrian crosstown thoroughfare; shy, small, and slightly built, he would have easily escaped my notice as I powered past at a brisk New York pace, paying little heed to sidewalk peddlers and their wares. A million lives can glance by one another in this town without intersecting.

But Amadou's life would intersect with four others, whose notice he did not escape. After he went back to his apartment in the Bronx around midnight on February 4, 1999, as he stood in front of his building, he would be approached by four white men with guns who emerged from a car moving slowly down his late-night deserted street. These men—who would turn out to be plainclothes police officers from an aggressive special division called the Street Crime Unit ("We Own the Night," their motto boasted)—would see this unarmed Black man with no criminal record, minding his own business on his own doorstep; witness him pull out his wallet and instead assume it was a gun; and fire a hail of forty-one bullets, nineteen of which would pierce his slender frame.

Amadou Diallo would not be going to college. Instead, he would be going home to his mother in a box.

The Coopers soon joined the front lines of the protests that followed. This was the forerunner of the Black Lives Matter movement, which would be born a dozen years later with the killing of Trayvon Martin in Florida and the acquittal of his killer; the Amadou Diallo protests shook New York City and the administration of its then mayor, Rudy Giuliani.

But the Diallo protests didn't kick into high gear until LGBTQ activists from a group with an appropriate name and a provocative acronym, Fed Up Queers, blocked traffic on Broadway. These white queer activists drew from the tactics of the AIDS activists of ACT UP, and in solidarity with the African American community they put their bodies on the line in protest. These would be the first arrests for civil disobedience in the struggle for police accountability for Diallo's killing, but not the last: Those peaceful acts of defiance spawned a daily ritual of arrests that moved to the police's own doorstep, One Police Plaza. Each day, coordinated groups of dozens of protesters planted themselves in front of police headquarters and got arrested to demand justice; arrestees, including luminaries from politics (for example, the former New York City mayor David Dinkins) and entertainment (for instance, the actors Susan Sarandon and Tim Robbins), eventually totaled more than twelve hundred. And always among the protesters were LGBTQ people, who got the ball rolling. I recall one of the protest organizers, the Reverend Calvin O. Butts—among New York's most prominent Black clergy—remarked in retrospect that he would never forget what the LGBTQ community had done for the cause.

The Coopers descended en masse on One Police Plaza on a sunny Tuesday, March 23: In what was very nearly a next-generation reenactment of the past, Melody marched with my young niece held by one hand while pushing my infant nephew in a stroller with the other. They moved to the sidelines (with the children in tow, Melody couldn't risk arrest) as Francis and I took our place in front of police headquarters with sixty-nine others, including Ossie Davis and Ruby Dee, a Black acting couple I'd grown up watching in the movies and whom my father idolized as much for their activism as for their talent.

"You are advised to clear the area immediately, or be subject to arrest!" a police sergeant announced through a megaphone, knowing full well from demonstrations yesterday and the day before that none of us would budge. Police officers flanked us, with plastic handcuffs at the ready. A moment later, at the sergeant's signal, they moved in.

It went down in a very professional manner, on the part of both the cops and us protesters. The police certainly had had plenty of practice in the preceding days, and under no circumstances would they be getting rough—not with the celebrity participation and the media glare. As for the protesters, none of us resisted; we *wanted* to get arrested, to keep that media glare exactly where we wanted it—on the inaction since Diallo's death, and the injustices of policing in Black and brown communities in general. Cops and protesters had become players in a Kabuki dance of civil disobedience, a performance designed to give voice to our outrage and move the needle on police misconduct with a mayor who refused to give an inch. Even knowing this, I still felt an urgent rush of adrenaline as cops cuffed my hands behind my back and led me, Dad, and the others away.

The police vans were ready and waiting, one for the men, the other for the women, bound for processing in separate precincts. As the van worked its way uptown, I slipped my relatively supple thirty-five-year-old wrist out of the plastic cuffs, retrieved the peanut M&M's I'd stashed in my coat pocket, and shared a conspiratorial grin with Dad as I snacked; it would take more than the NYPD's zip-tie restraints to come between this hungry man and his food. (Candy finished, I would wriggle back into my cuffs so the cops would be none the wiser, though I'd leave the wrapper for them to find on the van floor, a small token from the unbowed.) Surveying the van's dingy holding area, I saw almost exclusively brown skin crowned with gray, if there was any hair left atop at all. Conversation was light, the men mostly quiet. But that would soon change, and my father with it.

After our group was locked in a holding cell at the uptown precinct to await processing, one of those aging arrestees began to sing. It was some traditional spiritual, and for the life of me I couldn't say now which one it was. But that was all Francis had to hear; his eyes lit with a fire that was older than I was, and the voice that had sung in many a choir soared. I watched my dad transform into the man he must have been in his twenties, transported back to the civil rights days when he was always getting into good trouble; I watched it happen to all those graying activists as they sang together. And when the song was done, Francis started them up again with another one, and another. They took up words that had been sung in protest and struggle for as long as our people had been on American shores, words I didn't know well enough, if at all, to join in. I could only bear witness as the voices of these men filled the entire station house with a righteous sound, resonating through steel bars and brick and mortar.

It would be years later, and only once more, that I would find myself in the midst of the sound of such transcendence. Late in the spring migration one year in Central Park, Roger Pasquier, our friend Jared, and I all wandered into a clearing in the Ramble to find a mixed flock of warblers: males in their finest—Blackpoll Warblers in sharp charcoal lines, Cape May Warblers in tiger stripes and crimson cheeks, Bay-Breasted Warblers in rich tones of earth and clay, an American

Redstart colored as if for Halloween in May, and a Blackburnian Warbler whose throat glowed as if it were ablaze—each hailing from a
species with one of the highest-pitched voices of North American
songbirds. And they were singing.

They were singing as if with each phrase they were upping the ante;
as if we'd stumbled upon some insane warbler sing-off of sing-offs, a
battle of finalists to see who could go louder, stronger, higher. They
came down from the upper branches to where we didn't even need
binoculars, jumping into the judging stands to make their point, their
little bodies shaking with the raw power that emanated from them. To
this day, we have no idea why, no clue as to what factors in that specific time and place pushed these males to proclaim themselves with
such fierce urgency. But even Roger, the been-there-done-that-seen-it-
all Master Yoda of Central Park birders, was paralyzed as we were
blasted by waves of sound tuned so high that some human hearing
would find it inaudible. The ultrasonic chorus crescendoed in our
ears, a moment of revelation even if we couldn't fully fathom it with
our minds.

In both those moments, I could only appreciate that I was in the
presence of something mighty, and listen in awe.

My next arrest, a few weeks later as we activists continued to press
for justice for Amadou Diallo, was far more prosaic. I had come home
to my apartment building to find a protest starting a few blocks away
and joined in; far from the deliberate arrests at One Police Plaza, this
march was subdued: silent, so as not to disturb patients at a nearby
hospital, and circling picket-line style, confining ourselves to a part of
the sidewalk. Nonetheless, this quite legal and peaceful expression of
free speech prompted the NYPD to seal off the block and tell everyone
they had to leave that location immediately or be arrested. Then the
cops took advantage of the confusion their own illegal demands had
sown to nab some of the organizers.

Baffled and outraged, we marched down the sidewalks of the surrounding blocks, no longer subdued or in the mood for self-restraint.

"Take to the streets!" someone yelled from behind me. "Take the street!"

Dutifully, I spilled into the traffic of Second Avenue, holding aloft a borrowed sign with the damning illustrated message THIS IS A WALLET, NOT A GUN. But when I glanced behind me, I saw I was the only one in the street. A cop was upon me in an instant, smacking the sign to the ground and cuffing my hands behind my back.

Mr. Giuliani, it seemed, had had enough of peaceful protesters and decided to have the police crack down. I would learn just how hard when, instead of being processed at the local precinct and sent home with the usual desk appearance ticket for the later disposal of my case, I was taken to One Police Plaza. There I learned I would be spending the night in the notorious lockup in the bowels of police headquarters, before I could be processed the next morning. A few weeks earlier, in order to get arrested, I'd refused to leave the 1PP premises; now it seemed the police were determined to "honor" that intention.

In a dank, windowless anteroom lit only by fluorescents—as was the rest of the facility—my possessions were confiscated, including my belt, so that I couldn't try to hang myself in despair. The grim, dead-end environs were matched by the demeanor of the cops; they worked with a callous detachment fit for border agents and lifetime conscripts at the DMV. They didn't disguise their animosity toward us Diallo protesters, whom they perceived as anti-police. I heard another arrestee object when they took his AIDS medication away; there was no one-a-day pill in 1999, and anti-HIV meds had to be taken on a strict regimen. How his situation was resolved, I never learned.

By around 8:00 p.m., intake was complete, and I was locked in a large holding cell with about two dozen men, mostly substance abusers and others suspected of low-level crimes. Not my fellow activists this time; no songs of resistance would echo through these halls. Just the flushing sound of the lone toilet, exposed in the corner, with its attendant odor and the unwanted sight of a dumpy rump with the pants down. I claimed a spot on the hard, bacteriologically suspect floor and tried to sleep amid the occasional outburst. ("Courtesy flush!" someone shouted when one of the exposed rumps was slow to push the toilet handle—as we could all smell.) At 3:00 a.m. (why??) the cops clanged on the bars to wake us and hand us each a sandwich: two slices of Wonder bread with slivers of processed bologna between, as unsavory as the entire experience.

When I finally walked out around daybreak the next morning, Dad—who had been my one phone call upon arrest—was there to greet me, bearing the blessed relief of a bagel.

Since it was still spring migration, I hit the park the following morning, sharing the tale of my underworld journey with my fellow birders when they asked why I'd missed the day before. I half expected them—all white back in those days—to recoil in genteel shock at my "radical" Black activism. But instead I got nothing but kudos. Maybe it was just show for my benefit, or Manhattanite white liberal guilt at work, but it seemed genuine. One more reason to cherish our little birding community.

The arrests, like my first a decade earlier at the protest against anti-LGBTQ violence, were eventually resolved with an "ACD"—adjournment in contemplation of dismissal—after many months and constantly postponed court dates. (An ACD is effectively the judge's way of saying, "If you can stay out of trouble for six months, this all goes away.") Rudy Giuliani would be dubbed "America's mayor" in the wake of 9/11, and a national buffoon many years later as he serviced the one-term president Donald Trump; the defects the latter episode revealed about Giuliani's judgment and character were no surprise to New York City's Black community, with whom he'd cultivated an enduring antagonism before and after the Diallo shooting. The Street Crime Unit, whose members had pulled the trigger forty-one times, would not be disbanded until shortly after Giuliani's successor as mayor took office in 2002; the police who crowed with chest-thumping bravado that "We Own the Night" were ultimately disowned.

Diallo's mother, Kadijatou, continues to fight for racial justice.

With the wrongful death settlement she received from the city, she founded the Amadou Diallo Foundation, which among other efforts provides scholarships for immigrants and students of African descent to attend New York City colleges.

Even a force of nature can weaken and diminish with time. My grandma Elaine, born when the twentieth century wasn't even yet a teenager, started to slow down after the turn of the new millennium. She yearned to see *The Lion King* on Broadway, but when a pair of same-day tickets unexpectedly fell in my lap, the only way to get her from the row house where she still lived in Queens to the theater in time, what with rush-hour traffic, was the subway. I watched this ninety-year-old woman use sheer determination to power her way up the endless stairs to the elevated tracks of the station near her home, then fight her way up more stairs from the underground stop at the other end at Times Square. I saw her eyes glow like a little girl's as the theater went dark and giant puppet giraffes and gazelles streamed down the aisles toward the stage; I heard her clap along in delight during the rousing entr'acte; and I caught myself beaming at one of the best theater experiences of my life, not because of anything about the show, but because of what had happened in the seat next to me. When I poured my excited charge into a taxicab to take her home, I knew it had been more than worth the struggle to get her there. But it had indeed been a struggle for her. And she was going home to that row house where she lived alone, with all its stairs.

In her last year or so, the woman who had always been indestructible and indomitable declined precipitously, suffering from congestive heart failure. Her body, once so sturdy it had fended off the Spanish flu and turned innumerable patients in their beds, swelled from retaining so much water that it sometimes wept from her skin. The mind that had remained rock solid into her nineties was slipping, too, not just "senior moments" of forgetfulness, but repeating entire conversations she'd just had. She rejected the idea of a nursing home; we would have to pry her cold, dead fingers from the doorknob of that house she'd won for herself and maintained as her home against all odds. To prove it, returning from a hospital stint, she once pulled herself across the floor on her belly when her legs failed her, to show that she could still navigate her home. My too proud grandmother demanded we watch as she dragged her bloated body down the hall as if she were Jabba the Hutt, and for the first time ever I hated that *Star Wars* was in my head, to proffer that image and break my heart.

My mother, her only child, found an endless series of reasons why she could not help out by coming back for a while from the retired life in Tobago, which infuriated me. My anger mounted when I learned that she'd tried to save face with Elaine by lying to her; she'd told her that the small check I'd been sending to my grandmother every month for years was money that Margaret had been sending me to give to her. (Elaine knew better.)

Melody and I stepped in as we were able, overnighting at Grandma's house after work at times, when the home health aide wasn't there. As a nondriver, however, and working full time, I was limited in what I could do to help; and Melody lived in the suburbs with young children to care for. But through all of it, Francis was there: He and Miriam drove Elaine to and from appointments, brought her supplies, stopped in to see how she was doing, all for the mother of a woman he'd bitterly divorced a lifetime ago and who was herself AWOL from those duties. Francis respected Elaine his whole life, but more important, to him she was family. And in Francis's world, one goes above and beyond for family.

As Elaine's health continued to slide, I grew overwhelmed from seeing a pillar of my existence erode in close-up, robbed of her dignity. So on a Saturday afternoon in 2007, I chose my traditional escape route—a movie theater—not caring at all what movie it was, so long as I could lose myself in some silly reality for as long as the silver screen would flicker. "Silly" didn't begin to cover *Pirates of the Caribbean: At*

World's End, and I surrendered to its promise of nearly three hours of mindless bliss. Then, halfway through, the movie came at me sideways: a minor bit where a lost soul keeps repeating the same phrases and having the same conversation he had moments before, as if each time were the first. Suddenly I was sobbing in the back row, leaving those around me to wonder what kind of fool is moved to tears by a sequel to a spin-off of a Disney theme park ride. My grandmother died a few days later.

My mother had finally arrived in that last week of my grandmother's life. Margaret had a pileup of her own health issues to contend with: high blood pressure, a history of transient ischemic attacks (ministrokes), amorphous pains labeled as fibromyalgia and eventually diagnosed as multiple sclerosis—conditions that, though under treatment, affected her ability to function sometimes greatly, sometimes hardly at all. It was difficult to tell, since she was so far away, somewhat mendacious, and invested in the image of herself as an ageless beauty. She didn't have to sell that last one hard; before she'd left the States, whenever we went out somewhere together, my mother was routinely mistaken for my wife (which of course thrilled her to no end).

Several years after my grandmother's death, on my next-to-last trip to Tobago to visit Margaret, I was shocked at how time had finally caught up with her. She was frail and hardly mobile, requiring a walker to travel even short distances. Her constellation of ailments and symptoms had grown far beyond what one might expect for a woman of her years; everything but cancer—and that was only because her other illnesses made it impossible for cancer to survive in her body, I mused bleakly.

She was in denial about the help she needed, and so was I. I returned to New York with a litany of my own excuses about why I couldn't stay there for a while: I couldn't just leave my job, my partner, my life, to move indefinitely to a homophobic island, especially when my mother, knowing what the ramifications would be, had chosen to remove herself to a place so far away from her entire family. And I was still angry with her for abandoning Grandma. So I got back to my life, ceding keeping an eye on her to her strong network of friends—she'd been nothing but generous and an engaged member of her community since moving to Tobago—and I hoped for the best.

In my anger at her for neglecting her own mother, I ended up doing the same. At her time of need, I left the mother who had sheltered me from my father's storms all through childhood, who had always believed in me and supported me, to her own devices.

Her closest friend, Giselle, called a few months later.

"Christian, you and Melody should get down here. I don't think you'll have another chance."

My sister and I arrived in Tobago, surprising our mother at her hospital bedside. Margaret would rally and be released; we would spend a few days doting on her, to her delight, trying to overlook her diminishing prospects and the perfunctory care at the for-profit elderly home the way that facility overlooked the sea; and then we returned home, two thousand miles away.

I was out of town at a work conference only a week or so later, in August 2016, when Francis called me late at night with the news that my mother had died. I don't know how or why, but I went on with meetings the next day, mingling with my colleagues, keeping it all to myself, maintaining a flawless facade. At dinner, a co-worker asked around the table about comfort food from childhood, and I mentioned the bread pudding that my mother used to make, its raisins soaked in rum.

"Does she still make it?" she asked.

I hesitated. "No. She died last night."

Saying it aloud made it real, and my composure cracked, just for a second.

She laughed. She thought I was joking.

It took a few moments for the dozen people at the dinner to realize I wasn't. Shock fell over the table, and the poor woman was so distraught over her faux pas that I ended up trying to console *her*. But how could she have known? How could anyone? I'd treated the day after my mother's death like any other; who does that?

I was on emotional lockdown, trying so hard to be Vulcan that I'd turned into a piss-poor excuse for a human being.

"You need to have a talk with Francis," Tina's rueful voice implored me over the phone. My stepsister—Miriam's daughter from a previous marriage, and about the same age as me and Melody—loved my dad dearly, even though she hadn't grown up in the same household (or, considering what he was like when we were kids, perhaps *because* of that). She was acquainted with Francis's black moods, but they'd become more frequent and punishing on Miriam, who had to live with him 24/7, since his diagnosis of prostate cancer and then lung cancer in 2010.

This wasn't the first time I'd gotten this phone call. Miriam and Tina seemed to think I had some influence over my father that I just couldn't fathom.

"He listens to you," Miriam had said to me more than once; I was skeptical that that pigheaded man listened to anyone at all. But I knew if Tina was reaching out on her mother's behalf, things were bad.

"My mom will leave his ass if this keeps up," Tina continued in her characteristic unvarnished truth-telling style. "He's going to blow this family apart."

I knew how deeply he loved Miriam, and in that twisted Francis Cooper way the verbal and mental abuse aimed at her as he wrestled with his own mortality was proof. If she ditched him, it would be a terrible blow—akin to when his mother walked out—and leave him pitiable in his decline, left with nothing but rage. I had made a promise to myself to do better with my dad when he faltered than I had done with my mom, so I was determined to help however I could.

Reading him the riot act about his behavior, much as I'd done on our camping trip, was a given. Next I had to get him out of the house, and out of Miriam's hair, as much as possible. Birding was one way to do it.

Dad's lung cancer had been dealt with surgically, and his prostate cancer, although fourth stage, was being controlled by hormone therapy; he was slowing down, but he was still active as long as he didn't have to be on his feet for hours at a time. Central Park therefore offered the ideal setting to bird with him: paved paths, none of them especially arduous; plenty of benches on which to pause and rest; and restroom facilities located at key points, along with the Boathouse café where one could refuel. And spring migration beckoned with all its wonders. Dad still wasn't a birder, but as an outdoors and nature enthusiast he was birding adjacent, enough that he'd enjoy the outing—as he'd done when he used to take me birding on the South Shore Audubon walks when I started out as a little kid. We picked a day for him to trek in from Long Island and rendezvous with me in the Ramble, where I hoped to find a flashy species to dazzle him.

"There's a waterthrush here," I said as we neared the Azalea Pond; the bird's forceful call note, a sharp *speak!* alerted me even before we were in sight of that lovely woodland pool's banks. We'd had a decent enough morning so far—about a dozen of the more common warbler species—but for that knock-your-socks-off sighting I wanted to hand Dad a Hooded or Blackburnian bathing in the pond's shallows.

Bathing birds would be an easy catch requiring only modest binocular skills: no peering through leaves at the tops of trees for fast-flitting fliers. Though a waterthrush—a warbler with brown-above, streaked-below plumage—is about as far as one can get from flashy, it at least tends to stay on the ground, making it easier to spot. And its constant tail-bobbing behavior is a distinctive treat; my mind flashed to Marty Sohmer pantomiming the southern lady's sashay to differentiate the Louisiana Waterthrush from the Northern, and I chuckled internally.

Dad snorted. "You can't possibly know what that is just from that little tweet."

One of the Central Park regulars was standing nearby—trusty old Claude, whose own ears had failed in the upper registers with age. He couldn't help but correct Francis.

"Oh, he knows," Claude said.

The bird walked around a bend in the banks of the pond, at last in view, picking its way through the mud as its tail bobbed with not a hint of southern sashay. A Northern.

Even before we saw the waterthrush, Dad was smiling. Almost as if he were impressed with his son.

Birding Tip

In warm weather, staking out running water sources can be particularly productive as midday approaches, since many songbirds will take a splash to cool off as the morning heats up.

Accelerating our moviegoing partnership was another way to get him out of the house, and Miriam gladly handed him over to me for any film she wasn't interested in seeing, particularly science fiction. In a reprise of yesteryear, the entire genre-crazed Cooper clan—me, Melody, her kids, and Dad—waited on line for hours to see *The Force Awakens,* the first of a new trilogy of Star Wars films, on its opening night. (We younger folks took turns holding the spot in line so that Francis wouldn't have to stand all that time.) When at last we settled into our seats, I savored the aroma of the giant bucket of fake-buttered popcorn in my lap, ready to share with my dad next to me and his grandson next to him once the movie started. The audience hushed with anticipation as the lights dimmed; the sacred, conjuring words ("a long time ago in a galaxy far, far away") filled the screen; then a familiar fanfare filled our ears, starships hurtled through hyperspace, light sabers flashed in glowing fury, and we were young again. The movie played to mixed reviews among us, but the experience of reliving that seminal moment from childhood again with Dad along with his next generation of descendants, forty years later? That was the true magic of cinema.

An even grander reprise would follow. Francis called me with the crazy idea.

"A total solar eclipse, visible from North America!" Dad gushed over the phone. While this wasn't news—these things are known decades in advance—the astronomical spectacle was high on both our minds, now that it was only a week away.

"I know! Nashville is in the path of totality." Nashville wasn't the only place that met that criterion, but it was the nearest that wasn't in the Deep South.

"That would be amazing to see again."

Silence while we both had the same thought.

"You know, we could go," he continued.

"But every hotel will be booked by now, won't it?"

As it turned out, with some perseverance Dad was able to find a room with double beds in a motor lodge on the edge of town. From the dated decor to the faint mustiness of the carpet, the flimsy furnishings to the dingy walls, it was obvious why this was one of the last remaining reservations available in Nashville; one could safely say the heyday of this place was in its rearview mirror, receding fast. After some sightseeing downtown, we spent the night before the big event under a dim light fixture, binging on *Game of Thrones* episodes from my laptop—at least the Wi-Fi worked—while I eagerly gave a running synopsis of the backstabs and twists of fortune for each character to Francis, who had never seen the show before. Our dreary surroundings fell away, replaced by mythical lands of ice and fire; we howled in pain as a beloved dragon died, then gasped in horror as it was resurrected as an unclean minion of the walking dead. A typical Cooper idea of a great night.

The transformation of our surroundings the following afternoon was far more profound. We briefly considered driving to some pristine location as an eclipse viewing spot, but we chose to watch the sky right from where we were, on the grounds of the decrepit motor lodge; perhaps we feared we'd miss the eclipse regardless of where we stood—that the last-minute trek and shoddy accommodations we'd endured would be for naught—since the sky was obscured by considerable cloud cover that day. But as luck would have it, just before, during, and after the eclipse, the clouds near the sun parted. Through blackened, polarized film lenses designed specifically for the purpose, we watched the moon gradually gobble up the sun, and the sweltering southern light of August became a weak, silvery wash.

We'd both experienced a total eclipse previously, together on Prince Edward Island in 1970. And still we weren't prepared.

"Oh my God," I muttered involuntarily.

I'd pulled the blackout lenses away for the minute or so of totality, to see a hole carved into the sky.

It's not unlike the unicorn effect, when you at last see in real life a bird that until that moment has only existed in your imagination. Only in reverse: In an eclipse, something that's existed unquestioned for your whole life, the heavens above your head, is suddenly altered in a way that's hard to imagine. You are confronted with the magnitude of the cosmos, revealed for a few moments before your very eyes. In the parking lot of a run-down Nashville motor lodge, I stood side by side with my father as we had done nearly half a century earlier, and we stared into the divine.

That would be the last trip we would take together.

Near the end of the following winter, I'd booked a trip to the Galápagos. I was going with a group to bird in Ecuador and figured I might not ever be there again, so I splurged and added five days on a separate boat tour of the far-flung islands that inspired Charles Darwin to pen his theory of evolution. I'd be joining the Galápagos boat on my own, but I was paying double occupancy, because there was no rate for singles. So why not invite Dad along? The spot was paid for; it was exactly the kind of eco-adventure we not only both enjoyed but enjoyed doing together; and it was a chance for me to reciprocate for the Costa Rica trip he picked up the tab for all those years ago.

I could hear the glee in his voice over the phone when I proposed he come along. I was unaware until then that, as a former biology teacher and general science nut, visiting the Galápagos had been a lifelong dream of his. Preparing for the trip became an ongoing adventure for us in itself: planning what to pack, sharing the latest email updates from the tour organizer, making sure we had the right field guides.

And then, the day before our flight to Ecuador, I got a phone call.

"Hello, son. I've decided I'm not going."

I was stunned. Aside from all the planning and anticipation, it was totally unlike him to flake out at the last minute on something to which he'd committed. That was the kind of behavior he abhorred and excoriated others for.

"But wait—I don't understand. You've been nothing but excited about this!"

"I just don't feel up to it. I don't think I'll be able to keep up."

"It's on a *boat*, Dad! The hikes on the islands are minimal, and if you don't feel comfortable with any of them, you just decline it and stay on the boat."

I couldn't wrap my head around it. He was going to pass up his lifelong dream? The man who, even as he slowed with age, had always vested himself in being capable—including in all the days of preparation prior to this one—had at the eleventh hour of the eve of our trip developed clay feet? Something was going on, but he wouldn't elaborate.

"You insured the flights, right?" he added before he hung up, as if money were what mattered. "Just be sure to file the paperwork to collect on mine. Don't let them keep that cash." That, at least, was typical Francis.

I ended up embarking alone after all, making friends with the others in the tour group yet keenly aware of my father's absence the whole time. When a sea lion shuffled up to me on the beach and brushed me with its whiskers the way a friendly dog might sniff the back of your hand; when three juvenile sea lions saw me pass in a sea kayak and took it as a challenge to race alongside to see who was faster; when a curious Brown Pelican swam directly to me as I was floating offshore, until I was bobbing in the water nose-to-beak with it, no doubt both of us fascinated with how peculiar the other looked; as I struggled to ID each of Darwin's signature finches, bland in color but unique in its beak, shaped for its ecological niche by natural selection; as marine iguanas marched within inches (yes, the Galápagos wildlife really is free from any fear of humans); as I sorted through the foot color of boobies and marveled at the elegance of Swallow-Tailed Gulls, I had the same thought, every time: Dad would have loved this! But he wasn't there.

Others older and less able than Francis managed the boat trip just fine. And when I met the middle-aged lesbian woman (we had each other pegged from the get-go) traveling with her elderly father, I felt a pang at what might have been.

Back on the Ecuadorean mainland, while the birds lacked the fearlessness of the creatures of the Galápagos, they made up for it with dazzling diversity: tanagers in every conceivable combination of hues, a Plate-Billed Mountain Toucan dipped in astonishing blue, big Andean Cock-of-the-Rock males displaying orange helmets of feathers at each other amid the tangles of the deep forest, vastly bigger Andean Condors perched on the sheerest of cliffs at the highest of altitudes. And hummingbirds! So many, of so many different kinds, that they ran out of names for them and had to make up new ones: jacobins, hermits, coronets, sapphires, emeralds, trainbearers, racket-tails, saberwings, coquettes. At one hummingbird gallery (many of the locals have caught on that setting up a feeding station and charging a modest admission fee is a great way to bring in some dollars), the profusion of shining iridescent colors and radical feathers from a dozen species at once sent us birders into a frenzy, comparable to turning a glutton loose in a shop brimming with fresh-baked pies.

But when I got home, as the wonders of tropical American birding receded, I turned back to the mysterious behavior of my dad. I had a heart-to-heart with Miriam.

"It was weird," she said. "Your father was so excited about the trip; he'd even bought one of those special cameras for filming underwater to bring with him. For weeks he'd been laying out which clothes to take. The day before you two were supposed to leave, everything was packed. And then suddenly he decided he wasn't physically up to it."

Soon we learned why. His lung cancer was back and had metastasized. He was being treated at Memorial Sloan Kettering Cancer Center in Manhattan for both cancers; ever since his initial diagnosis, I'd accompanied him and Miriam to as many appointments as I could. He'd asked me to come, because he thought it was important for me to know what I as his genetic heir would likely be facing, at least in respect to prostate health, as I aged. That was the reason he gave me, anyway.

Within a year, he'd run through all the viable treatments for a man in his eighties. His decline over that time was rapid, and he grew ever nastier to Miriam as he became more and more dependent on her. He spent his days in his favorite recliner, falling asleep in front of the TV; at night, she barely got any rest, because she had to wake repeatedly to help him to the bathroom, or else he would try to do it alone and fall. Her son, who lived nearby, had to race over, pick him up off the floor, and try to talk some sense into him more than once after he'd done that.

To give Miriam a break and let her get some sleep, sometimes Melody or I would come out to Long Island and sleep next to Francis in their bed while Miriam spent a desperately needed night in the guest bedroom. It was sobering, seeing the fearsome beast my father had been my whole life, laid low; he was a shell of himself—gaunt, weak, skin sallow—though he still had the Francis Cooper booming voice, if backed with less fire. He could barely walk the short distance from bed to bathroom or clean himself properly after defecating; I had to help with that too. That was all nothing compared with the daily physical and emotional brunt Miriam had to bear, and I was glad to relieve that even a little, difficult as it was. You're not meant to see your parents naked and helpless, yet as it turns out for so many people my age with elderly and infirm parents, that's what has to happen. He and I made a joke of it, in that buddy camaraderie we'd established in my adult years, and at least he was comfortable enough with me to let me help, with a minimum of patented Francis Cooper stubborn resistance. One night we stayed up talking in bed when he couldn't sleep, and I took the opportunity to thank him for fighting the fight and getting into "good trouble" in his youth, for passing on that righteous demand for justice to me and Melody, for giving me a passion for the wild world and nurturing my love of birds, and for embracing my gayness without so much as a flinch.

Without making light of what I'd said, he shrugged, as if it were all in a day's work. Especially the birding.

"Taking you birding on Sunday mornings was easy," he said. "I loved that. Getting outdoors, sharing nature with you."

Eventually, we fell asleep, hand in hand, nothing left unspoken between us. I'd said it, and I'm so glad I said it.

By the late winter of 2019, he was on home hospice care and completely bedridden. Melody, her mostly grown children, and I paid a visit together, so he could have his whole family around him while he was still lucid. Being Francis Cooper, he had to carp about something, and my trip to Boston a few days earlier to attend a twenty-four-hour science-fiction movie marathon was the easy target.

"I might have *died*," he said melodramatically, half-joking, halfaccusatory. That phrase had long ago become a refrain.

"But you didn't," I replied, continuing to snack on nuts unperturbed.

"Stupid movies that you've seen a hundred times are more important than your father."

I rolled my eyes. Speaking of stupid movies, we were watching one together, because TV viewing was one of the few things left for him to pass the time in bed. The mindless entertainment we were largely ignoring was 2004's *Troy*, starring Brad Pitt, Eric Bana, and Peter O'Toole in the legendary tale of the Trojan War. The drama pierced our conversation from time to time long enough to hold our attention, one such moment being as Hector is about to go to his certain death in single combat with Achilles. Hector's father, King Priam, struggles for words for the brave, doomed prince of Troy.

"No father ever had a finer son," Peter O'Toole's Priam tells him through tearing eyes.

"I do," my father said clearly. No almost-as-ifs about it.

It was so unexpected Melody gasped. The rest of the family turned their eyes on me.

I kept my mouth busy eating the nuts and my gaze glued to the TV, although I can't say what happened in the rest of the movie. Something had gone wrong with my eyes, like Peter O'Toole's.

Fate had one final twist in store for Francis Cooper.

My eldest niece used one of those genetic testing services to find out the mix of her ancestry, and she checked the box that allows those who may be in some way related to contact you. Lo and behold, in the final weeks of my dad's life, she got an email from a woman who turned out to be Francis's first cousin. Her mother was the sister of Thelma Burke—the woman who walked out on my dad and his three sisters when they were children.

Unsurprisingly, their side of the family had a completely different story. In their version, the tyrannical Henry Cooper kicked Thelma out of the home and banished her from the lives of her four children. This cousin noted that their family knew never to mention children around their aunt Thelma; otherwise she would become quiet and very sad.

With all parties long gone, it's impossible to know where the truth lies, but it's probably safe to say it's somewhere in between the two versions. That Henry was an abusive monster, I have no doubt, just from the little I remember of my grandfather and more important my father's behavior around him. Yet it's also true that Thelma never made any attempt to contact her children ever again, even when they were grown and Henry was no longer in the picture.

The cousin forwarded family photos: In one, Thelma's sister happened to strike a pose identical to that of one of my aunts in a photo taken years later; the two were dead ringers. The eldest of the Cooper siblings, my aunt Aleta, was old enough when Thelma left to retain clear memories of her; now, as Aleta passed ninety years old, she saw pictures of her long-lost mother for the first time. I can't imagine how staggering that must have felt.

It was in consultation with Aunt Aleta that Melody and I decided not to share this new discovery with Francis. He had only a matter of days left as the cancer made its final push through his heavily medicated body, and his periods of lucidity had become unpredictable and few. He had spent his entire life with the hatred of the woman who had abandoned him as an article of faith; it seemed pointless and perhaps even cruel to upend those underpinnings as everything else slipped away from him. So I kept silent.

We had been told by the hospice care staff what to expect: that near the end, he would thrash around vacantly, but that this was normal. Still, as I sat on his bed next to him one evening, I tried to calm him.

I told him he was at Jones Beach, where we used to go as a family when Melody and I were young. I named everyone who was there with him at the beach picnic: Miriam; all his sisters, including his closest, Audrey, who had died many years ago; his children, stepchildren, niece; all his grandkids and his beloved great-grandchild. The sand was fine and white, the ocean clean and calm with the sun sparkling off it, the air tangy with salt, with only the slightest sea breeze. I told him what everyone in the family was doing on the beach, each consistent with their quirks and foibles; I was birding, of course. He was enjoying watching the children play in the surf, lying on a beach blanket while indulging in that pleasant exhaustion that comes at the end of a day doing nothing. I had him look up, past the umbrella, to a sky with a few scattered cumulus clouds, which are very important to someone who flies gliders, as the sign of warmer, rising air to provide lift. Sure enough, there were gulls overhead, soaring high in looping arcs on white motionless wings, their paths through the blue sketching out the shape of the warm air bubble they were riding.

I have no way to know if he heard and understood me, but his thrashing slowed as I added more and more detail to the description. Once he was calm, I took a break from sitting with him and went downstairs for a meal with Miriam at the kitchen counter. When the barstool I sat on nearly collapsed, I grabbed some tools and tinkered with the stool to pass the time, and to my absolute shock the guy with the construction skills of a toddler actually fixed it.

"The spirit of Francis Cooper was definitely moving my hands tonight," I said, as Miriam laughed and went upstairs to check on Dad.

"*CHRIS!*" she cried out a moment later.

I had never heard Miriam's voice like that; I sprang up and thundered up the stairs.

Francis lay sprawled on the bed, his eyes open and unmoving.

"He's gone," she said.

I like to think he was on that beach when he left.

12

Another Incident in Central Park

MANY PEOPLE HAVE asked me what was going through my head in the decisive moment when I was confronted with weaponized racism while birding in Central Park. My thinking at that moment is impossible to understand without first recalling the killing of Philando Castile.

Castile, a thirty-two-year-old African American man known to his friends as Phil, worked as a nutrition services supervisor in a school district in the suburbs of Minneapolis–St. Paul (a region that would figure fatefully into events again). He knew all the kids' names, roughly five hundred of them, and memorized their food allergies. On a warm July evening in 2016, he had picked up his girlfriend and her daughter and was driving near the Minnesota State Fair when a police officer pulled him over for a traffic stop.

Castile dutifully did all the things that Black mothers tell their sons to do to survive an encounter with the police: He complied with the officer's instructions. He was respectful in his tone. He volunteered to the police officer that he had a gun in the car, a gun he was licensed to carry, so that there could be no misunderstanding.

The police officer nonetheless shot Castile dead with seven shots as the young man sat behind the steering wheel complying, with his girlfriend next to him and a four-year-old child witnessing from the backseat. The events might have escaped public attention, except that Castile's girlfriend live streamed video of the immediate aftermath of the shooting to the world, as Philando drew his last breaths.

As in the Amadou Diallo case—and as has become numbingly routine—the police officer was later acquitted of all charges.

It's also necessary to keep in mind the nation's explosive racial legacy right in Central Park, and right from its beginning.

The park's very existence was contingent upon Black suffering. Before the graceful lawns and wooded slopes of the landscape architects Frederick Law Olmsted and Calvert Vaux, a community comprised mostly of African Americans thrived on that land between what is now West Eighty-second and West Eighty-ninth Streets. Known as Seneca Village, in the early nineteenth century it was a refuge for New York's downtrodden: Black folk and a smaller group of Irish immigrants, the "Blackest" white folk in America's social hierarchy of the day.

"Before the park, there was a whole shantytown of squatters who had established a home for themselves here," I told a group of mostly Black birders I was leading on a walk through the park one morning.

Crystal, one of those Black birders, interrupted: "That's actually not correct."

I was taken aback; there *hadn't* been a mostly Black community here?

"It wasn't a shantytown," she continued. "And they weren't squatters."

Upon further investigation of her correction, I learned that the residents of Seneca Village in fact owned their land. Many built two-story homes, where they dined from chinaware and lived relatively comfortable, prosperous lives as tradespeople and laborers. "Downtrodden" isn't synonymous with "dirt-poor"; though oppressed by society at large, in Seneca Village, Black people had carved out a place of their own (including three churches and an African American school) where they could live in dignity. The shantytown notion had been promoted by leaders of the all-white establishment of the nineteenth century to serve their own interests, and it lingers to this day, to the point that I was repeating that falsehood some 175 years later and might still be doing so, if not for Crystal sharing her superior knowledge of Seneca Village's history. The establishment of that era had an agenda, so they crafted a narrative to suit it.

That agenda was the creation of a grand park that would eventually stretch from Fifty-ninth Street to One Hundred and Tenth Street. Seneca Village stood in the way, so the "shantytown" had to go. Using the power of eminent domain, the city bought the landowners' property, regardless of whether they wanted to sell. With little surviving documentation, it's left to the imagination whether these powerful princes of the city paid fair market value to a bunch of undesirable Blacks and a smattering of equally undesirable Irish. The stability and accumulation of wealth across generations that home ownership provides were stripped from these families, and since little is known about where they scattered, none can say how long it took them to recover, if they ever did. By 1857, Seneca Village was gone.

Today, people of all races and ethnicities enjoy the sprawling urban oasis of Central Park. As a birder I cherish its glories more than most, yet I remain mindful of what its creation cost and who paid the price. Its origin fits the depressingly familiar pattern of "progress" on the backs of Black and brown people; to this day, our communities disproportionately house sewage-treatment plants, emissions-spewing power generators, highways that cut off our neighborhoods from key downtown areas, and other infrastructure improvements that do anything but improve the health and welfare of the people who live next door to them.

The calculated destruction of Seneca Village would be followed by eruptions of violent destruction: New York City's draft riots in 1863, in which Irish immigrants, some of whom had shared Seneca Village with African American New Yorkers, went on a rampage against them that left 120 dead and the Colored Orphan Asylum burned to the ground; the 1921 Tulsa, Oklahoma, massacre of residents of its prosperous Black community of Greenwood, sparked by rumors of an incident between a Black man and a white woman; the 1923 massacre and destruction of the Black town of Rosewood, Florida, also sparked by an alleged incident between a Black man and a white woman. Separate events with sometimes disparate causes, yet united by a common thread: The end of Seneca Village needs to be understood in the context of Black communities and Black lives swept away, by violence or by design, because they were the most vulnerable, the most expendable.

Fast-forward 132 years in Central Park, and not much had changed in who was deemed expendable. I remember the Central Park jogger case vividly; nobody who lived in New York in 1989 could forget it. It dominated the headlines for months after the April attack: A woman on her regular nightly run through the park was raped, beaten, and left for dead. Though she survived, she suffered severe and permanent brain damage that left her with no memory of the attack and facing months of rehabilitation. (It's worth noting what did not make the headlines: a similarly horrific rape in Brooklyn less than a month later, in which the attackers threw the victim off the roof of a four-story building. She too survived, but with severe injuries. The Central Park jogger was wealthy and white; the Brooklyn victim was Black.)

I also recall the prevailing sentiment in my family and broadly in the African American community that the five Black and Latino teenagers who'd been rounded up by the Manhattan Special Victims Unit and charged with the crime were being railroaded. But the cry for swift justice in the city at large deafened most ears to such sentiments—particularly after a rich and uncouth real-estate developer, Donald Trump, ever eager to grab some attention, published a full-page ad in all four of the city's daily newspapers calling for New York to reinstate the death penalty, with the implication that it should be applied to the five teenagers.

After that, their convictions were inevitable. The Central Park Five spent years of their lives incarcerated for a crime they didn't commit, before they were finally exonerated. And Donald Trump went on to become president of the United States.

Into this woeful history, tangled like poison ivy through the beauty of the park, a cocker spaniel named Henry rushed off the leash, headlong.

By Memorial Day 2020, the variations in my spring habits had become routine—changes wrought by living in the American city at the center of the raging COVID epidemic. Transit workers were falling to the virus at an unprecedented rate, and since I didn't feel justified riding the subway and potentially putting them at further risk just so I could bird the Ramble, I'd taken to biking to the park. With office buildings shut down, I cruised through the eerily deserted streets of midtown unimpeded by the usual traffic menaces to cyclists. And I'd learned the spots on the park's perimeter where I could lock my bike without the worry of its theft gnawing at me the whole time I was birding. Its wheels and frame secured to a sturdy lamppost, I pulled out my binoculars and dug into the new day to see what treasure it might bring me.

It was nearly the end of the season, and it showed: The plantings throughout the park had fully leafed out two weeks earlier. The aesthetic pleasure of a lush landscape was tempered a bit for me, since small, active songbirds would be that much more difficult to spot amid all the foliage. Besides, I always savor the first blush of spring, when the tree branches knit a delicate filigree of pale green and the world is full of promise, after weeks of cold and dark. I gave a mental shrug; the progression held its own comforts and satisfactions. Only a fool bemoans lost beauty while still in beauty's embrace, just of another sort. Something inside me, content, returned the park's hug.

The Ramble was mostly empty. The overnight winds had failed to bring a fresh influx of birds, or else they'd blown what birds we'd had to their next destination north; this late in the migration, it could be both. As for other birders, their absence was particularly acute, and had been all season; I'd been seeing less than half the usual number. Because of COVID, nearly all birding groups had suspended their organized outings, walks that could draw forty or more. And because birder demographics skew toward the elderly—one of the populations most vulnerable to the coronavirus—many birders simply stayed home. Claude, still a Central Park regular even now in his nineties, skipped the spring 2020 migration entirely, as did many others. Combined with the exodus from the city, either from COVID or for the holiday weekend, this Memorial Day capped a quiet season for seeing other Central Park birders.

Not so for dog walkers. The city's padlocking of the dog runs (to prevent congregating that could spread COVID), combined with the decimated ranks of birders, led a subset of dog owners to think they had free rein in the Ramble. The off-leash situation had always been bad, but in some thirty-five years birding the park, I had never seen it like this. Dogs were routinely left to run roughshod over sensitive areas, to the point that dog walkers who might otherwise be compliant with the park's regulations were beginning to think that this was no big deal, one of those rules like jaywalking in New York that no one cares about, and if everyone else is doing it, why not me and my pooch? It had become its own kind of epidemic.

Dogs off the leash in protected zones is hardly a problem unique to Central Park, or even New York City. They can be devastating on beaches, where endangered shorebirds like Piping Plovers and Least Terns that nest on open ground are especially vulnerable. But in places like Central Park and Brooklyn's Prospect Park that serve a dense urban population, a large number of dogs becomes concentrated in a limited space. If they were allowed to roam free in the leash zones, wildlife, including migrants in desperate need of rest, would be constantly disturbed, and the habitat would be ruined as the turf is torn up and plantings destroyed. (The next time you're near a dog run, take a look to see if anything grows there.)

Birding Tip

We love your pets. But Man's Best Friend is a hungry wolf to a bird, no matter the harmless, playful little scamp Fluffy may seem to you. And Athena, with her retractable claws, silent stalking, and high-jump pounce, is a bird-killing machine engineered for that purpose by millions of years of evolution. The American Bird Conservancy estimates that in the United States, where the domesticated feline is a non-native predator disrupting the natural balance, cats slaughter 2.4 BILLION birds EACH YEAR. Keep cats indoors, and dogs on the leash in protected areas, if they are permitted there at all. The birds—and other birders—will thank you.

For decades we birders had pleaded through our organizations to the Parks Department for enforcement that almost never came. Small wonder: A city government perennially strapped for cash rarely adequately funds its parks. In 2020 the number of urban park rangers would be cut by more than half, leaving fewer than 50 to cover the more than 28,000 acres of parkland in New York City. And while the uniformed police in the park are relatively plentiful, the idea that they'd do anything about dog owners flouting leash laws in the Ramble is laughable; we knew that, because we saw them ignore it, time and time again, when it was right under their noses. Their enforcement might is reserved for serious crimes like murder, robbery, rape, and the occasional Black fellow selling loose cigarettes outside a Staten Island bodega. (The man's name was Eric Garner.)

If our precious patch of the park and its wildlife were to survive, it was up to us birders, the problem being that birders are, by and large, insanely nice people. When we'd say something to the dog owners, in the nicest possible terms—even going so far as to explain why keeping the dog leashed in this area is so important—what we got back ranged from the dismissive to the offensive:

"Oh, not [insert dog's name]. S/He wouldn't hurt a fly!"

"The birds are in the trees. My dog doesn't bother them."

"Mind your own business."

"Are you a park ranger? A cop? No? Then I don't have to listen to you."

"Go fuck yourself."

To be clear, the problem is not the dogs; they can't be faulted for wanting to run free and do all the things that dogs naturally do. The fault lies with the irresponsible dog owners. To further clarify, about a third of dog owners are respectful of the park and their fellow park goers, keeping their dog on the leash in protected areas. Another third will leash their dog when asked, either resentfully or claiming they didn't know the rules. (In fact, they almost always know; the signage is everywhere, except where it's been pulled down by the Fido Über Alles crowd.) The other third is that special breed, common to the zip codes flanking the Ramble, who are accustomed to having things their way and who see their dog as an extension of themselves and their privilege. Their sense of entitlement is matched only by their apparent delusion that a leash is strictly a fashion accessory to be draped artfully about one's own neck, rather than attached to their dog's.

And then there's Amy Cooper.

I didn't know her name then, and we had never met. Her voice calling out to her dog was the first I'd ever heard of her.

"Henry! *Henry!!*"

The sound was unmistakable, in both decibel level and stridency; nobody would take that tone with another human being. It split the morning's tranquility and made me wince like nails on a chalkboard. I didn't have to see it to know: yet another dog off the leash in the Ramble. That voice could portend only bad news. I never imagined just how bad, how consequential coming events would be—the random intersection of the lives of two unrelated Coopers, in turn intersecting with a far weightier event halfway across the continent later that same Memorial Day.

I took a deep breath. I hadn't gotten up before 5:00 a.m. so that I could spend my time in the park dealing with leash scofflaws; I was focused on the end-of-season hunt for a Mourning Warbler, which I hadn't seen yet that year. But the Mourning Warbler is a ground dweller, skulking through low growth, and sure enough, as I approached the planted area where I'd hoped to find the bird, just northeast of the Ramble's Tupelo Meadow, a cocker spaniel bounded through that patch. If there had been a Mourning there before, there certainly wasn't one there now.

A young white woman, a brunette in an open hooded sweatshirt, top, and leggings—and a leash that wasn't attached to her dog—came into view, walking north on the path that skirts the Tupelo Meadow's eastern side; I stood on the intersecting path on the north side of the field, facing east, and waited. I knew there was a sign on the fence where her dog was running, right where the two paths intersected: DOGS MUST BE LEASHED AT ALL TIMES IN THE RAMBLE, complete with a little human-with-leashed-dog icon for the reading-impaired. In a moment, she'd cross right by it.

"Excuse me, ma'am," I said in a voice just loud enough that she could hear me clearly over the twenty or so feet between us. "Dogs in the Ramble have to be leashed at all times. The sign is right there."

I pointed toward the green placard that was now next to her. When bringing the regulations to someone's attention, I find it always helps to have them spelled out incontrovertibly in official ink.

"The dog runs are closed, and he needs his exercise," she said.

"I get that," I replied, "but all you have to do is go about a hundred yards that way"—and I gestured eastward on the path where I stood—"and cross the drive, and you'll be outside the Ramble, where you can let your dog run off the leash to your heart's content until 9:00 a.m."

"That's too dangerous."

Too dangerous? She'd crossed the drive with her dog to get into the Ramble; she'd have to cross the drive again to get out. It is, in fact, nigh impossible to get in or out of the Ramble *without* crossing one of the park's drives. Of necessity she and her dog would pass through the areas I'd recommended beyond the Ramble anyway, no matter what route she used to go home. If she needed her dog off the leash so badly, why not go there? It was as if her hoodie were woven of a unique cotton/polyester blend impervious to reason.

But her meaning was clear enough: She couldn't be bothered. She was going to do what she wanted, and that was that.

"Look, if you're going to do what you want, I'm going to do what I want, but you're not going to like it," I said.

She looked at me sharply. "What's that?"

So I called to her dog.

"He won't come to you," she said with complete certainty.

"We'll see about that," and I pulled out a bag of dog treats.

I had started carrying dog treats many years before, one of a suite of countermeasures I could deploy in response to the off-leash problem. Treats were the nuclear option, an escalation reserved for the worst of the worst, because their use is admittedly not a very nice thing to do, and as noted earlier, we birders tend to be a nice lot. But I'm also an activist from a family of activists, someone who's spent a lifetime getting into "good trouble" fighting for LGBTQ rights and justice for African Americans. ACT UP didn't change the course of AIDS treatment by being polite; civil rights leaders didn't shy away from provocative actions if they helped bring Jim Crow to its demise. The long-standing situation in the Ramble didn't come close to that moral stature, but the principle was the same: Being nice is secondary to being effective. I didn't seek conflict, but neither was I afraid of it. Faced with a threat to wildlife, the park, and my right to enjoy it just as much as anyone else, I had effective ways to push back.

And the treats are indeed incredibly effective. (But not for the faint-hearted: I was assaulted twice that spring by seething dog owners—one man riled by the dog-treat tactic, another guy simply because I called his dog to get it out of the woodland wildflowers when he wouldn't. In neither case did it go beyond them thumping me on the chest in apelike challenge, because I didn't engage. I don't do physical violence—never have, hopefully will never have to. As Isaac Asimov wrote in his science-fiction classic *Foundation*, "Violence is the last refuge of the incompetent.") With treats, one can coax a dog out of sensitive plantings, and more important, one can compel the owner to leash their animal. They don't like it when a stranger feeds their dog against their will, and because a dog is a dog, eager for whatever scraps it can get from whomever, the only way to get it to stop eating the treats is to put it on the leash.

Or at least, that's usually the case.

"DON'T TOUCH MY DOG!" Amy Cooper took one look at the bag of treats and zoomed from unperturbed to panicked in 0.5 seconds. Before I had a chance to toss a single treat, she scooped up her dog by the collar and started dragging it around off the ground by the neck, to the dog's obvious dismay.

This was not the desired response. Aside from the fact that the moment she set the dog down, it would be running around off the leash again, she was hurting the animal. It was the beginning of a downward spiral for her, one that would lead to a very dark place.

In the hopes of getting a more appropriate response, I switched to a different countermeasure, one that a number of us birders had been using to document the problem in the Ramble. Away went the treats, and out came the smartphone. I was determined to record video of her scofflaw behavior until that dog was on the leash.

Thus, the infamous video recording was born. A common misconception is that I recorded the video to document racist behavior; in fact, I had no way of knowing what was coming next. Indeed, it might not have happened if I wasn't recording, because as she unraveled, it was the recording that set her off more than anything else.

"Would you please stop. Sir, I'm asking you to stop," she said as she simultaneously wrangled her dog and marched in my direction.

"Please don't come close to me," I said, mindful of the constant COVID messaging that we should keep at least six feet of distance.

"Sir, I'm asking you to stop recording me, because you are," she repeated, continuing to approach with a raised finger gesturing for me to get gone. Her dog was still off the leash, so I kept my camera running. I wondered if she'd try to snatch the phone out of my hand.

"Please don't come close to me," I said again.

"Please take your phone off of me."

"Please don't come close to me." My stress level was heading skyward, but I was determined to stand my ground.

"Then I'm taking a picture and calling the cops." Out came her cellphone.

"Please—*please* call the cops. *Please* call the cops." She didn't have a leg to stand on, while her dog was about to be loose on all four, untethered, if she ever stopped choking it by the collar. If she wanted to bring a two-hundred-dollar fine down on her own head, I was 100 percent down with that.

"I'm going to tell them that there's an African American man threatening my life."

Whoa.

A part of me froze, deep down inside.

So she was going *there* with this. Until that moment, this had been just another dustup between a birder and a dog walker—the second-oldest story in the Ramble. But now she'd decided to take it to a whole other place, a place where brown-skinned bodies swung from trees, a place where we lie shattered by a hail of police bullets.

I have lived my whole life as a Black man in the United States. I don't have to go all the way back to Tulsa and Rosewood and Emmett Till to know what it means for a white woman to accuse a Black man, and who would likely be believed. This was potentially a world of trouble heading my way. Her fingers were already dialing; in a split second of self-preservation, I considered that if I just stopped recording, maybe this would all go away.

Which of course was her intent. I can't say whether it was a conscious choice or the product of unconscious bias when she grabbed that bloody, blunt object, of the White Damsel in Distress Threatened by the Black Menace, to try to club me into compliance with her wish not to be recorded; I don't know her at all, can't know why it was so easily within her reach, when she was grasping for something to give her leverage in our confrontation. In the weeks that followed, several right-wing mouthpieces would seek to excuse it, justifying her injection of race into the situation as merely her giving a full and accurate physical description of me to the police. (Never mind the falseness of the accusation in the first place.) Except at that moment, she wasn't speaking to the police; she was talking to *me*. People who think their life is in danger don't pause to inform their supposed assailant, in a rather triumphal tone of voice, that they're about to call the cops and inform them of your race; if they're genuinely scared for their life, they punch the digits, period. Her intent, in saying it to me, was to use the long history of Fear of the Black Man, and the resulting unjust police violence against us, to intimidate me into submission.

That's when my split second of hesitation gave way to thoughts of Philando Castile.

Philando Castile's death had been a turning point for me; I'd considered what I might have done in his situation, and yet nothing Castile or any Black man could have done would have changed the outcome one iota. "They're going to shoot us dead no matter what we do," I thought at the time. "In which case, I'm going out with my human dignity intact." I would not twist myself into a pretzel to cater to some white person, cop or otherwise, and their irrational fears of any complexion darker than Coppertone sun bronzed; I will *not* comply in any manner other than what might be expected of a similarly situated white person. (Having since witnessed how little compliance is expected of white people, as evidenced by the antics of COVID anti-maskers and January 6 insurrectionists who with lone exception somehow still don't end up dead at the hands of police, we can all attest that it's a pretty low bar.)

That resolve informed my decision, in the face of Amy Cooper's attempt at racial intimidation, to keep on recording as anyone might whether they were white, Black, brown, Hulk green, or Andorian blue. Under no circumstances would I make this easy for her by capitulating to her threat. I would not be complicit in my own dehumanization.

"Please tell them whatever you like," I said. My camera would keep rolling; she would have to do whatever she was going to do, and it would be on her alone.

"Excuse me," she said incongruously; presumably to me, as if she needed to apologize for disengaging with me so that she could report me to 911. And further indicating she wasn't necessarily thinking things through, she proceeded to remove the COVID mask covering her nose and mouth—even though she knew she was being recorded— exposing her full face for easier subsequent identification.

The rest of her words that the video captured were directed to the person on the other end of the phone line (all the while, her cocker spaniel continued to dangle like a piñata):

"I'm sorry, I'm in the Ramble, and there's a man, African American, he has a bicycle helmet, he's recording me and threatening me and my dog." Her tone was relatively calm at first; after a pause during which she was no doubt being prompted for more information by the 911 operator, she continued, slightly more agitated:

"There's an African American man, I'm in Central Park, he's recording me and threatening myself and my dog." Another pause; upon failure to receive the urgency of response she believed she merited, her throat constricted to inject a terrified rasp into her voice:

"I'm sorry, I can't hear you either! I'm being threatened by a man in the Ramble! Please send the cops immediately!"

The problem being, the Ramble comprises a sizable area. One can only guess that the person on the other end of the line asked her to specify where in the Ramble she was; any birder could have told her, including me, but like hell was I going to help her out. By now her histrionics were full-blown.

"I'm in Central Park in the Ramble! *I don't know*—!"

Simultaneously, she took pity on her dog: Instead of hauling it by the collar, she attached the leash. Finally.

"Thank you," I said, and turned off my camera. With the dog on the leash, I had no further interest in her.

What happened next was therefore not captured on video:

"So now that I've called the cops, you stop recording," she said to me; her 911 call finished, the terrified rasp was gone, replaced by a reprise of her triumphal tone.

"No," I replied, "now that your dog is on a leash, I stopped recording."

I briefly considered waiting there at the Tupelo Meadow for the police to arrive, to clear up the matter, and promptly rejected the idea. I had come to the park to bird, not to deal with the likes of her, and that's exactly what I was going back to doing. She does not get to further deform my morning with her mess. Done with her, I started to walk away.

Just then, a white guy came up the northern path toward us; until then, it had just been me and her, with no one else around. She took one look at him and slipped back into performative mode, rasp and all.

"Please get help!" she said while doubling over in apparent distress. "That man threatened my life!"

"I just asked her to leash her dog," I said with a shrug and kept walking.

The poor guy. He looked at me, looked at her, at me, at her, only his stricken eyes visible above his mask. I have no idea what I would have done in his shoes; I have no idea what he ended up doing. I didn't stick around to find out. There were birds to be found.

I wish I could say that when I walked away, the whole thing rolled off my back like water off a duck; that my emotional control was so Vulcan-like, I was able to immediately return to my birding norm: alert and engaged, simultaneously tranquil and excited with possibility.

But the truth is, I was unnerved. As I birded my way out of the park as I had planned, I kept waiting for a police cruiser to pull up, and then, like every Black man accused by a white woman, or at least the ones not immediately set upon, I'd have some explaining to do. In the meantime I did my best to focus on the bird-finding task at hand. An American Redstart sang, drawing my attention to the warbler's black-and-orange beauty; the green expanse around me, reliable as ever, worked its soothing magic, and my stress level gradually dropped below stroke inducing. By the time I reached my bicycle, no cops had descended on me, and I breathed a sigh of relief.

My custom after a morning birding during spring migration has long been to post the most notable sighting of the day on Facebook, to let my non-birding friends know what they're missing and why they don't see me for six weeks. The incident in the park, while not a sighting, was certainly notable; so as soon as I got home, I posted the video to my FB friends, including a description of the events leading up to the video, to put it in context. Sharing what had happened helped relieve the last of my tension, and I figured my pals had to see the crazy crap from the morning for themselves.

Had to see that crazy crap indeed: Almost immediately, several friends messaged me to ask that I make the post public so that they could share it with others, and I agreed. Next, my phone rang.

"What the—?" my sister said. Melody was understandably out-raged. Any Black relative would be; considering the long history of reckless police enforcement against Black bodies, it was all too easy for her to envision the worst-case scenario of what might have hap-pened to her brother. It took some doing, but I reassured her that I was fine, though she was still fuming. "Can I post this on Twitter?" she asked.

I hesitated; Melody is plugged into Black Twitter, the informal but active network of African Americans on the Twitter platform venting on everything from A-Rod to Jay-Z. (I, on the other hand, am the least social-media-savvy person I know. To me, tweets are for birds, literally and figuratively.) Black Twitter could give the incident broader exposure than just my friends and their friends, and I wasn't sure what the ramifications of that might be. But I knew that the video spoke volumes: Here was an urban sophisticate (so sophisticated she used the politically correct "African American," never any slur) in liberal New York City who consciously or not was aware of the pervasive ra-cial bias in policing, so pervasive that she felt confident in weaponiz-ing it. She knew that mentioning that a suspect is Black, particularly in relation to a white woman, could bring the cops whistling down on that suspect with special vengeance, and she didn't hesitate to use that ploy. If that could happen in this place, with these two people, in such relatively mild circumstances—a leash law dispute—then how deep does this bias go? That reality of race today needed to be understood, and perhaps, as captured in sixty-nine seconds of digital video, it could be.

So I gave Melody the okay. After all, how much attention could it get?

"Your video in Melody's tweet is getting a lot of hits," Arturo said that afternoon as he peered at his smartphone. He and another friend had joined me and my boyfriend, John, for a Memorial Day cookout. Of course we'd discussed the incident; I was determined to drown the ridiculousness of it in healthy rounds of margaritas. Arturo was obsessed with monitoring the Twitter response.

"*Oh my God—Kathy Griffin just retweeted you!!*" he whooped about an hour later; to him the edgy comedian seemed to be the ultimate validation. I blinked, unsure what to make of this, having remained in my own social-media-free bubble since posting on Facebook in the morning.

Things only snowballed from there.

"Dude, you've gone viral," Arturo said in awe after another half hour, looking at a number of hits somewhere north of astonishing; to date, the video has gotten more than forty-five million views. "Never before have I been there with someone as that happened."

And I'd never had it happen to me. Melody pressing Send had thrust me into a national frenzy. I was still processing when my phone started to ring: The press had somehow gotten my private cell number. I made as if I hadn't been dosed with margaritas and tried to sound coherent as I fielded their calls. Maybe that impaired judgment, combined with an ignorance of the media landscape, accounts for why I agreed to meet a reporter from *Inside Edition* the next morning outside a park in my neighborhood.

At first, the interview followed a standard trajectory, though the reporter's skintight jeans and stiletto heels had set off alarm bells when we'd initially met. Then she mentioned something that for me came out of the blue.

"What's your reaction regarding the African American man in Minneapolis who died yesterday after a white police officer kneeled on his neck?"

I don't follow the news very closely during migration; this was the first I'd heard of it. When I told her that, her eyes lit up.

"You haven't seen the video? I can call it up on my phone and you can watch it right now" *as the camera records your reaction.* I don't recall if she said it outright, but she didn't have to.

"No."

"Why won't you watch the video with us?"

Why won't I allow the raw nerve of Black pain to be exploited as a performance on cue for the titillation of your audience?

"We won't be doing that," I said flatly.

A few more questions, and the interview was a wrap. That was the last time I ever spoke to *Inside Edition.*

And that was how I learned about the murder of George Floyd, though at that time his name had not yet been released to the public. By some strange twist of fate, my run-in with Amy Cooper and the far graver, lethal encounter between George Floyd and his murderer, the police officer Derek Chauvin, had occurred on the very same day. Both incidents would be captured on video for the world to see—the latter by the teenager Darnella Frazier, who had the presence of mind to record the events unfolding before her. If she hadn't, one can only guess what line of bullshit (sorry: fabrication offering plausible deniability) we African Americans would be expected to swallow in the aftermath of Mr. Floyd's death. (To that point, in findings published in September 2021, *The Lancet*—one of the most respected medical journals in the world—revealed that about 55 percent of fatal encounters with the police in the United States between 1980 and 2018 were listed as another cause of death. This discrepancy disproportionately involved Black victims.) For once, all Americans could witness for themselves, in moments adjacent to each other by a few hours, what we African Americans have been saying for decades: in the morning, the underlying bias affecting police perceptions; and in the afternoon, its fatal consequences.

George Floyd's murder epitomized a blatant disregard for Black life in policing—not just in Chauvin's casually merciless deed, but in the three other cops on the scene who stood by and did nothing to stop it. It was the straw that broke the camel's back: It came rapidly on the heels of the police shooting of innocent Breonna Taylor as she slept in her own Louisville, Kentucky, home; and the case of Ahmaud Arbery, shot dead by a pair of white vigilantes for daring to jog through their Georgia neighborhood—a case police only took seriously months later after public outcry when, once again, video emerged. (The take-away for us African Americans is clear: Use the power that technology has put in your pocket; grab your smartphone and record, record, record.) The final fuel to the George Floyd response was the shutdown due to the coronavirus pandemic, which had left many people frustrated, cooped up, and with the opportunity to turn out in numbers, if they dared to brave the disease.

They dared. The wave of protests was unprecedented, defying convention in composition (these were the rare racial protests where white people often outnumbered Black people), in scale (by the thousands), and in scope, in that the protests took place in cities and towns nationwide and were sustained over many weeks. Black Lives Matter moved from the margins to garner that ultimate badge of mainstream approval, corporate embrace.

Meanwhile, I was grappling with a firestorm of attention. I was so overwhelmed with media requests that Melody, as the person who had posted the video to Twitter, ended up taking on almost as many as I did. It felt surreal to have my phone chime with the latest *New York Times* news alert and discover it's about me; to hear my name issue from my own TV as I was eating breakfast and watching my usual morning cable show. Even stranger was when John called me from a protest and held up his phone so I could hear: In the same breath as George Floyd and Breonna Taylor, the crowd was chanting my name. (That made me really uncomfortable, not the least because I'm not dead.) It crossed into the absurd when the *New York Post,* a conservative rag useful only for its colorful headlines, sent a photographer to stake out the front of my apartment building; I rushed past him into the lobby as if I were Princess Di fleeing the paparazzi.

And if it was like that for me, I can only imagine how it was for Amy Cooper, who was the focus of an entire nation's scorn. What she did was unmistakably a racist act; there's no mincing words about that. Yet I refrain from labeling her a racist, because I don't know her at all and am not privy to how she conducts her life beyond that one incident. Only she herself can tell us whether she's a racist, principally through what she does going forward.

Many find it odd that I could have a measure of empathy for someone who did something so crappy to me. Scores of people have told me how sorry they are that I had to endure such trauma, to which I can't help but think, what trauma? The dustup in the park was certainly unsettling at the time, but it would take a lot more than that to traumatize me; Amy Cooper's antics in and of themselves simply don't wield that kind of power. Similarly, for those who worry whether I'll ever be able to bird the Ramble again, I just laugh at the notion that her bad behavior could somehow erase decades of incredible birding experiences that are embedded in this locust tree or that bend in the path, sense memories that linger years later so that you can recall just how you felt at the moment you saw that special bird in that exact spot. I'm sure that if I'd actually had to deal with the cops, let alone if I'd been roughed up or locked up, my view would be different and my attitude toward Amy Cooper more harsh. But the fact is, I suffered no real or lasting harm. (I recognize that I'm very fortunate in that regard, unlike George Floyd.)

Moreover, it's easy to render someone a cardboard villain from an item in the news. As the person who was actually there, I can't help but see Amy Cooper as a human being—a deeply flawed human being who did something incredibly racist, but a human being nonetheless. I can't deny to her what we insist cops must keep in mind in their encounters with African Americans. (Melody was unsurprisingly unforgiving. Don't mess with a Black woman's family.)

I'm loath to pass judgment on someone based on a few minutes of their life. We've all had our worst moments (though hopefully not as bad or racially biased as that one); most of us are just lucky enough to not have those moments captured on video. Amy Cooper's luck was so bad that the video of her worst moment synchronized with one of the most depraved police murders of an African American ever lensed; it amplified her error so as to extend its shelf life indefinitely. Throw in her on-camera abuse of her own dog to generate extra outrage from animal lovers, and she was caught in a perfect storm.

None of this excuses what she did; the storm was largely of her own making. Indeed, she made things worse by calling the police to reiterate her false charges when she got home; when the stress of the moment had passed and she'd had time to consider her deeds, she doubled down. (I only learned of that weeks later, putting what empathy I had for her sorely to the test.) Still, it must be a hard thing to swallow: to start your morning with the everyday act of taking your dog for a walk, only to blow up your whole life in a few minutes of poor choices.

She soon offered a tepid apology in the press (she never reached out to me directly), which I accepted as far as it went. It showed little indication that she understood the nature of what she'd done. As the *Washington Post* columnist Michele Norris perfectly observed,

> How refreshing it would have been if Amy Cooper had said, "Yep, that was a pretty clear act of racism on my part," instead of apologizing to "that man" and insisting that she was not really a racist.

I have seen the power of such an open acknowledgment of racial error. It gives everyone else permission to examine their own failings on race and to determine to do better. That would be a response on her part that I could get behind. But it's not the path she would choose, as would become clear months later.

After several days of the media whirlwind, I was ready to hide under a rock until I could have my life back. And that, I realized, would be a mistake; for better or worse, I found myself in a place where I could try to articulate where this moment in the nation's ongoing train wreck of race relations had come from, what it meant for Black people and the nation at large, what was and wasn't happening, and what we all might do to get on track and move forward. George Floyd, Breonna Taylor, Ahmaud Arbery, and Philando Castile couldn't do it; they'd been robbed of that ability. But I could.

I do not hold any special wisdom in that regard, beyond that which comes from living in a Black body in the United States for more than half a century. But there are things I've stood up for, for the better part of my life: fairness and justice for Black people, equality for queer people, the sheer joy of birds and the need to protect them and their wild places. If microphones and cameras were going to be stuck in my face, then I would use them to push those very things, to say what I thought needed to be said.

First, it's not about Amy Cooper. What's important is what her actions revealed: how deeply and widely racial bias runs in the United States. (Ironically, she was born in Canada, yet she still tapped into that dark vein that carries its poison to every part of this land.) Focusing on her is a distraction and lets too many people off the hook from the hard, ongoing examination of themselves and their own racial biases that needs to happen if we're ever going to get this country out of this wretched place we're stuck in. If you're looking for Amy Cooper to yell at, look in the mirror.

Second, the unjust deaths and brutalization of Black people at the hands of police officers is absolutely *not* a situation of "a few bad apples," the canard tirelessly repeated by nearly every person in a position of authority. Racial bias infects American society in myriad ways, and cops are a part of that society, ergo the police suffer from racially biased perspectives just like everybody else, from homemakers to retailers to hiring managers to CEOs. The difference is that cops are given weapons and license to use deadly force; so when they act on their biases, Black people end up maimed or dead. Compound that with a culture of policing that prioritizes the "blue wall" of silence over truth and accountability, a culture that is increasingly militarized; add the undue influence of reactionary police unions, who block reasonable reforms at every opportunity; and the broken Black bodies start to pile up.

To be sure, there are the Derek Chauvins, rotten to the core. But there are also their enablers: the ones who did nothing, who looked the other way, who moved the bad apples from department to department. And then there are the cops who would probably never consider themselves among the rotten fruit. Yet, witnessing a blond boy running around with a gun, they would see a child like their own and take the time to ascertain that the "weapon" is a toy; put that same toy in the hands of a brown-skinned child and they've shot the twelve-year-old dead in under two seconds. (The boy's name was Tamir Rice.)

Third, contrary to the loudest mouths at some protests, every cop is not evil. Yes, they have all spent their lives in the same subtly and not-so-subtly toxic racial stew as the rest of us, but some in the performance of their duties manage to transcend those shackling preconceptions. If not, I would not be here today, but rather would have been lost in a pool of blood on a subway platform in 1980, just another headline, just another source of Black outrage. The two white cops then and there did their jobs right, protecting public safety, including that of the foolish Black kid they sent home intact to Long Island. When I'm told that I'm lucky I was never confronted by the police in Central Park, that I would have ended up roughed up or dead, I acknowledge that distinct possibility; and then I also remember that moment in 1980, and I acknowledge that the police might have arrived at the scene in Central Park, found me there, and done their job as professionally as the two officers forty years earlier. I know the police can get it right, because I've lived to see it. That's why we can and should demand better of them.

Fourth, Defund the Police is a worthy idea with the most idiotic branding ever. The name sows confusion as to what the approach really involves: shifting significant resources (but by no means all) away from cops, who are being asked to perform a growing range of social interventions for which they're ill-equipped. Those resources would then be redistributed to social service providers as responders who can handle such situations more successfully and without the risk of the use of deadly force. But most people's understanding of Defund the Police never gets that far; it was weeks before I grasped the concept hidden behind the misleading name I'd shrugged off as a nonstarter. The real nonstarter—Abolish the Police—may be a favorite slogan of mostly white radicals at the fringes of protests as they scream it in the faces of the police present. But I suspect it has about as much support on the ground in communities of color, where crime takes its heaviest toll, as abolishing the air we breathe: It may reek at times, but it's still necessary. Presenting our options as brutal policing versus no policing paints a false choice.

Finally, to the surprising number of white people who look at the video of the Central Park incident and whose primary reaction is "That poor dog!": You are in dire need of sensitivity training not conducted by PETA.

In the wake of "the incident," as I had come to call it, I decided that if I was going to have fifteen minutes of fame thrust upon me, I was going to use it to best effect. The spring and summer of 2020 were the height of perhaps the most consequential presidential campaign of my lifetime, and the white nationalist occupying the White House needed to be ousted. So through Harvard connections, I was tapped while my name recognition was still high to endorse the Democratic candidate, Joe Biden. If, as the spokesperson of the moment against racial injustice, I could help deliver critical Black voters with my endorsement, I was eager to do it. So a Zoom meeting was set up where I was to have a conversation with Biden one-on-one.

The morning of the Zoom, I waited for my phone to ring with word that the meeting was canceled; surely the Democratic nominee for the presidency had more important things to do than spend half an hour chatting with me. But suddenly there was Joe, the man who would go on to become the next president of the United States, on the screen of my laptop! We talked for a good forty minutes, uninterrupted (he did most of the talking; politicians truly have the gift of gab), and the campaign chopped the recording into useful bits and placed them online in targeted ads. I have no idea if it moved the needle for him, but I was thrilled both to talk to him and to do my part, as so many others did in ways large and small in that election. Those efforts put Joe Biden where he needed to be and where a dangerous, grifting narcissistic real-estate developer didn't belong.

I also endorsed Ritchie Torres, a Black, openly gay, progressive candidate facing tough odds against one of New York City's most notorious homophobes, in the Democratic primary for an open seat in the House of Representatives. Ritchie, too, prevailed and now represents a section of the Bronx in Congress.

About that time, my phone rang—this time, not a reporter.

"Christian."

"Bobbie!"

"And Marie," added a third voice on the line. My old Marvel buddies, who I knew were now both high-muckety-mucks at DC Comics, had a startling proposal.

"How would you like to do a comic story drawn from your experience in Central Park?" Bobbie teased.

I hadn't even remotely considered it. I'd been out of comics for twenty years, and I didn't see how the issues involved lent themselves to a superhero context. I turned the idea around in my head for a while, but every angle I came up with felt contrived.

Marie called me back a few days later.

"Well, you don't have a story yet, but we have an approved title: *It's a Bird*."

It took me a second, maybe because for me Bobbie and Marie are still associated with Marvel, rather than DC and its high-flying signature character, Superman.

"Ah! I get it." And from that title, suddenly the story took shape in my mind: a foray into magical realism, as I'd pursued in Latin America in my youth, with the world of superheroes only obliquely referenced. No literary tradition was better suited to communicating realities so extreme, so unbearable. And while I couldn't give the story a happy ending, I could at least offer a glimpse of grace for those gone by.

"It's a Bird," with art by the awesomely talented Alitha Martinez and Mark Morales, became the first story published in DC's new *Represent!* series, which gives a voice to often overlooked perspectives and communities. After so many years away from comics, I was full of trepidation when I started writing. But the old muscles were still there, eager to stretch their graphic storytelling wings again. I couldn't be prouder of what they let fly.

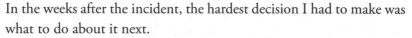

In the weeks after the incident, the hardest decision I had to make was what to do about it next.

The first move, concerning protection of the birds and their habitat, was easy. About a month prior to the incident, I and a handful of other birders representing various organizations had appeared via Zoom before Community Board 7 to plead for some enforcement of the leash regulations in Central Park; a community board is the most local and immediate level of civic authority in New York City, its members unpaid representatives drawn from the neighborhood, and CB7 shared jurisdiction over the park. The powers of a community board are extremely limited, but as the voice of area residents it at least prompts lip service from those who do have real power. We'd gotten on CB7's agenda, but as is typical for community boards, often rife with divisions between clashing interests and personalities, any action on a resolution about leash enforcement had been deferred to the next meeting. Now the second meeting had arrived, with the incident—sparked by the very problem we'd asked them to address previously—having made international headlines.

When my turn came to address the meeting, again via Zoom, I pointed out that if the leash rules had been enforced, the clash between me and Amy Cooper would never have happened. Others spoke their mind, mostly in support, until one white board member made my jaw drop: He opposed the resolution because it asked the police for more enforcement, and that "sent the wrong message" in light of the problems with policing highlighted by Black Lives Matter.

Note that the leash scofflaws in the Ramble, because of the neighborhoods surrounding it, are almost exclusively white. So this board member was effectively saying that his takeaway from the murder of George Floyd and the surging BLM movement was that there should be less police enforcement on *white* people.

It took everything I had in that moment not to scream.

That "logic" swayed a few votes, but not enough; the resolution passed.

What to do about Amy Cooper was a tougher call. The Manhattan district attorney's office was hounding me to get involved in some action against her, and I was doing my level best to avoid them, because I found myself conflicted about that. On the one hand, I understood there was an important principle at stake: that in a country with a history of Black people being falsely accused and the accuser getting away with it, holding the accuser accountable in this case, with its clear-cut evidence, would set a meaningful precedent. It would act as a deterrent to others who might try making false accusations in the future.

On the other hand, I was utterly repulsed by the bloodlust aimed at Amy Cooper in social media; she merited strong rebuke, yes, but not death threats. I was left to wonder—particularly with the Manhattan DA facing an election year—how much of his office's eagerness to prosecute was to appease a mob's thirst for vengeance.

"Eagerness" is one way to put it: I was about to start a Zoom meeting for work one day when I was startled by a relentless, Gestapo-like pounding on my apartment door; at first I thought racist crazies had tracked down my home address, but it turned out two people from the DA's office had gained access to the building and were displeased that I'd failed to return any of their calls. I refused to respond, and when my neighbor intervened, they tried to pull rank and bully her with "go back inside, official business" tripe. Big mistake; she's a pit bull of a lobbyist who has handled worse than them for years. She kicked them out of the building, God bless her. I can't say that their approach to contacting me helped their cause.

I was also constrained by a sense of proportionality. Amy Cooper's life had already imploded—job gone, reputation destroyed, past indiscretions splashed on the front pages. Wasn't that punishment enough, especially since I'd suffered no significant harm? Criminal charges seemed like piling on. And if someone contemplating making a false accusation could look at the outcome for her and not be deterred, I doubt any legal precedent would stop them either.

And to be honest, I felt somewhat guilty. I didn't want to be responsible for destroying somebody's life, and even though intellectually I know that's not the case—that she brought about her own downfall by trying to leverage race to her advantage—I still *felt* responsible. I had never sought her head on a pike; I just wanted her dog on a leash. But we'd both chosen to escalate our conflict, and the result was ruin: ruin she'd tried to bring down on me that instead had landed on her.

Up to a year in jail was on the table if she was convicted, and while that kind of sentence seemed highly unlikely for a first-time offender, it wasn't inconceivable with such a high-profile, politically charged case, in the midst of an election cycle, and with the public's mood. I couldn't countenance being part of that.

Moreover, it wasn't my case to make; this was never a matter of me filing charges, or else the case goes away. The DA's office was prosecuting regardless.

So despite the important principle, I had to err on the side of compassion and my conscience. I declined to be involved in the prosecution. If the DA required my participation, he could subpoena me, and I'd comply.

The blowback from some in the Black community for that decision was swift and severe. I can't say I blame them; part of me felt the same way. This was personal for many, even within my own family: One relative by marriage was angry, only later sharing with me that her brother had spent years in a South Carolina prison when a white woman had falsely accused him of rape to cover up their affair. Some felt betrayed. Others seemed to want Amy Cooper punished for Emmett Till and every other outrage African Americans have suffered, as if this one individual should bear the brunt of all the wrongs done to us. I understand the sentiments, but could only follow my conscience. In all that happened with the incident in Central Park, this part was the most painful for me.

Conversely, some folks seem to have read that act of conscience as an opening to a feel-good resolution. The number of people—almost exclusively white—who approached me about a reconciliatory meeting between me and Amy Cooper was staggering. Not just journalists, who of course saw such a makeup session as potentially great television; ordinary white people seemed invested in the idea that the incident somehow needed to be "made right," that my bestowing of forgiveness was the next step. Never mind that Amy Cooper had gone into hiding, had never made any overture or apology to me directly, and had never indicated that she was open to such a thing.

I'm certainly not interested in it. I have no need for a face-to-face with Amy Cooper, whether as a Jerry Springer–style hair-pulling fight or a hug-it-out kumbaya moment. If such a meeting would advance fairness for Black people facing the criminal justice system, or otherwise help root out deep-seated racial bias, I'd consider it—though you'd face a high bar to convince me that was true. Besides, it has become clear that Amy Cooper still doesn't appreciate the dimensions of what happened on that Memorial Day, and without such an understanding on her part, such a meeting would be worse than pointless—a useless photo op.

About a year after the incident, Amy Cooper filed a wrongful ter-

mination suit against her former employer. Presumably to support
that claim, she resurfaced a few months later to speak to a reporter for
the first time since the incident, offering her recollections. I saw little
advantage to a "he said, she said," so I held my tongue, and will only
point out now that my description of events surrounding the video
was written down on Facebook the same day they happened. That,
and one other thing jumped out at me.

Amy Cooper claimed she was afraid that I would harm her or her
dog with the bicycle helmet I held in my hands, implying that I was
brandishing it menacingly. There's only one problem with that; I'm a
birder, and there's one indispensable tool that birders use: binoculars.
The only way to effectively use binoculars is with *two* hands. If I've
biked to the park to bird, my bicycle helmet is *always* clipped to a belt
loop of the pants or shorts I'm wearing, or, if that makes walking awkward, to the strap of my shoulder-slung satchel. Holding the helmet
in my hands would make birding impossible.

I can't say whether her claim is a deliberate falsehood or the product
of memories distorted by time and an unconscious need to conform
them to a desired narrative. But more important, it once again speaks
volumes about bias: A Black man can't have a bicycle helmet without
it being regarded as a potentially deadly weapon, brandished in poly-
styrene menace. One wonders what one is supposed to do if one has
biked to the park while Black. I imagine if I'd taken the subway, she'd
worry that my MetroCard could be converted into a shiv.

I'm sorry to say that since the incident Amy Cooper has, apparently, learned nothing.

Exactly one day shy of the one-year anniversary of the incident, I was
in the Ramble again, close to wrapping up another season. The 2021
spring migration in Central Park was winding down, and it had proved
to be the polar opposite of the year before. Where birders were scarce

during COVID's height, our numbers had not only recovered but soared; the pandemic had created a bumper crop of newbies, folks who needed an excuse to get outdoors or who had started watching birds from their window while on lockdown. With vaccines available and transmission rates down, birders new and seasoned had descended on the Ramble in droves. It reflected an explosion of birders almost everywhere.

More Black birders are among them. Where decades earlier I used to joke that you could do a North American census of us on one hand, over the past year I'd met more fellow African American birders than in the previous twenty. The incident had prompted the scientists of Black AF in STEM to respond with Black Birders Week, a series of live and online events celebrating who we are and what we do; it was about to happen for its second year. Participating in it, I was dazzled by just how many of us raise binoculars to the sky nowadays. We're still a small fraction of the birding populace, particularly compared with our proportion in the general population, but we're no longer as rare as a Kirtland's Warbler.

My own life had taken unexpected turns in the last year as well. As masks came off, I had to adjust to a minor bit of celebrity; sometimes I'd get recognized in the oddest contexts, but always in the nicest way. Black people who told me I'd inspired them and young people who told me I'd turned them on to birding melted my Vulcan heart. Folks from across the country (and even a few from other countries) sent me moving notes, more than I could ever reply to, and a few even sent original artwork; the woman who knit a doll of me in my birding getup, complete with binoculars and an accompanying tree of birds, took pride of place. And I'd had a celebrity thrill of my own, hanging out in the park with Spike Lee to be a small part of his sprawling documentary about New York City in the twenty-first century.

Over the course of the year I'd fielded speaking requests from a score of organizations, primarily birding and conservation groups, most of which I simply couldn't manage to take on. Always glad to boost birding with the youth, I'd recorded bits for PBS—for online *Nova* projects and for the kids' TV show *Cyberchase*—and by that October I'd quit my desk job of nearly twenty years to pursue an intriguing new possibility: hosting a birding TV series, perhaps the first of its kind for a major channel. I figured if *Law & Order: Special Victims Unit* could bring a fictionalized version of me and the incident into millions of homes (as a longtime guilty viewer of the show, the meta moment of watching Captain Olivia Benson talk to "me" in the season 22 opener, "Guardians and Gladiators," made my head explode), those millions may as well get the real me extolling the feathered creatures I adore.

Yet with all that had happened in that year, spring migration remained sacrosanct, and I'd spent the last six weeks exactly where I belonged. Now that it was late May, the park was in full leaf out, right on cue. The Blackpoll Warblers were singing their high-pitched squeaky-wheel song from the dense foliage in multiple parts of the Ramble, the yearly sign of the migration's imminent demise. The vast majority of dogs in the Ramble were on the leash, a stark contrast to last spring. Nobody wanted to be the next Amy Cooper.

Well, almost nobody.

As I walked up from Oak Bridge toward the Humming Tombstone, I saw a medium-large dog bound off the path and into the plantings. Determined not to stir up trouble, I decided to do only what we'd been instructed to do for the Parks Department: document the off-leash encounter with cellphone video.

As I recorded, a young white woman came walking into frame: the dog's owner.

"Ma'am, dogs in the Ramble have to be on the leash at all times," I said in my gentlest possible tone. I was *not* going to cause a ruckus today.

"I don't even know where I am!" she said with a confused smile, throwing her arms in the air.

"Well, you're in the Ramble, so you might want to put your dog on the leash."

"Oh, okay, I'll do that."

And she did. I thanked her, stopped recording, and moved on, happy to have avoided any unpleasantness. I went back to scanning the trees for birds.

"Sir! Sir!" her voice called out to me, about two minutes later.

I turned around; she'd followed after me. Her dog was on the leash.

"Were you recording me?" she asked.

"I was recording your dog, yes."

"Why?"

"Because we've been asked to document dogs off the leash in protected areas for the Parks Department."

"Was I in the recording?"

"Probably, yes."

"I'd like you to delete that, please." Her tone made it clear she expected compliance.

"No."

"But it's a violation of"—I could see her searching mentally for some law that doesn't exist—"my personal self."

I didn't know what to say to that, so I was just brutally honest.

"I'm not concerned with your needs."

"But I didn't know!"

"Okay, well, now you know."

She was getting a bit frustrated. "Why won't you delete it?"

"Because we've been asked to document dogs off the leash in protected areas for the Parks Department," I repeated.

"Do you have a letter that says that?"

"I have emails."

"I'd like to see those emails."

I was astonished. I kept it simple: "No."

She took out her cellphone and started recording.

"Well, how do you like it when I record *you*?" she snapped.

"Have at it." And I shrugged.

So she upped the ante.

"What if I show this video to the police and tell them there's a man re-cording people?"

I just stared at her. Was she for real? Does she not watch the news? It was all so preposterous I was about to burst out laughing. We were standing on the edge of the Tupelo Meadow, about twenty feet and almost exactly one year from the Amy Cooper incident. I began to wonder if I was cursed to repeat this *Groundhog Day* for an eternity.

"Okay." It was all I could muster.

"So you're going to go home and get off on my picture, is that it?"

I recoiled. I try to be sensitive to women's concerns about privacy and safety in public spaces, but you don't get to play that card when you're the one violating park rules. Besides, her accusation was rather presumptuous. You'd think the giant rainbow flag on the front of the T-shirt I was wearing that day might have been a tip-off.

"Have a good day," I said and turned away, ignoring her thereafter. I was glad it was late morning this time, with plenty of people around. Hopefully, somebody else was seeing this, because it was crazy.

"What are you, some kind of perv?" she shouted after me. "Are you going to jack off to my picture?"

All I could do was shake my head and throw my eyes skyward, wondering who up there I had pissed off. And laugh. Or maybe weep.

Looking across the sweep of it, from 59th Street to 110th, from 1857 to Memorial Day 2020 and beyond, from the first Kirtland's Warbler I ever saw to the last echoes of ugly accusation hurled at my back, I can honestly say, with both elation and frustration, Central Park will never cease to amaze.

13

Out of Alabama

A HAZARD AWAITS BIRDERS: We know too much. It can trip us up at the movies with laughable effect, as with *Blood Diamond*'s North American birds singing in Africa. But the birds-and-movies mixed message I most remember—especially now that I'm here with an Audubon chapter on my first trip to the deepest of the Deep South—caught me even more by surprise. And it felt like a knife to the heart.

The moment came near the end of the director Steve McQueen's *12 Years a Slave*—one of many hard moments juxtaposing gorgeous imagery with despicable acts of horror to indict the antebellum South. Melody and I sat in the sold-out crowd on opening night, feeling the air leave the room as those moments piled up, one against the next. By the climactic scene, when trauma is enacted upon a Black woman's body and a Black man's soul, you could sense every heart in the theater pause on the edge of breaking. But what broke mine was not just what I saw, but what I heard.

Behind the cries of pain and rage, in the background, I'd swear I heard a singing Blackburnian Warbler. I couldn't help it; for an ear birder, that skill never turns off, even with a sound as high-pitched and nearly inaudible as that one. But to me, that particular song is a summons, demanding that I stop to witness my most beloved of the American warblers; as the seven notes spill from its fiery throat, they somehow convey everything that's glorious about the world. That this sound of all possible birdsongs should frame the film's most crushing moment doubled every blow, and I became desperate to hear anything but that. I tried to deny my ears, unwilling to cede this last terrible juxtaposition. But the song's signature final note kept repeating, rising with urgency, as if the bird were trying to scream as it and the world's joy were being strangled.

I feel something like that at this moment, standing on the corner of Sixteenth Street and Sixth Avenue North in Birmingham, Alabama.

It's August in the Deep South, but the afternoon has so far managed to avoid being oppressive. The sunny skies are dappled with a few clouds that offer shady relief on occasion; I'm sweating a little as I walk, but a personal tsunami hasn't yet soaked my shirt, my brow. When a cloud pulls away, a robust light shines on this pleasant corner of town: on the arches at the entrance of a stately Baptist church; on the rich greens of the well-tended Kelly Ingram Park opposite. At the park's edge there is a statue of four little girls, one with her shoes off beside her, in various states of play and repose. I fixate on those empty shoes. The absence speaks volumes.

I wonder, as I walk through the park, how such a spot can be so pretty and ordinary today, considering what lies buried underneath the rubble of its past. On the morning of September 15, 1963, at the height of the civil rights movement, in this city that was widely considered the most segregated in the United States, white supremacists set off a bomb in the Sixteenth Street Baptist Church—the center of African American worship and organizing in Birmingham, and the very church across from which I was now standing. More than a dozen people were injured, but Addie Mae Collins, Denise McNair, Carole

Robertson, and Cynthia Wesley, all fourteen years old or younger, died. They had gathered in the basement that morning to prepare for the church's Youth Day. They weren't supposed to be martyrs, the explosion that killed them searing the conscience of a nation. They were supposed to grow up and have complicated, messy lives, like the rest of us. Instead, they left behind empty shoes.

Here in the park, no Blackburnian sings incongruously. Instead, I hear a mockingbird, just as one sang at the grave of my birding mentor from childhood, Elliott Kutner. Now as then, it offers its own eulogy, its many voices having much to say about all this.

I'm glad to be here, to confront this difficult history—finally. Having visited Paris (France) and Paris (the hotel in Las Vegas), danced until dawn in Buenos Aires, trysted in Sydney, trekked the Himalaya, safaried in Tanzania, and sailed the Galápagos, if you'd asked me a year ago, I'd have ranked Alabama near the bottom of the list of where to go next. I'm a northern guy, New York City born and New York City suburbs raised, and tales of the very real oppression Black folks suffered down south loom large in the northern consciousness. "My people left there for a reason," I would often demur at the mere suggestion of a trip below the Mason-Dixon Line. Add to that the fact that I'm openly gay and a non-Christian, and visiting a conservative Bible Belt state became a complete nonstarter.

For a Black birder, this calculus is all too common. All African American outdoor enthusiasts share an awareness of racial geography; for birders of color it dictates, in ways big and small, where we will and won't follow the birds. We write our own sort of Green Book— the segregation-era travel guide that listed the establishments where Black people on the road could hope to find safe lodgings and a meal—keeping a mental map of where we do and don't feel we can bird, camp, hike, or climb, safe from possible harassment and harm. There are areas, sometimes entire swaths, of the United States where we won't venture—alone or at all. As J. Drew Lanham, a professor of wildlife at Clemson University whose books and essays have long articulated the soul of African American birders, wrote in his essay "Birding While Black," "In remote places fear has always accompanied binoculars, scopes, and field guides as baggage."

To my northern Black mind, no place in the States was as remote or fear inducing as Alabama. Yet here I am, in a strange twist of fate. The spotlight from the Central Park incident has made me, at least for a time, the most well-known birder in America (a feat not hard to achieve, since birders are hardly household names). The fact that that birder is Black turned heads; plus, unlike George Floyd, I am lucky enough to still be alive to relate my experience. I had to decline most of the resulting participation requests from various organizations out of sheer volume. But one in particular had jumped out at me: Alabama Audubon was hosting its first Black Belt Birding Festival, and would I be interested in being their guest?

I had only a vague notion of what "Black Belt birding" might entail. (It is not, it turns out, indicative of some birding initiate's martial-arts-style level of skill.) But the idea of being able to get some southern specialties was exciting; those species had been inaccessible to me, because the Deep South had long been one of my no-go zones. Though I wouldn't dream of visiting on my own, it would be a whole other matter to be shepherded by the folks of Alabama Audubon, like-minded birders who know the lay of the land: which trees might harbor the birds I want, and which trees I might end up swinging from by the neck.

Further, the other invited guest to the Black Belt Birding Festival was none other than Professor J. Drew Lanham, with whom I'd only communicated remotely. Participating in Alabama Audubon's event would present the opportunity to meet one of my admired icons face-to-face. (Alas, the COVID situation forced Lanham to cancel his travel plans at the last minute, so such a meeting would have to wait.)

But I also had a very personal reason to visit Alabama. My mother's side of the family is African Caribbean, and my father's is African

American, and regardless of where our families live today, virtually all African Americans ultimately trace their roots to the South. Beginning around 1910, the Great Migration saw some six million Black people surge northward out of the states of the former Confederacy, spurred by the same thing that lies behind the yearly migration north in the spring for so many bird species: improved prospects for a next generation. For the birds, the draw is food—mainly insects and other creepy crawlies, but also nectar, fish, and other prey—resources that are abundant in temperate latitudes only seasonally. The bird that makes it to the North has the opportunity to exploit that summertime abundance to raise healthy young. For African Americans, the opportunity was economic in the North's industrialized cities, with the added benefit of escaping harsh racial oppression; presented with the prospect of a better life for their children, millions took it, in waves over the next half a century. The Coopers were among them, coming not just out of the South, but specifically out of Alabama. When I would say, "My people left there for a reason," it could very well mean the ground I'm standing on.

So in a sense as strange and foreign to me as when I, an American, set foot in Africa, being here in Alabama represents a homecoming for this northerner. Similar to my thoughts on visiting Africa, I have no illusions that a sweet-home-Alabama revelation is brewing for me; no warm reunion with long-lost relatives is in the making. I wouldn't know where to start looking for kin, and besides, the one time twenty years ago that I'd met a distant Alabama cousin (he had looked up my dad on Long Island), the gulf between us was simply too great for any bond of kinship. We talked differently, saw the world differently, and though in our brief encounter we never got that far into our personal lives, I suspect he woke up with a very different sort of person on the other side of the bed.

Yet I remained curious about a place that figured so prominently in my family's history, and if the gulf between me and someone like my Alabama cousin could be bridged, I was betting it was through a shared interest in birds. When Alabama Audubon's invitation arrived, I seized the opportunity.

My host, Alabama Audubon's executive director, Ansel Payne, takes me to a late lunch before we leave Birmingham for the southern part of the state, closer to the festival; I can't help but notice the rainbow flag in the café window as we enter, with a bit of surprise. Ansel isn't a native Alabamian, but we're joined for lunch by two of his bird conservation colleagues and allies, both of whom are. One is a twenty-something white lesbian with multiple piercings (in her ears; the rest, I wouldn't know) who fled her rural small town for the social freedom of the big city; the other is a respected elder presence in her Black neighborhood who is only now discovering birds as she discovers the connection between the health of their habitats and the health of her community. As different as their life experiences are, these two people are united by birds in common cause. I couldn't be more pleased. Nor more surprised as even in our short trek through this trendy Birmingham neighborhood, rainbow flags pop up with regularity.

I'm beginning to grapple with a reality more complicated than what I'd imagined. It's not that my fears of a place my forebears left behind are unjustified; rather, my assessment lacks nuance and draws from a knowledge base that needs updating. Birmingham in particular has evolved into a relatively progressive enclave; the pattern of urban liberalism versus rural conservatism repeats here as in most regions of the nation. And undoubtedly the South as a whole has changed on race since the 1950s and 1960s for the better, albeit not as much as some like to claim; white nationalism and Confederate flags are still colors flown unabashedly by some.

But I regret to say, that makes the South little different from the North. When my boyfriend, John, and I spent a summer day at the beach on Long Island, a concert at the adjoining Jones Beach Theater featuring the country singer Luke Bryan on his Proud to Be Right Here Tour drew hordes tailgating in the parking lot; their Trump flags (even though he was many months out of office) and Confederate flags (even though they're illegal on state property in New York) fluttered in the ocean breeze. Northern neighborhoods can be as segregated as any from the South, and Amadou Diallo, Patrick Dorismond, Tamir Rice, Eric Garner, Philando Castile, and George Floyd all died at police hands in the North, not the South. I of all people should know that bias knows no latitude: My own notorious run-in with racism took place in New York and was with a Canadian, for heaven's sake. It doesn't get more northern than that.

Granted, my interactions in Alabama are somewhat curated, as I'd intended. Plus I'm a tourist here, getting only surface impressions over three days. Nonetheless, what I've experienced so far departs pleasantly from what I'd expected.

Soon Ansel is at the wheel, ferrying his non-driving New York City guest from place to place without complaint. It makes for a reverse *Driving Miss Daisy:* The Black guy is the one being driven around, by a white person nearly half my age, leaving me feeling old and useless. (But at least this Miss Daisy rides in the passenger seat, not the back!) By dusk, we reach our home base for the Black Belt Birding Festival: Selma.

"Oh, wow," I murmur as we round the corner of Broad Street and Water Avenue, Selma's two main arteries.

Casting its shadow as much in my imagination and in history as it does over the somewhat faded charm of downtown Selma, the Edmund Pettus Bridge rises into view. A more notorious spot in the nation's civil rights struggle could scarcely be found, and here it stands before me, a solid reality: the place where a young John Lewis and more than six hundred others were savagely beaten by white state troopers on Bloody Sunday in 1965 for trying to peacefully march across that bridge toward Montgomery and equality. A thing of interlocking steel, its girders painted white, the bridge dominates the landscape. As the day ends, I make a mental note to return here.

The next morning, Alabama Audubon's Chris Oberholster, an amiable white guy originally from South Africa, joins Ansel and me on a quest to get those southern specialties.

"Listen for a dog's squeaky toy," Chris advises as we scan a stand of pines on a wooded lakefront.

Sure enough, within a few minutes it sounds as if someone's Chihuahua has been treed while gnashing at its favorite plushie. This crazy-cute sound signals the presence of the Brown-Headed Nuthatch—a miniaturized version of the stout, trunk-hugging birds found throughout North America and an adorable addition to my life list.

Our next quarry, my big target of the trip—the Red-Cockaded Woodpecker—presents a far greater challenge. This robin-sized black-and-white bird whose males sport two tiny red spots (the "cockades"; probably the only time you'll see that word in your life), one on each side of the head, once roamed the South. But their habitat needs are so specific—habitat that human activity has reduced to next to nothing—that the bird has been sliding toward the grim fate of another southern woodpecker, the Ivory-Billed. Red-Cockaded Woodpeckers are now endangered and found only in very specific local spots, so rare that many lifelong Alabama birders have never seen one. I get to witness the forest management under way to prevent extinction for the species, and then, through luck and the skill of my companions, I get the bird!

Having noted this woodpecker in my field guides since childhood (who could read the name and not wonder what it meant?), I find it shortens my breath to finally see it, and my binoculars shake in my hands a little: side effects of the Seventh Pleasure of Birding, the "unicorn effect." What a privilege, to be a person for whom, every once in a while, a unicorn comes to life! Most people don't inhabit a world with such magic, but we birders do.

Along the way we score a Scissor-Tailed Flycatcher, whose extra-long tail split down the middle makes it one of the drama queens of the bird world, but we fail to find a Painted Bunting, a sparrow brought to you in Technicolor. Having seen their vibrance before, I'm more keen for kites: the same family as the raptors soaring over the rooftops of Kathmandu, and the star attractions for tomorrow's Black Belt Birding Festival. Happily, we get a preview: My first Mississippi Kites pass overhead as we lunch outdoors at a sandwich shop. Which leaves the Swallow-Tailed Kite—a drama queen much in the way of the Scissor-Tailed Flycatcher—as the outstanding major target of the trip.

The term "Black Belt" describes a region spread across the southern states that was known geologically for its rich black soil and historically for a high density of Black people there to work that soil, first as slaves, later as hands earning slave wages on white-owned farms. In Alabama, the Black Belt comprises a line of eighteen counties stretching east to west across the southern tier of the state. It is almost certainly where the Coopers came from. Today, the Alabama Black Belt is majority African American, with many of those communities impoverished.

But not everyone is broke, and not every farm is white owned. By the afternoon of the festival, I'm standing on the cattle ranch that for multiple generations has belonged to the Joe family. Christopher Joe, a tall, strapping Black man in his thirties with a thick beard framing his killer smile, greets us festivalgoers at the gate; without going into detail, he tells us how those generations struggled to keep the land, even when the Klan rode to their doorstep to try to force them to give it up. The Joes still struggle, as every farming family does, but they have a new ally to help them make ends meet, and this is where the birds come in.

Chris Joe has always been aware of the natural world—part of being a farmer. But until recently he didn't know about the growing ranks of birders eager to see the birds the Joe farm attracts. The festival is a step in bringing farmers and birders together.

In the steamy Alabama sun of an August afternoon, I get a firsthand taste of what that's like. Nearly two dozen of us festivalgoers pile onto a waiting tractor bed to trundle out to the edge of the farm's hayfields, open green expanses framed by grand, old trees that have had the better part of the summer to grow lush. Once there, we line up along the low fence bordering the field, and we wait.

The moment Chris turns on the mower, they start to fly in: multiple kites, soaring down to feast on the big bugs the mowing of the hay scares into their waiting talons. To the kites, the sound of the mower's engine starting up is the ringing of the dinner bell, and we birders have a seat right there at the table to watch. During the festival visit in the morning, that group had both Mississippi and Swallow-Tailed Kites swooping in front of the tractor and their very eyes, Corina Newsome tells me; an outgoing, young Black biologist visiting from Georgia, she was so thrilled that she skipped other festival sessions—a mix of birding offerings typical of these events, in this case outings to other farms, a lakeside park, and a former state cattle ranch—to return to the Joe farm a second time in the same day. This afternoon, for whatever reason, it's all Mississippi Kites. (I blame Corina; her greediness for a second helping jinxed us!)

Both the morning and the afternoon prove that in soil that two centuries ago was soaked in the blood and misery of slavery, something new can grow: an opportunity for Black landowners to deepen their stewardship of the land; a population of migrant and resident birds with a better chance to thrive; and the enthusiasm of birders from across Alabama and even from out of state, of all stripes, who come to savor the experience, their ecotourist dollars helping to keep multigenerational Black-owned farms in Black hands. The impact of this first Black Belt Birding Festival hasn't been quantified yet, but considering the number of people I've seen at food carts and eateries, and festivalgoers I've talked to who booked hotel rooms to be here, it can't help but be a positive jolt for this economically challenged region.

Witnessing this win-win-win for myself, now I truly couldn't be more pleased, unless I'd seen a Swallow-Tailed Kite! But the unpredictable nature of birding is part of what makes it so much fun. I'll see those kites eventually; what I've seen unfold today is far more important.

At the end of a hot, satisfying day in the field, Ansel takes Miss Daisy back to Selma. There's still plenty of sunlight in these early August evenings, so after thanking Ansel profusely for doing all the driving, I peel off on my own, walking down Broad Street toward the intersection of Water Avenue and the Edmund Pettus Bridge. I have a lot to think about: not just the marvel the day turned out to be, emerging from all the complexities of this place, but also the marvel of the life I'm privileged to lead, emerging from all the complexities of its past—a life that, at this juncture in particular, is on the cusp of becoming something new. I look back at my tortured teen years when I considered putting a final end to my misery, and that act is almost unfathomable from this perspective; my sixtieth birthday is racing toward me like a freight train, and still the future seems full of promise. I feel the way I did just before graduating from Harvard to start a new chapter in life, when I was compelled to visit "my" grave before leaving Cambridge. I can't leave Selma without walking across that bridge.

As that hulking span comes into view, I scan the skies above me, hoping to see a Red-Tailed Hawk: a sign of my dad. He'd idolized the Black pilots who'd borrowed the bird's name, and as a pilot himself, of gliders, he'd yearned to soar effortlessly under his own power as they do. He'd even gone so far as to say that if he could come back as any creature, it would be as a red-tail, and upon his death Melody and I have seen him in every soaring red-tail ever since.

There are no red-tails in sight as I set foot on the bridge, and I'm okay with that. I know Dad is with me; I don't think he ever came here himself, and he wouldn't miss this. My mom, who fought every bit as hard for civil rights, is here too; I can practically hear her voice retelling yet again how she pushed me as an infant in a stroller at marches, and she's going to march with me again, right now. I can feel my grandmother's arms around me; that indomitable force of nature, who did things a Black woman wasn't supposed to be able to do on her own, is in the air I'm breathing.

As I start across the bridge, I think of them and the things they did that allow me to be taking this walk; about what those marchers on Bloody Sunday in 1965 went through, and what my ancestors from somewhere in this very land must have endured, for me to be able to be here, free to live a complicated, messy life. In that context, my incident in Central Park is just an asterisk. More than a year later, it remains exceedingly strange for me—the notoriety, that I'd even be mentioned in the annals of the nation's racial strife. I'm uncertain as to where my now somewhat more complicated mess of a life is headed, and I'm okay with that too. I have a lot of help to get me across the bridge.

I am a Black man running through the streets of Selma, Alabama, as if my life depends on it. And it's all Ansel's fault.

After I'd returned from walking across the bridge, a small group of us celebrated the success of the festival with a drink at a local hotel bar. As we emerged from the bar into the last of the long day's light, we immediately heard the chitter-chatter from on high, and our gaze shot skyward: Chimney Swifts, hundreds of them.

Small, uniformly dark birds that flutter like bats and look like flying cigars, Chimney Swifts live in the sky; they spend their days almost constantly on the wing swallowing bugs out of the air. But at night, they settle into communal roosts and have adapted to using human structures for that purpose—hence their name. These Chimney Swifts, having finished the day's aerial patrols, had begun massing in preparation for nightfall.

"We have to follow them to the roost!" Ansel cried excitedly. With many chimneys capped these days, swifts are on the decline, and Alabama Audubon monitors them in a project that tries to help the species. "They must have a roost nearby—come on!"

And we're off. Half a dozen of us, Black and white, women and men, run around like chickens with our heads cut off, trying to follow on foot as hundreds of birds zigzag through the air every which way. The flock seems to be heading in one general direction, but wait, no, really it's *that* way. Also, we're a bit tipsy from the bar, and giddy with the excitement of the chase.

In other words, we look ridiculous. And we're loving the moment so much we simply don't care.

As twilight dims, Ansel thinks he's located the roost somewhere behind the roof of a brick building off Broad Street. We stake it out, watching the birds disappear one by one into crevices along the roof, but not before they do something I've never seen in my life.

The swifts, birds that more than any other in North America live in the sky, touch the ground.

We're dumbfounded. Collectively, we who are gathered on this Selma street corner have known these birds for decades if not centuries, yet we've never even heard of such a thing. The swifts alight in the middle of the asphalt for just a moment, fluttering wing beats caught in the beams of the streetlamps, and then return to the sky. There's no discernible reason why—no water pooled on the street that they might be drinking, no insects to feed on that we can see—and besides, snatching bugs from the ground, as opposed to midair, contradicts everything we know about swift behavior. We're at a loss to explain it.

It's a moment when as a birder I'm reminded: We know so very little. I'm not just okay with that; I'm thrilled by it. I'm thrilled that I can hear the sounds of ravens, the bird geniuses, and have absolutely no idea what they're communicating. I'm delighted that I'm hopeless (for now) at puzzling out which little "peep" sandpiper is which, and that when something utterly unexpected happens, like a hovering Costa's Hummingbird running her bill up and down my calf because she's checking out my leg hair as potential nest material, it's more than just my skin that tingles with excitement. It means my whole life through I'll still be learning something new from birding, right until they pry the binoculars from my cold, dead hands. What a terrible, wonderful curse we suffer from, to find joy in chasing flying cigars through town to witness the impossible by the light of ordinary streetlamps; what ridiculous fools we must be.

What birders.

Acknowledgments

Writing a memoir is akin to taking off one's clothes in public, and as I learned years ago in the amateur strip contest as Darren and the go-go boys cheered me on, success at such an endeavor can only happen when you've got a lot of people pulling for you. First among those people is my agent, the irrepressible Gail Ross, without whom this book simply wouldn't exist, and I've got to tip my hat to journalist and commentator Van Jones, who introduced us. My heartfelt appreciation goes to my editors, Chayenne Skeete and Mark Warren, who wouldn't accept my attempts at a Vulcan's emotional reserve. As skillfully and mercilessly as a dentist extracting a stubborn tooth, they coaxed what I was really feeling onto the page. (Ignore the screams still echoing from the metaphorical dentist's chair.)

The family of Elliott Kutner generously shared him with the world when he was alive, and I'm grateful they were willing to share their thoughts and remembrances now that he's gone. Vincent Wright's insights on my father's early years proved similarly invaluable. A big shout-out goes to Roger Pasquier, Claude Bloch, and all the Central Park regulars, my birding kin, who are woven into these pages as the birds are woven into our lives. May we have many more rarities together!

And speaking of kin, I give gratitude and love to my entire family, who have been nothing but patient and helpful as I tackled this project. My debt especially to Miriam Cooper and my sister, Melody Cooper, for their wise counsel cannot be repaid. As for my partner, John Zaia, with any luck I'll be working off my debt to him for his loving support for many more years to come.

ABOUT THE AUTHOR

CHRISTIAN COOPER is a science and comics writer and editor and the host and consulting producer of *Extraordinary Birder* on National Geographic. Cooper was one of Marvel's first openly gay writers and editors and introduced the first gay male character in *Star Trek,* in the Starfleet Academy series, which was nominated for a GLAAD Media Award. He also introduced the first openly lesbian character for Marvel and created and authored *Queer Nation: The Online Gay Comic.* Based in New York City, he is on the board of directors for NYC Audubon.

ABOUT THE TYPE

This book was set in Garamond, a typeface originally designed by the Parisian type cutter Claude Garamond (c. 1500–61). This version of Garamond was modeled on a 1592 specimen sheet from the Egenolff-Berner foundry, which was produced from types assumed to have been brought to Frankfurt by the punch cutter Jacques Sabon (c. 1520–80).

Claude Garamond's distinguished romans and italics first appeared in *Opera Ciceronis* in 1543–44. The Garamond types are clear, open, and elegant.